D1061456

CHIEF CRISIS OFFICER

CHIEF CRISIS OFFICER

Structure and Leadership for Effective Communications Response

JAMES F. HAGGERTY

Cover design by Amanda Fry/ABA Design.

The materials contained herein represent the opinions of the authors and/or the editors, and should not be construed to be the views or opinions of the law firms or companies with whom such persons are in partnership with, associated with, or employed by, nor of the American Bar Association unless adopted pursuant to the bylaws of the Association.

Nothing contained in this book is to be considered as the rendering of legal advice for specific cases, and readers are responsible for obtaining such advice from their own legal counsel. This book is intended for educational and informational purposes only.

Printed in the United States of America.

21 20 19 18 17   5 4 3 2 1

ISBN: 978-1-63425-175-4

e-ISBN: 978-1-63425-177-8

Discounts are available for books ordered in bulk. Special consideration is given to state bars, CLE programs, and other bar-related organizations. Inquire at Book Publishing, ABA Publishing, American Bar Association, 321 N. Clark Street, Chicago, Illinois 60654-7598.

www.shopABA.org

For Elyse, Liam, and Conall:
Ar scáth a chéile a mhaireann na daoine.

Contents

Introduction

Why in the world would my company need a Chief Crisis Officer?

Good question; here's the answer: In the modern, media-saturated business and social environment, "crisis response" is most often dominated by communications concerns, i.e., ensuring the public, media, employees, and other stakeholders know (1) what has happened; (2) what may happen next; and (3) what you are doing about it. And the stakes have never been higher. In this new web and social media-dominated era, a fumbled, ineffective public response can mean the difference between a crisis you manage and one that manages you. In ways not imaginable previously, a public-facing crisis can have devastating and long-lasting consequences for an organization's goals, success, and even its existence.

Chief Crisis Officer *is built on the premise that every company and organization must identify a leader and a structure for effective and efficient crisis communications response. Using real-life examples, analysis, and tactical guidance, this book will break down crisis events into their component parts and provide both a strategic approach and proper tools to enable a Chief Crisis Officer to assemble his or her team and respond when an inevitable crisis occurs.*

❀ ❀ ❀

Shit happens.

When it does, you need the right plumbing in place to deal with it. And you need a plumber who knows how the system works, and how to clear a drain when things get clogged.

This, in essence, is what *Chief Crisis Officer* is all about.

"Eww!" my wife remarked upon hearing this comparison. "No one is going to read a book that starts off talking about poop!"

I hope she's wrong, and that you'll excuse my vulgarity. I'm not someone who throws around such language casually, but in all honesty, there's no more apt analogy to describe the main theme of this book . . . and no reason to sugarcoat it. A crisis—whether it's an accident, workplace incident, product recall, data breach, lawsuit, or investigation—is, more often than not, what we call in the old neighborhood a "shitstorm." Effectively cleaning up the mess is what this book is all about.

But let's put my thesis in more dignified, business-like terms: In *Chief Crisis Officer*, we will examine two premises that are essential to public response when negative events or issues threaten to do reputational harm to you, your company or organization, or your personal or business goals:

First, you need systems and procedures in place that respond when a crisis hits (the plumbing).

Second, you need a Chief Crisis Officer who understands those systems, how they work, and when to use them (the plumber).

In the chapters to come, we will explore the structure and protocols you need to respond appropriately when a crisis occurs, and the particular skills and expertise of the Chief Crisis Officer to ensure you come through a crisis or other sensitive reputational event in the best possible shape.

Reached for Comment, Company X Could Not Get Its Act Together

We've all seen it before, whether on local television, in your daily newspaper, or in the pages of The *Wall Street Journal:* "Company X could not be reached for comment."

The story in question is often highly negative in nature, involving either an immediate crisis event (product recall, workplace incident or data breach, to name a few) or, perhaps, a longer-term crisis like an investigation or lawsuit. The lack of response only makes things worse. The audience doesn't know the facts, so they speculate; they don't know the company's side of the story, so they assume the worst. Allegations or unexplained negatives just hang out there, crying for some sort of explanation, some sort of context that would help the public understand why the company, organization, or individual is the subject of such unflattering publicity. Readers or viewers think: "Why isn't the company available for comment? Don't they know how bad this story looks? Don't they care?"

I've been doing this for more than 20 years, so I can tell you the following with a high degree of confidence: When you see a lack of response during a crisis, it is often *not* intentional, and it is usually *not* because there was nothing to say, no way to manage the spiraling negatives that threaten both reputation and livelihood. Rather, in most situations, that lack of public response happens simply because the party in question couldn't get its act together in time enough to respond. And more often than not, that's because they didn't have the structure or protocols in place to make such a response efficient and effective, and because no one was identified to lead the effort before media and other audiences.

This is the problem that *Chief Crisis Officer* is designed to help solve. Although this is a public relations book, it is less about the "creative side" of

PR—cute soundbites and images, branding campaigns, media tours—and more about process, leadership, and message.

The Curious Profession of Crisis Counselor

> *"You have a corpse in a car, minus a head, in the garage. Take me to it."*
>
> —Winston Wolfe, *Pulp Fiction*

> *"It's handled."*
>
> —Olivia Pope, ABC-TV's *Scandal*

There is a mythology around the crisis manager—the fixer, the spin-doctor, the operative—forged through movies and television programs over the past few decades. The shady Svengali, moving in the shadows to bury facts, getting the right people to say the right things; the fixer who knows what strings to pull and buttons to push to make a problem go away; the sleek operative dropping an envelope with incriminating photos on a reporter's desk, or trading a good story for a *better* story not involving their client.

I'd love to say that my business works that way—not only would my job be easier, but I personally would seem a lot more interesting.

But that's not what we do in the crisis communications business. Rather, consider this quote, from the 2013 George Clooney movie *Michael Clayton:*

> *There's no play here. There's no angle. There's no champagne room. I'm not a miracle worker, I'm a janitor. The math on this is simple. The smaller the mess, the easier it is for me to clean up.*

Janitor, plumber . . . very similar concepts. And this quote is an effective distillation of what crisis counselors do: We take steps to make sure the mess is smaller, so it is easier to clean up.

Which is why every company over a certain size needs to have a plan for responding to unexpected public events that can do reputational damage. And a Chief Crisis Officer and team to execute that plan. Only then can you ensure the right response when things get dirty.

There's nothing tricky, or sly, or cinematic about it . . . most of the time.*

---

* Ok, I guess it would be wrong to suggest that there's *nothing* interesting about the work we do. Over the years, I've been involved in many situations that seem like they're pulled from the pages of a movie script, but even in these situations, our advice tends to be more strategic than sensational.

This Book Is for You!

"This book is not for me," you think. It's for General Motors. Or Toyota. Or Target. Tylenol. BP in the Gulf of Mexico. The Exxon *Valdez*. Three Mile Island. These are the types of companies and events that need crisis communications: Big companies, with big problems. Companies with oil rigs in the Gulf, ships at sea or thousands of potentially deadly vehicles on the road.

Not me, you think.

Respectfully, you are wrong. Crisis communications planning and execution are vital for every company that interfaces with the public and worries about the negative implications of unforeseen (or at times, perhaps, foreseen) events on their organization and its reputation.*

Want proof? Consider the following crises that occurred in March 2015, over a span of less than two weeks, involving organizations of all sizes. Each of these incidents were high profile enough that the organization in question had to issue a statement to the media in response:

- On March 3, pharmaceutical firm Orexigen accidentally released preliminary clinical trial test data prematurely, endangering FDA approval;

- On March 4, TFC National Bank responded to an employee's lawsuit over wage violations;

- On March 4, Ateeco, Inc., announced a voluntary recall of "Mrs. T.'s Pierogies" due to plastic shard contamination;

- On March 4, the Mandarin Oriental Hotel experienced a credit card breach;

- On March 5, Cedars Sinai Hospital in Los Angeles responded to a "superbug" outbreak linked to a brand of endoscope;

- On March 5, Allstar Marketing Group entered into an $8 million settlement with the Federal Trade Commission (FTC) over deceptive marketing practices;

- On March 5, the police department in Las Cruces, New Mexico, responded to media reports that it used excessive force that hospitalized a suspect;

---

* You'll notice I bounce back and forth between the terms "organization" and "company" throughout this book. To be honest, this is not intentional . . . I just chose whatever term sounded better in that particular sentence. But to be sure, some of the lessons contained herein are probably more applicable to for-profit companies than to nonprofits, government agencies, and other organizations (or high-profile individuals with their own reputational needs). Rest assured, however, that this book is designed for organizations of all types and sizes—business, government, nonprofits, educational institutions, the arts . . . you name it.

- On March 9, Canadian National Railway faced two separate train derailments in Northern Ontario;
- On March 10, the Houston Port Authority responded to events surrounding the collision of two ships in the Houston ship channel;
- On March 11, five high school students were killed in a car crash on the way to a high school basketball game;
- On March 12, Exide Technologies announced it was closing a lead battery recycling facility in Milton, Georgia, after entering into a non-prosecution agreement with the U.S. Attorney's office;
- On March 13, five patients at Via Christie Hospital St. Francis in Topeka, Kansas, contracted Listeria after eating tainted ice cream; and
- On March 16, Texas A&M University accidently posted students' and faculty's Social Security numbers online.

And again, this is just in a two-week period!

From the list above, you see small manufacturers, regional hospitals, local retailers, government bodies, police departments, high schools, community banks, and universities. All are moderately sized institutions for their industry or segment, yet all are facing the types of issues that, while perhaps not likely to land them on wall-to-wall coverage on CNN, will nonetheless portray them negatively to their respective audience. These companies and organizations were not household names, and the issues involved were not necessarily front-page news. Each incident, however, was critically important to the organization in question; each organization's response, therefore, is vital to its perception in marketplace and ultimately, its business or organizational mission.

Thus, the critical question is: Were they prepared? Even more critically, are you?

There were other, more major crises in this two-week span as well, involving name brands that are in the headlines every day. During this period:

- McDonald's responded to national labor issues over the payment of its minimum-wage workers;
- Novartis Pharmaceuticals was fined $12 million for giving Medicare inaccurate pricing data;
- Quantas Airlines battled fake Facebook pages;
- Hedge fund honcho William Ackman faced an investigation over potential manipulation of Herbalife stock;

- Toyota issued a recall of more than 11,000 vehicles; and
- Apple's iTunes had a day-long outage.*

Here's the point: Although this book is for McDonald's, Novartis, Apple, and Herbalife to be sure, you don't have to be a name brand to face an issue or event that will put you or your company under the unflattering glare of the media spotlight. You only need to have a public—and care about what that public thinks about you, your product, service, or issue.

Crisis Communications Is Not Just for the PR Team

It is important to recognize that a thorough understanding of crisis communications is not just for your public relations department or outside PR firm. For that reason, although this book provides an excellent roadmap for planning and executing a crisis communications program, it is *not* a technical treatise accessible only to those who already have an in-depth understanding of the communications or public relations field. And there's an

---

* These lists were compiled using the innovative software CrisisResponsePro—a tool you'll learn more about later in this book.

important reason for this: because planning and decision-making during a crisis involve many functions and operational levels of an organization—from the executive suite, to the legal department, corporate security, the IT department, and more.

Indeed, as you read the lists detailing crises that befell companies and organizations of all sizes, many of you who are not in a traditional PR role might have thought of the issues you are currently facing in your position and how you may assist in the response—because crisis communications touches everyone.

Thus, I've written this book with many audiences in mind, including:

- **Business owners:** Ultimately, it's your business and reputation on the line. Depending on the size of your business, your personal reputation is often entwined with that of your business, so much so that it may be hard to know where one ends and the other begins. Regardless of the size of your enterprise, though, you will need crisis communications leadership and protocols reasonable to your particular organization, its culture, and the issues you may face.

- **CEOs and other senior executives:** Whether you work in a for-profit company, a nonprofit, or a public sector entity, you know from experience that you are on the front lines of the decision-making process, and the decisions made during crisis communications planning and execution can have a huge impact on your organization's reputation and performance . . . and therefore your own. You cannot be involved in every aspect of the crisis communications effort, but you must have an understanding of how to put the right people and protocols in place to ensure the machine is running smoothly when a crisis occurs.

- **General Counsel:** Increasingly, as the chief legal officer for your organization, you are finding yourself and key members of your team involved in decision-making in many areas that go beyond tradition legal roles. As you'll learn in Chapter 6, with regulation and legal issues now central to nearly every area of business operations, it is more common for the General Counsel to be tasked with managing certain sensitive PR concerns.*

---

* There is a small but growing trend in Corporate America for the PR function in an organization to report directly to the chief legal officer, and not only in highly regulated fields: For example, in fall 2015, Twitter announced that their General Counsel Vijaya Gadde was also assuming the role of head of communications for the company (see http://www.corpcounsel. com/home/id=1202739500003/Twitter-GC-Swoops-Into-Dual-Role-as-Communications-Bos s?mcode=1202617073467&curindex=4&slreturn=20150914073435).

- **Law firm lawyers:** Particularly in small organizations, an outside lawyer is often called upon to work with an organization's internal communications resource to help formulate a response when a crisis or other issue arises. As the organization seeks your guidance on a number of sensitive company concerns, they will likely turn to you for advice in this area as well.*

- **Top public affairs or public relations executives:** Top PR and/or public affairs personnel in an organization are generally tasked with managing all manner of public response that could impact the overall reputation of the organization, including crisis communications. But crisis response is likely not the central component of your job, and you must have the proper mindset, tools, and team to do this job well.

- **High-profile individuals:** You are a top athlete, entertainer or other figure who lives their professional life in the public arena. You are very much a business and a brand of your own. All of those around you—your agent, lawyer, publicist, business manager—need to be skilled in the management of crisis events and you should have a personal crisis response plan in place for that Tweet, social media post or other public action that can threaten your brand and your livelihood.

The point is: this book is for you. Crisis communications planning and techniques are not merely for the largest of companies, facing the biggest of issues, in the most major of media outlets. Nor is it solely the domain of the public relations practitioner who specializes in the crisis field. Effective crisis communications is for everyone involved with issues or events that could negatively impact their organization.

Thus, while big companies, their executives, and their advisors will find enormous value in this book, it is not solely for them—or even primarily for them. If you're a $5 million manufacturing company whose facility has caught fire or a small software startup that just experienced a breach and the theft of several thousand credit card numbers, crisis communications

---

* Major law firms are now entering the crisis management business, including Washington, DC, heavyweight Covington & Burling, which created a "crisis management" practice group in 2011 that included former Homeland Security Secretary Michael Chertoff and former NFL Commissioner Paul Tagliabue, among others (see http://prcg.com/law-firm-unveils-crisis-management-specialty/), and Holland & Knight, which created its own crisis communications group in 2015 (see https://www.washingtonpost.com/news/powerpost/wp/2015/06/10/powermoves-holland-knight-starts-crisis-communications-team/).

suddenly becomes very relevant to you, your company, and your future. So read on.

Who Am I?

Why take advice from me? Let me give you a bit of my background: I've been doing this work for more than 20 years. I started in politics, became a lawyer, entered PR, and eventually got into crisis and litigation communications. I run a specialist PR firm in New York and recently became a software entrepreneur, launching a separate company, CrisisResponsePro.com, which offers an innovative crisis communications software product. (You'll learn more about the role of technology in crisis communications response in Chapter 7.)

For more than two decades, my crisis communications consulting firm has been involved in high-profile, sometimes explosive crises, including industrial accidents, facility fires, truck and airplane accidents, data and IT issues, product recalls, discrimination and sexual harassment complaints, workplace violence incidents, class action litigation, labor disputes, business lawsuits, investigations and indictments, and so forth.

Along the way, I wrote a book called *In the Court of Public Opinion* (now in its second edition), which specifically discusses the types of reputational issues that arise during litigation and legal disputes. *In the Court of Public Opinion* was well received in both legal and non-legal communities, earning nearly unanimous accolades. (*Financial Times*, for example, called the first edition "the perfect handbook for this age of show trials.")[1] My book was cited in textbooks and law review articles (and even in an Indiana state Supreme Court ruling),[2] spawned more than a few imitators, and helped ease the acceptance of communications consulting as a legitimate tool in the modern litigator's arsenal.

If you like this book, in fact, I encourage you to read *In The Court of Public Opinion* as well. It's full of valuable lessons for lawyers and non-lawyers alike. Indeed, as the discipline known as "litigation communications" continues to become intertwined with traditional crisis communications, it can be hard to tell where one ends and the other begins. Or as crisis communications expert Harlan Loeb puts it in Chapter 8 of this book: "There is not a corporate crisis I've seen that was not either preceded by or generated litigation. So it's either on the front end, the middle end, or the back end, but litigation hovers quite closely."

This is an important point, and one that we will revisit throughout this book. The interplay of legal and crisis communication issues informs both the approach an organization should take when preparing and executing a crisis communications plan, and who should take the role of Chief Crisis Officer to lead the organization's efforts.

Toward a More Expansive Definition of Crisis

Much of the study of crisis communications fails in one significant regard: Research and discussion primarily focuses on only the most high-profile crises of recent years, such as the BP oil spill, the Target data breach, or the GM ignition switch recall, to cite just three examples. Other studies examine notorious crises of past decades, such as the "cyanide-in-the-Tylenol" case or the Three Mile Island nuclear power plan disaster of the late 1970s. In other words, the type of wide-scale, "center-stage" crises that tend to dominate news coverage and—in recent cases—light up social media for months at a time.

That's fine, and we'll look at these big cases in the pages of *Chief Crisis Officer*, too, since there are many lessons that can be gleaned from such case studies. But I believe more is needed, since we all don't work in major, Fortune 100 multinational conglomerates, and we won't all face a "cyanide-in-the-Tylenol" style crisis. If we are only focusing on the most famous crises, involving large corporations and multimarket products or services, we're missing something. And if you write a book that only examines "name brand" crises involving the largest companies in the world, not only will you have a very small audience for your book, your readers will have a somewhat skewed perspective regarding what crisis communications is all about. Thus, a more expansive definition of crisis is required when considering examples of crisis events, with case studies drawn from many types of companies of all sizes and shapes, and in all industries.

There is, for example, tons written in both general business media and the trade press regarding the handling of the 2010 BP Deepwater Horizon oil spill in the Gulf of Mexico. This coverage includes stories in both the general business media and the public relations trade media, analyzing the overall response and the steps that were taken, or not taken, at each stage in the crisis. As a result, there were ample opportunities to analyze every public utterance made by all of the actors involved—and there is value in that.

But the truth is this: A small crisis to a large multinational corporation may be a big crisis, or a very big crisis, to a midmarket company with a half-dozen locations across the United States. As such, if we study only the biggest of the big, you wind up with a wonderful set of recommendations for these companies and little else for the rest of us.

So, while still focusing on some of these big-name cases at various points in *Chief Crisis Officer*, I'm going to try to avoid just rehashing the biggest events, impacting the largest companies. Throughout this book, I'll draw broadly from my own experience handling crises of all sizes—from those involving large multinational corporations and product recalls to those involving small and mid-market companies. This scope allows us to draw lessons from a variety of issues and events, thus giving a more comprehensive view of the discipline and best practices that ensure crises are managed properly, regardless of company size or the nature of the event.

I think what is great about this field is that there are lessons to be found for every organization in all types of crises. It's not my intent to say that the BP oil spill and Toyota sudden acceleration cases cannot provide lessons for organizations of all sizes, but, rather, that we need balance. In the pages of *Chief Crisis Officer*, that's exactly what you get.

The Road Ahead

As you'll learn further along in this book, a good crisis plan provides you with a roadmap of where you are going and how you are going to get there. So does the Introduction to good business books. With that in mind, let's take a look at what you are going to learn in the pages of *Chief Crisis Officer*.

First, in Chapter 1, we'll break down a crisis event and draw lessons that form the basis of our discussion throughout. We'll examine the big-name crises that have made news over the past several years, as well as less well-known events involving small and mid-sized organizations, with the goal of developing a real sense of what happens during a public-facing crisis and why effective leadership and proper structure for crisis communications response are important.

In Chapter 2, we'll discuss the Chief Crisis Officer position—who this person should be, the particular skills and capabilities he or she will need for the role, and the characteristics that make an otherwise talented professional a bad crisis responder.

In Chapter 3, we'll create a crisis plan and explore how the Chief Crisis Officer and his or her core crisis communication team can put together a plan that is actually useful during the heat of battle.

In Chapter 4, "Rapid Response: Where BP and Target Went Wrong . . . and Where You Can Go Right," we will examine our trademarked methodology for responding to crises to ensure you understand the proper systems and protocols that should be triggered as a crisis unfolds.

In Chapter 5, we'll look at messaging and why it is so important to avoid clichés, corporate-speak, jargon, and other ineffective language when communicating about your company's issue or crisis. I'll give you my take on what makes a good message during a crisis, information on what the message *shouldn't* be, and how you can work to create a message that resonates with your audience, even as the crisis is unfolding.

In Chapter 6, we'll consider litigation communications, a particular subset of crisis communications that is increasingly prevalent in an era where legal issues and regulation reach into every aspect of business operations.

Technology and social media are everywhere, and in Chapter 7 we will examine the role of technology in crisis communications response and the particular tools that can help create a more efficient and effective system in the event of a crisis.

In Chapter 8, we bring these themes together by looking closely at a hypothetical example of a well-managed crisis—showing what an effective crisis communications response looks like when you're "hitting on all cylinders."

I've also included Action Points at the end of each chapter to give you of quick summary of the main points of the chapter.

Finally, in an Afterword called "Perspectives on Crisis Communications," I've collected interviews with leaders in various aspects of the crisis communications field to give you a sense of what works and what doesn't in the real world from variety of different perspectives.

It's important to note that this is not a book discussing the nuts and bolts of PR practice, such as how to write a press release, how to call a reporter, or how to arrange a press conference. There are very good books out there that will give you a grounding in these areas. My goal is not to create a simplistic, paint-by-numbers manual—since, obviously, managing the modern crisis is decidedly not a paint-by-numbers process. Rather, although plenty of "how-to" is found in *Chief Crisis Officer*, I want to give you a way to *think* about crisis communications response and the leadership, teams, planning, and tools you need to get the job done right.

In examples from my own work, I've tried to use as many of the facts of the actual crisis as I can while protecting client confidences. As a result, these examples will tend to be amalgams of various crisis matters and situations I've been a part of in the past—all are "based on true events" and the names changed to protect the innocent. My clients should take note: I'm not talking about you! Rather, I'm providing lessons drawn from various crises involving hundreds of clients over the course of more than 20 years.

I hope you find this book interesting, informative, and even a little fun. And when you are done reading, I hope this book leaves you with the following takeaways: *First*, that organizations of all sizes can face crisis events that subject them to public scrutiny in a manner that might negatively impact both their reputation and overall strategic goals; and *second*, that smart organizations must take the steps outlined in this book to ensure that they manage the crisis, rather than have the crisis manage them.

Anatomy of a Crisis

In my view, the best way to learn how to respond to a crisis is to live through one. So we'll start Chief Crisis Officer *by doing exactly that—or, at least, as close an approximation as you can get in the pages of a book—using a fact pattern and details based on an actual crisis my company worked on several years back. There's no better way to teach than by example, using a blow-by-blow description of what really happens when a crisis hits and how the Chief Crisis Officer and his or her team must act quickly to coordinate a proper response. We will also draw lessons applicable to all types of crises and consider examples that emphasize the "need for speed."*

Most basic crisis communications principles are universal in their application, so as we move along, we'll also contrast this example with lessons learned from some of the best-known crisis events of the past several years. The goal is to show that elements of crisis communications response are applicable whether you are a middle market industrial facility in the shadow of the Statue of Liberty, or one of the largest companies in the world.

> *"Statue of Liberty clouded by smoke as fire rages . . . "*
> —First AP wire service stories

I am sitting at home eating breakfast when the first email comes in:

> *Jim,*
>
> *We have a fire at the Mills Point facility. It's pretty big—heavy smoke. There's already media on the scene and at least one newscopter overhead. Can you call John Smith immediately? He's the manager. We're going to need a lot of help on this one!*

It's 6:20 a.m.

I push my breakfast aside and hop on Google News. Two stories are posted already: one is on the website of a local newspaper and the other is an Associated Press (AP) story. (AP, as many readers know, is a wire service distributed to other media outlets and websites around the world.) From the AP story, I learn that smoke from the facility, which is on the waterfront facing New York Harbor, is so heavy that it has totally obscured the Statue of Liberty as the dark plumes drift east across the harbor. A quick check of Twitter reveals a slew of Tweets from early morning commuters, some with pictures of thick, dark smoke moving ominously toward the New York City skyline.

This is going to be a busy day.

I send a quick message to two members of my team through our crisis response software—one is a New Jersey guy who knows the media outlets there and can help coordinate the response to reporters. The other will handle research, including social media monitoring, so that we know what is being said about the fire in real time. She'll also draft the messages we'll need to send as a response to the media, elected officials and regulators, employees, and other key audiences.

First, I've got to make sure they are awake and available.

To their credit, I receive return messages almost immediately:

> *"On it," from my man in New Jersey.*

> *"We're setting it up now," from my researcher.*

It's 6:24 a.m. Welcome to the wonderful world of crisis communications.

❋ ❋ ❋

A few things to point out about this example, which we'll come back to in a bit: First, as you can see, although we are outside consultants, in this case, my firm worked so closely with the company in question that we were default members of the crisis communications response team. The company, a $2 billion-plus industrial outfit, was a long-time client, but not particularly public-facing; therefore, it had no dedicated internal PR staff to handle such crisis events. So my firm, so to speak, was it.

The second point is equally relevant: the company had no crisis plan in place. As you'll learn in Chapter 3, the lack of a crisis communications plan is not uncommon in companies, regardless of size.

Third, the company relied on the fact that my team would all be available and ready to go to work at the moment the crisis occurred. If I had been on a plane instead of sitting at my kitchen table eating Cheerios with fruit, the crisis response would have floundered. In other words, they got lucky. This serves to highlight a key point: one of the most important steps in crisis communications preparedness is ensuring you *institutionalize* and *mechanize* the crisis response function, so that it can be triggered even if some of the key actors aren't available when a crisis occurs.

This is why I am highlighting the *timing* of the crisis in the example above, using the records and emails available regarding the real crisis that serves as the basis for this example. Rapid response was critical to handling this crisis, and it more than likely will be critical to handling yours—whether you are a Fortune 100 "name brand" or a relatively obscure company known mostly in your own industry.

Crisis Defined

A crisis is when you can't say: "Let's forget the whole thing."
— Unknown

It takes 20 years to build a reputation and five minutes to ruin it. If you think about that, you'll do things differently.
—Warren Buffett

No company or organization is immune from crisis. Regardless of size or industry, whether for-profit or nonprofit, any organization that faces the public and has an interest in the way it is perceived must be prepared for the crisis events with the potential to negatively impact the reputation of the organization, and, as a result, markets, profits, or other business or organizational goals.

Sounds perfectly simple, yes? Of course. However, in practice, I think it's fair to say that most organizations, regardless of size, are ill-prepared when a crisis hits. In this chapter and the chapters that follow, we're going to consider why that is and what to do about it.

But let's start at the beginning: What is a crisis in the organizational context?

"Crisis" can mean many different things, of course, depending to whom you are speaking. Some may apply the label "crisis" to only the most extreme of negative events: bet-the-company episodes like the BP oil spill or the 2014 crash of Malaysia Airlines flight 370, the Ford/Firestone SUV tire saga of the early 2000s, or the "cyanide-in-the-Tylenol" crisis of the early 1980s.

Others might use the term crisis to apply only to those incidents requiring emergency notification—i.e., hurricanes and other weather events, oil spills, terrorism or other criminal or national security emergencies and the like.*

---

* Indeed, it should be pointed out that this book is not primarily focused on the emergency notification elements of crisis response—which although sometimes also called "crisis communications" is a distinct, though at times related, discipline.

As discussed in the Introduction, my definition (which we'll come to in a moment) is broader. To me, a range of events can fall into the category of "crisis," including the following:

- Accidents or facility fires;
- Accidents involving company vehicles or transportation;
- Data breaches and other issues involving information technology;
- Workplace violence;
- Other attacks and incidents of violence (including terrorist incidents);
- Disasters, both natural (such as a hurricane) or man-made (such as a power outage);
- Regulatory investigations;
- Incidents of discrimination or harassment;
- High-profile lawsuits, including the more sensational variety (e.g., a CEO divorce or a tawdry sexual harassment allegation) or those of a more commercial nature (e.g., a patent lawsuit or contractual dispute with a joint venture partner);
- A product issue, which includes everything from a product recall to isolated incidents of health or safety concerns involving your product or service;
- Financial matters, which could include embezzlement by a senior member of the organization, insider trading allegation, or a U.S. Securities and Exchange Commission (SEC) investigation;
- Personnel-related changes that could impact business operations or continuity—from the illness or sudden death of your CEO to the abrupt resignation of a star up-and-comer who represented the future of your organization.

And so on. Here's my point: These are, perhaps, not BP-oil-spill or cyanide-in-the-Tylenol moments for the organizations involved, but they are crises nonetheless. From a communications standpoint, they should be treated as such.

Why treat all of these events as crises? My rationale is as follows: If you take a limited view of what constitutes a crisis, you won't prepare for the myriad other events that could be considered crises . . . and that, if ignored, might do just as much damage over the long term.

Moreover, don't be fooled by complicated distinctions between a "crisis," "incident," and "issue." Label a developing crisis merely an incident or issue and you run the risk that it will be ignored or downplayed as it is developing, until it is too late to control the matter properly. That *thing*—that event, issue, incident, whatever—if you are not giving it proper gravity, it's going to come back to bite you. From a risk management standpoint, an incident or issue should be managed with the same seriousness and care as a crisis, since it may just be a crisis that hasn't exploded yet.

This doesn't mean you call the fire department for every grease fire in your kitchen. Far from it. The key to effective crisis communications is to know what to react to and what to simply keep an eye on. The overall point is this: You are taking all of these events and analyzing them with seriousness, care, and proper attention. With some of these events, the need to respond is obvious—such as during a natural disaster, for example, when you need to communicate as much information as possible to as broad an audience as possible. In other cases, you may not respond at all. Some are potential crises for which you prepare in case a response becomes necessary. Others you watch to see how they develop. In all of these cases, you carefully consider the proper level of response given the event unfolding in front of you. This is the essence of effective crisis communications.

I owe you a definition of crisis communications, don't I? First, let's consider the definition of "crisis," courtesy of the online edition of the Merriam-Webster dictionary:

> *An unstable or crucial time or state of affairs in which a decisive change is impending; especially: one with the distinct possibility of a highly undesirable outcome*

or . . .

> *A situation that has reached a critical phase*

These definitions are actually pretty good, aren't they? Let's adapt them into a workable definition of crisis communications that will serve as the anchor for the rest of this book:

> *Crisis communications can be defined as the process of ensuring an effective communications response to an unstable or critical state of affairs that threatens to have an undesirable or negative impact on an organization's reputation, business or goals.*

Our definition of crisis does not parse or split hairs regarding what type of event qualifies as a crisis, as opposed to an "incident," "issue," or "event." Thus, we make preparations for *all* of the various scenarios that could become a crisis. We treat them carefully, not overreacting or charging blindly into an unnecessary full-court press when none is needed, but we watch, monitor, analyze, and plan for all of the issues that may become full-fledged crises in the weeks or months to come.

This theme runs through this book: Do the work. You won't regret it, even if you never have to use it. In my view, the essence of effective crisis communications falls back on the old Boy Scout mantra: Be Prepared.

The Two Types of Crises: Exploding and Unfolding

So now I've implored you to stop calling crises other things, no? But there many types of crisis? Shouldn't there be more than one definition, or at least, various categories of crises, given the list of many different negative events that could befall a company or other organization?

Perhaps, but another recurring theme throughout this book is *simplicity*: If you want to respond effectively during crisis situations, you must keep it simple.

So for the sake of simplicity, therefore, I would identify only two major categories of crises—the "exploding" crisis and the "unfolding" crisis. They can be defined as follows:

1. **Exploding:** an immediate, event-related crisis that explodes onto the scene (e.g., an accident, fire, or explosion).

2. **Unfolding:** the long-term, unfolding crisis; the type of crisis that bubbles up over time, like a lawsuit or investigation.

As we'll learn, significant differences exist between exploding and unfolding crises. Indeed, we'll devote a whole chapter in this book to the proper management of a legal crisis. My overarching argument, however, is that, in this age of increasing regulation and legal liability, far more similarities can be found between these two types of crises than in the past. It comes down to training, preparation, and messages—whether it's an explosion that rocks your manufacturing facility or a slow-moving lawsuit that threatens to crack the foundation of your business. The physical elements of the damage can be quite different, but in both cases the reputation of the company is very much at risk.

And speaking of "explosive" crises, let's return to the example that opened this chapter . . .

❈ ❈ ❈

It's now 6:29 a.m., five minutes after I first learned of the New Jersey fire.

I receive a call from the company's General Counsel, who also has the company's head of security and internal PR director on the line. I've worked with them all before, so they know me well. We dive right in.

Despite the thick smoke, the report I get from this team is good: there are no injuries or fatalities at the site, and the fire is expected to be under control within approximately 20 minutes. No nearby properties are threatened. A lot of smoke, yes, but it is being blown into the harbor (hence the smoke cloud that obscured the Statue of Liberty) where it will dissipate without causing problems to local residents. There will be physical damage and lots of cleanup, but the situation is definitely manageable.

"The problem is this," says the General Counsel, "We now have three television cameras sitting outside our facility, God knows how many other reporters and photographers, and two newschoppers overhead."

"And I think we've gotten at least a half-dozen calls to our headquarters from media asking about this incident," the PR director adds.

I wasn't 100 percent familiar with the facility, so I ask the group: "Can you give me a sense of this place? Where can you get onto the grounds, and how open is the entrance? Is it fenced in? Is there a security guard? Is it just one entrance, or several?"

The security director responds: "It's right on the waterfront, so the only way in or out is through main gate—which has a guardhouse."

"But to tell you the truth," he adds, "I'm not sure how closely our security guard is watching the gate right now, given everything that's going on. I assume he's stopping media, but we need clarification on that."

"We've got to give media a place to go," I say.

The PR director knows where I'm headed with this comment.

"You know," she says, "next to the main entrance is a small building used as a breakroom for workers. Nice size room . . . chairs . . . refreshments . . . "

"That's great," reply. "Ok, first thing we need to do is make sure the access to the facility is restricted. Let's ensure security is letting no one in. At the same time, we need a media staging area. The building by the entrance sounds perfect—that's where the reporters and cameramen can go, sit down, and have a cup coffee, even as they're waiting for more news on the fire. They'll also be less cranky if they're out of the cold and have someplace to go. Let's direct them there."

Just as I was saying this, one of my colleagues in New York posts on our crisis communications portal:

Jim, you need to look at this.

Indeed.

The message contains a link to a news report from the AP that includes a picture from well within the facility—a close-up of a firefighter battling the blaze, taken from directly behind, with rubble all around and the flames practically leaping toward the camera. We just learned the fire was manageable and coming under control, but from the photo, you would have thought the gates of Hell just opened.

Not a great thing for my client. I explain to them what we just found and get the full story from my client.

As it turns out, in the early stages of the fire, an AP photographer simply walked onto the grounds while the initial fire trucks arriving at the scene took the full attention of the guard. The result was a photo from the site that, while dramatic, was not representative of what was occurring.

And just as I'm pondering this information, a new email comes from the security director (who was still on our call, but was multitasking): The fire is now indeed under control.

I post back to my colleague:

> Get on the phone with the Associated Press. Tell them that if they're going to run a photo like that, they at least have to include a caption that states that the fire is now under control, and that there have been no injuries.

Back to the teleconference line: "Okay," I say, "we need someone on that scene to find the photographer who is on site. Speak to him or her, explain the fire is now under control and ask that they update their photographs in the web version of the story—even if it's not hardly as dramatic—in the interest of good journalism." (Journalists usually respond to appeals to good journalism . . . most of the time.)

"Then ask the photographer if she'd like some coffee," I add, "and very politely get her into that media staging area."

It is now 6:46 a.m.

❋ ❋ ❋

In Chapter 4, you will learn about a system of responding to crisis that we call the CIR approach, which stands for Control, Information, Response®. It is a system we felt so strongly about that we registered the service mark—hence the® symbol.

For the purposes of this inaugural chapter, as we move through our example (and others), you can see the outlines of the CIR system taking shape. As the fire raged at that industrial facility in New Jersey, we needed to get *control* over the crisis site and proper *information* about this crisis, in order to formulate the appropriate response.

Ensuring the proper information flow takes two basic forms:

- We needed information from the scene in order to accurately understand the situation at the site. This information came directly from the

General Counsel and the PR director for the company, via teleconference and email.

- We needed to understand what the rest of the world was learning, thinking, and feeling about this crisis. Hence, at the same time I was on the phone with my client, my colleagues were collaborating through our crisis communications portal to ensure that a steady stream of information regarding public reaction to the fire was collected, analyzed, and understood.

I will discuss these topics again later in this book, but the important point to remember is that by quickly establishing control over the crisis site and information about what is happening on-scene, we gave ourselves time—and time is of the essence in virtually every form of crisis communications response. This statement is true whether you are in the midst of a sudden expected crisis like a fire at your facility or a growing crisis like an Internet rumor campaign or legal investigation.

The Fumbled Response

Why is the element of time critical? Because in nearly all cases, it is not the crisis but the response in the initial stages that determines whether the event will cause long-term damage to a company and its reputation.

Specifically, without **Control** over the crisis scene (whether real or virtual) and without the proper flow of **Information** to inform a coordinated **Response**, you create an atmosphere that allows a crisis to flourish. Hence, those key initial moments determine whether a crisis blows up, or the initial flames of crisis are blown out.

This is not just opinion: There is remarkable evidence to back this up. Consider recent "big name" crises that have dominated the news over the past several years: the BP oil spill, Volkswagen's diesel emissions scandal, Toyota's sudden acceleration case, the GM ignition switch recalls, and Target data breach. What all of these crises have in common is that the initial response by the organization was . . . well, awful. The fumbled response was like pouring gasoline on a fire: It fed the flames of public outrage, allowing the heat surrounding the event to rise to uncontrollable levels.

Now it is true that each of these events was big, with widespread damage and a large universe of victims. These crises certainly would have attracted attention regardless of the company's actual response. But what becomes startlingly clear when you look closely at these examples is that, in each case, the company in question dropped the ball at the outset. They fumbled the initial public response, which allowed the crisis to gain momentum and ultimately thrust the events squarely into the center of public consciousness.

Then, after a week or two or three of inept response, each company got its act together and began to repair the initial reputational damage (including, in some cases, by bringing in a new outside crisis communications team to help).

In fact, I would posit that, in each of these cases, the initial fumbled response was the *determining factor* in the crisis becoming a sustained national news event.

Need proof? Consider these news excerpts, each appearing in major media stories in the first weeks after the initial event triggered the crisis:

- "Target, the nation's No. 2 retailer, was initially caught flat-footed, several analysts say, when a computer security blog broke news last week that thieves had stolen credit card information from an estimated 40 million customers. Since then, the Minneapolis-based company has launched a fierce public relations counterattack . . . "[1] (written eight days after the crisis);

- "Senior executives from the Canadian and U.S. operations of Toyota Motor Corp. will take to the television airwaves this morning . . . Toyota has been criticized by safety groups and consumers for not acting quickly enough and not providing enough information about when the vehicles will be fixed"[2] (again, written eight days after the news breaks of Toyota's sudden acceleration recalls);

- " . . . after an initial bobble in which the company downplayed the size of the leak at about 1,000 barrels a day, BP appeared to be doing many things well"[3] . . . (written 11 days after the explosion); and

- "Volkswagen . . . said on Wednesday that Stephan Grühsem, head of communications for the group, would leave the company immediately . . . Hans-Gerd Bode, previously head of public relations at Porsche, will take over as head of communications for the parent company"[4] (written 12 days after scandal broke).

Indeed, the more you look at large, headline-grabbing crises—the types of events that are thrust to the "front-burner" in the days and weeks after the initial flashpoint—the more you realize that the dominant characteristic of such crises is not the nature, or even the severity, of the event itself, but rather the disorganized, inept initial response. *It is the case virtually every time.*

Perhaps, though, you still argue that, given the severity of the events, even the best response wouldn't have made a difference. The problem with this view is that—both in my experience and based on our research—it's just not true. For example, in the automotive field, for every Toyota sudden acceleration or GM recall, there's another crisis that didn't generate nearly the same amount of public attention. Although the GM ignition recall is the largest recall in history, for example, you may be surprised to learn that the Toyota sudden acceleration recall is only the sixth largest. What is the second largest? A 2009 Ford recall over a cruise-control switch prone to spontaneous combustion, which was under way even as the Toyota crisis was unfolding on CNN and in the pages of *The New York Times* and *The Wall Street Journal*.[5] Never heard of it? Neither had I until I started writing this book.

Or consider the 2013 Target data breach, which cost the CEO his job and became the poster child for data breaches worldwide. In the months after news of that crisis broke, Home Depot announced its own data breach, which was more than 40 percent larger. The Target breach occurred first, of course, which added media interest as a result, but this doesn't mitigate the fact that Home Depot's proper handling of public communications during their data breach crisis kept that crisis from spinning out of control.

Indeed, I've searched and am unable to find a full-blown crisis in recent years that didn't have, among its initial elements, a fumbled response. Maybe one exists, and maybe someday there will be a more empirical study on the relationship between a fumbled response and the severity of a corporate crisis. In the meantime, all evidence points to a dramatic connection between the two.

Further to this point: I can tell you with complete certainty that there are many, many sensitive situations and crises—including those my firm has been involved with—that you haven't heard about. Not because these crises didn't warrant your attention or that they didn't rise to the right "level," but because the situation was handled so well during the initial stages that public interest was tamped down. It just never went anywhere.

Yet, it seems that, in each of these big, front-page crises, the company in question fails to learn the lessons of those that have gone before. These companies think they can continue doing things the way they have in the past, the way BP did, the way Volkswagen did, the way General Motors did, and so on . . . and so on . . . and so on.

You'd think large companies would be smarter. I can also tell you, though, based on my experience working with companies of all sizes over the years, that larger companies don't necessarily do things better than smaller companies. In fact, for reasons of both organization and cultural inertia, sometimes they do things much worse.

What can a company and its Chief Crisis Officer do? Step One, I believe, is to *learn*. Learn the ways in which your organization is susceptible to doing things the wrong way. Learn that there are better ways to do things: strategies that can minimize the chances that a crisis will spin out of control. Learn to put the leadership and structure in place to do things better.

At its essence, this is a risk management issue: To minimize the risk of a crisis that can do long-term, sometimes permanent damage to a company, its reputation, its valuation—sometimes even its existence—organizations must develop the systems and structures *now* to effectively respond during the initial phases. In the same way you wouldn't neglect insurance coverage as a way to mitigate risk, you must take steps now to ensure you don't fumble the initial day . . . two days . . . two weeks . . . of that institutional crisis that is, inevitably, on the horizon. Learn the lessons of those who have gone before.

Yet I suppose there will still be doubters, and on one level it's a very difficult thing to prove—that perhaps things would not have been as bad for BP had they not handled the initial stages of their crisis in such a fumbling manner. After all, oil was spilling into the Gulf of Mexico at an unprecedented rate. The truth is: We'll never know for sure. But here's what we do know: The one constant we have in all of these cases is an initial response that allowed the crisis to fester. And the lawyer in me says that's persuasive evidence of a causal connection. Case closed.

❄ ❄ ❄

Now back to our regularly scheduled crisis.

It was now nearing 7:00 a.m., and while the fire at the New Jersey facility was technically considered under control by officials at the scene, flames could still be seen from the newschoppers circling overhead, with heavy smoke wafting over New York Harbor during a busy morning commute. Even as I was still on the phone with the company's General Counsel, the head of public relations, and the company's security director, my colleagues were speaking with other personnel in the company's public relations department, collecting the relevant facts to create a public statement. This statement would serve as the core of our initial public response, and in various forms be sent to media, uploaded to the company's website, converted to talking points and an email to employees, and boosted on social media. This response would ensure that the public would have at least some basic facts and information about this very prominent event blanketing the harbor with a dark, smoky cloud at the start of a Monday rush hour.

Our audience for this message included media, regulators, politicians, customers, company employees, and local fire officials (who we were sure to thank). Everyone needed to know that, while the situation was certainly dramatic and visual, it was under control. There were no injuries or loss of

life. That all would return to normal shortly. And that the company understood the seriousness of the incident and was doing everything in its power
to respond.

Thankfully, after years of handling these types of incidents, we have statements like these on our servers and readily available. Moreover, given that
we often are thrust into crises at a moment's notice, we've become very adept
at tracking down a template and quickly editing it for the current purpose
when the need arises.*

Again, the need for speed predominates effective response: By 7:00 a.m.,
four different media outlets had posted web reports on the fire. Thanks to
our contacts and media databases, we knew exactly who these media outlets
were and how to reach them. On our crisis response portal, a draft of the
public statement my team created had been uploaded. After reviewing the
final draft on my smartphone, I called the CEO directly, read it to him, and
got a quick approval. After a few changes, we were off.

By 7:10 a.m., the Associated Press and each of the other news outlets that
initially covered the story, including the three media outlets that sent cameras
and/or newschoppers to the scene, received our statement. They now knew
that the fire was under control. They knew that no one had been injured
or killed and that we had publicly thanked the local fire department for its
quick response. By about 7:15 a.m., all four news outlets were reporting this
information prominently in their stories.

In the end, it was all about *rapid response*: understanding before the event
occurred what needed to be done—and who needed to do it—and executing quickly and efficiently despite the chaotic nature of the crisis unfolding
before us.

Everybody Knows Better; Everybody Starts Too Late

Why aren't companies more skilled at this? In my experience, hubris is certainly one reason.

If you examine a crisis that's spinning out of control, you'll often find a
situation where two things happened: (1) The company in question thought
it knew better and didn't need a plan . . . didn't need advice . . . didn't need

---

* As you'll learn in other parts of this book, we also recently created a separate software company,
CrisisResponsePro, which provides many of the functions laid out in this example. Included in
our software, for example, is a database of more than 10,000 public statements issued by other
companies in crisis situations, easily sortable, searchable, and available at a moment's notice.

to be ready; and (2) as a result, they started too late with a sharp, cogent and effective response.

In fact, many successful organizations I work with in these situations started out the process feeling that preparing for a crisis and responding quickly and effectively out of the gate didn't apply to them. They all had some type of reason:

- The company isn't big enough, or didn't face these sorts of crisis situations often enough, to be concerned about effective response.
- Their issue is just too complex for pre-planning.
- Their industry is already too maligned; therefore, effective crisis communications wouldn't have any real impact (or, alternately, their industry is so highly regarded that they can withstand any attack).
- The company or executive in charge was once in a similar situation—a year, or 10 years, or three jobs ago—and it went away on its own. So they think that, because they got lucky once, it's far more effective to bury issues like these rather than confront them. Hell, it worked before!

Yes, many, many companies out there have believed this . . . and they've all been wrong. In my experience: Every. Single. Time.

- They were wrong about what was needed during the initial stages of the crisis.
- They were wrong about being proactive and heading off negative stories.
- They were wrong about the impact that being proactive could have on the course of events.

They were wrong about all of it.

The fact is this: You *can* prepare effectively. You *can* anticipate scenarios that might affect your particular organization. You *can* explain even the most difficult issues successfully to your target audience.

In other words, you *can* do it.

Too many companies take the approach that if a crisis is going to occur, it's going to occur. It's our turn. We'll just keep our heads down and suffer through it and see what we can do to rehabilitate ourselves afterward: Maybe we'll sponsor a golf tournament or make a donation to a children's charity.

This begs the question: Why? Why is there an unwillingness to accept that proper crisis communications techniques are worth the effort? Why don't companies believe that sending such messages to the right audiences, in the right way, and at the right time can have a real impact, often making the difference between a crisis contained and one that spins out of control?

Part of this willful ignorance is basic human nature: Company leaders don't want to be going through a crisis. They want the crisis to go away. There is a natural human tendency to think that if you ignore something long enough, it will go away. You want to put the issue to the side, say and do as little as possible, and go back to the positive stuff—the things you like to work on. Maybe you'll get lucky and you won't have to deal with the issue at all. Maybe that smoldering ember won't turn into a raging fire. Maybe it will be extinguished before it spreads.

Well, maybe . . . but are you really going to build your organization's risk management strategy on *maybes*?

This type of thinking is the equivalent of not going to the doctor for fear the doctor might find something wrong. Clearly, this is not a great way to safeguard your health or the health of your family members and loved ones. Yet, in the organizational context, sometimes we don't take some simple preventative steps to ensure long-term health.

In the end, I can only assure you to the best of my ability, based on a quarter century of experience: This stuff works. Crisis communications planning and proper execution during a crisis can make a tremendous difference. It won't solve all your problems, but if you are properly prepared, you'll put your organization in a better position for handling them. You'll be ready to give the proper level of attention to crises as soon as they crop up (or, even better, when they appear about to) rather than ignoring them until they spin out of control. Again, I emphasize that this doesn't mean you come out guns-a-blazing for every minor issue facing your company. Sometimes you can do more harm than good that way. But it does mean you take the situation seriously and put the proper protocols in place to ensure the appropriate level of response to minimize the crisis event.

The Myth of Absolute Control

My nine-year-old son is extremely bright. Sometimes there are downsides to this.

Recently, for example, he's become aware of mortality, and consequently, my mortality. He's obsessed, in other words, with me dying. Constant questions about heart attacks, lung disease, and family history.

Finally, I had to have a talk with him, and since I couldn't tell him definitively that I wasn't going to die any time soon, all I could do is appeal to his actuarial side.

"Conall," I said, "you've got to play the odds. I'm still relatively young, relatively in shape, have never smoked, no history of cancer in the family. While there's no guarantee, it's highly unlikely I'm going to die anytime soon."

His face brightened as I said this and I knew I was getting through.

I saved my best point for last.

"In fact, I'd say it's far more likely I get struck by lightning leaving the house than die of some disease in the near future."

He stared at me for a moment.

"Wait," he said, "you can get struck by lightning just leaving the house?"

Back to square one.*

Here's my point: You can't control everything in life, but you can play the percentages. The more you set up conditions where things will naturally move your way when bad things happen, the more likely you are to get a proper reaction from your various audiences and emerge from the crisis relatively unscathed. Hence, the importance of establishing some level of control over what is happening during the earliest phases of the crisis by:

- Selecting a leader—a Chief Crisis Officer—to lead a company's response as events unfold (you'll meet your Chief Crisis Officer in the next chapter);
- Surrounding your Chief Crisis Officer with the best possible core crisis communication team, ready to respond when a crisis hits;
- Deciding to create a crisis plan—a structure and roadmap for responding in times of crisis; and
- Preparing templates, messages, and other resources so you have a playbook to work from when action starts.

In the end, you are using effective crisis communications response to minimize risk and limit the long-term reputational damage from a crisis, whether an exploding crisis that thrusts you immediately into the public spotlight or an unfolding crisis that builds up over time. This is exactly the structure we had in place for the example I've weaved throughout this chapter. By being ready and having the tools at hand to respond, we created conditions where reputational risk could be minimized through a combination of speed, structure, and leadership.

---

* Now, in the off chance I am, in fact, dead as you are reading this, know two things: I lived a very good life...and that my last thought probably was: "Damn, that kid was right!"

Inevitably, you will find this foundational structure present in all good crisis communications response, and absent in examples where a crisis is mishandled.

❄ ❄ ❄

Back in New Jersey, it took a full day for the fire to be completely extinguished and a few days after that for fire investigators to determine the cause. We used the company's website to periodically update the public as the fire was being doused—preparing a total of three additional web updates in the first 24 hours, then reporting back when investigators reached their conclusion: A faulty switch in recently purchased industrial equipment was the culprit. Many of these core messages were converted to communications that could be used to reach out directly to local community leaders, nearby residents, and other "stakeholders" whose perceptions would be formed based not on the event itself, but by how forthcoming and helpful the company was in response.

This effort didn't end when the flames were snuffed out and the investigator's report was delivered. It continued for several weeks, as new facts came to light regarding our company's response and new parties became involved in the accident's aftermath. Specifically, those parties included regulators, politicians, and plaintiffs' lawyers in the surrounding community. And there's a lesson in this as well.

As you will learn in Chapter 6, even with the most "physical" of crises, such as an explosion, a plant fire, an industrial accident, or similar incident, there tends to be a legal element that can continue the story for weeks (if not months and years) after the initial event takes place. Sometimes, parties only peripherally related to the crisis itself want to keep the fire raging (metaphorically, of course) because it serves a broader political or policy interest they are trying to advance.

In our New Jersey example, the first inkling of trouble came after a short news report on a local website suggested that the company did not call the fire department quickly enough after the fire occurred. The publication speculated that this was because employees were trying to put the fire out themselves so they wouldn't get in trouble. This, it was alleged, is what allowed the fire to burn out of control for so long. Nearby community groups, who were never keen on the idea of an industrial facility in their town in the first place, seized on this information as evidence of the company's malfeasance. They started fanning their own flames with town officials, state prosecutors, and anyone else who would listen.

The problem for our client was that none of these new reports were true. In fact, the plant employee on the ground called 911 immediately from his cell phone. Unfortunately, he lived in Brooklyn, whereas the fire was in New

Jersey. The 911 operator, from another state, failed to relay the information in a timely fashion to local dispatchers in New Jersey. There was no intent to cover up the fire.

Local politicians will always try to score a few points if they can. In this case, they tried to make it seem as if there was some sort of duplicity by the company in the initial reporting of the fire. It took us several days to tamp down this false story through a series of personal meetings with elected officials in the region and by speaking to key reporters and editors in local media to explain the facts and dispel the rumors. Eventually, this erroneous story was corrected, and the controversy went away.

Then there was the OSHA investigation of the fire and the threat of a lawsuit by a local environmental lawyer alleging that the company's fire safety protocols were not up-to-date before the fire occurred. That lawsuit, as it turned out, was never filed—primarily because our public relations efforts convinced the plaintiff's lawyer that there was little to gain. After more facts came out, it was clear that not only had the company been keeping up with its fire protocols, but that fire officials from the local town were at the facility several weeks earlier conducting inspections that went quite well. (I believe the act of thanking the fire department early on paid benefits in this regard, since they backed the company quite publicly on this point). We then pushed this angle of the story hard in local media reports, so that the public—and the plaintiff's lawyers itching to force a big settlement—would realize that this argument was a nonstarter.

The overriding lesson here is that the core crisis communications response team remained vigilant and effective even after the initial crisis subsided. The rapid response protocol remained in place and handled each of these issues effectively and efficiently as they occurred. As we learned more substantive information regarding each element of the controversy, we updated our core messages regularly. We made this information available to stakeholders, including the general public, to ensure that no one felt the company was hiding anything. We described the cause of the fire when fire investigators finished their work, explained that air quality tests of the surrounding area indicated there was no lasting impact, and that all damage was to company property and not to employees, outside property, or firefighting equipment. Significantly, we were careful *not* to do this in a way that would create more issues and make the story bigger. Rather, we made this information public in a nuanced manner. In other words, we got the information to the right audiences, in the right form, and at the right time to ensure maximum positive impact without broadening the overall reputational risk.

It was an intense few weeks for the company, but because we were able to marshal the facts early, we could prepare the right response quickly and get it to important audiences early. This ensured that the crisis had no "legs," despite the follow-up news and threat of a lawsuit.

Structure, Leadership, Logistics

I use this example to make an important point about crisis management, a lesson that is applicable whether you're a midsized company whose plant has just caught fire, or BP, whose oil rig just blew up in the Gulf of Mexico. We will explore this point throughout the pages of *Chief Crisis Officer*, and it can be best summed up as follows:

> *Structure, leadership, and logistics make the difference between a crisis that is contained and one that spins out of control.*

What is clear in our example is that the damage to the company was minimized primarily because: (1) We had worked with company executives for quite some time—we all worked well together and knew our respective roles and gelled seamlessly when the crisis broke; and (2) We all happened to be available to devote our time to the issue as it was breaking.

Thus, if you look at this example, you begin to see the outlines of what is necessary to effectively respond in the event of a crisis:

- First, you need someone to respond: your **Chief Crisis Officer.**
- Your Chief Crisis Officer needs a team around him or her: your **core crisis communications team**, with resources ready to respond effectively (which is why the **crisis plan** is so important).
- Your team needs **Control** over the site of the crisis, be it real or virtual, and **Information** from the front lines that provides them with an accurate picture of what is actually occurring.
- Your organization also needs the right messages for an effective **Response** to the various public audiences that have an interest in your issue or event.

These are the basic elements of crisis communications, and the types of things that you are going to learn about in this book.

Now in the example above, the organization had no dedicated internal person to serve in the role of Chief Crisis Officer, so it fell to me and my team. The company also didn't have an approved crisis plan in place. Again, they had us. We had the knowledge regarding how to respond, as well as the tools and resources at our fingertips to construct both an effective response plan and effective messages. We had the lists of media, local officials, and other key audiences and the appropriate methodologies to disseminate the company's response quickly and efficiently. Because we work closely with this company on other matters (and we have worked with many other companies on similar crises), we were a living, breathing crisis communications plan at their disposal.

That said, here's where the company in question took a huge gamble: In this example, we succeeded in no small part because we all happened to be available and ready to jump on the assignment when the crisis occurred. Additionally, my crisis communications team already had the technology in place to collaborate and start the flow of information immediately. It didn't hurt that we been through events like this dozens of times and had access to archives statements, checklists, and other materials to ensure that we had the right response, the right messages, the right talking points, and other materials . . . right out of the gate.

To a certain extent in this situation, my client got lucky. But as Branch Rickey, famed president and general manager of the Brooklyn Dodgers once stated (I believe quoting the British man of letters John Milton): "Luck is the residue of design."

So as we move further through this book we will design structures to ensure good luck. We will institutionalize the processes I've described, so that a positive crisis response is not left to chance or to the right people being available at the right time. This is the goal of *Chief Crisis Officer*: to put the plumbing in place now to ensure that when it is time to respond, you're ready.

Because what I really want you to know about crisis communications is this: It's all about structure, organization, and leadership. It's not about spin-doctoring, cute slogans, Twitter campaigns, putting your CEO in a YouTube video, or finding a sympathetic reporter who will write a puff piece about your company. These are all good tactics in certain circumstances, of course. But not a strategy.

And strategy, structure, and leadership make all the difference.

Action Points

- Crisis communications can be defined as ensuring an effective communications response to an unstable or critical state of affairs that threatens to have an undesirable or negative impact on an organization's reputation, business, or goals.

- There are many different types of organizational crises, but for simplicity's sake, it is best to define a crisis as either "exploding" or "unfolding."

- Strategy, structure, and leadership are key elements of crisis communications response: You need a Chief Crisis Officer and a core crisis communications team in place well before a crisis occurs.
- Speed of response is often the determining factor between a crisis that is managed and one that threatens to cause widespread reputation damage to the organization, its mission, and its goals.

The Chief Crisis Officer
and the Team

The premise underlying this book is that putting together a proper system for pub-lic response in the face of crisis events requires not only the right tools and cri-sis communications team, but also the right leader for the task: the Chief Crisis Officer.

Who should serve in the role, and what are the ideal qualifications? Is this person a member of the internal public relations team, a lawyer, or someone else? Is the Chief Crisis Officer the same person every time?

Well, here's the bad news: It depends. Each organization is structured dif-ferently, has a different culture, and is home to many types of professionals with differing skills, experience, and temperament. The Chief Crisis Officer may not always be the head of PR or assistant General Counsel . . . but it could be. Therefore, one of the key challenges lies in identifying the right person within your organization for the role and giving that person the tools and authority to act. The good news? In this chapter, we're will discuss precisely how you should evaluate your team to decide who might be the ideal candidate for Chief Crisis Officer in your organization and who, despite outward appearances, is ill-suited for the role.

The client, a major manufacturer in Phoenix, was in big trouble. The company's crisis communications response was floundering in the face of a particularly sensitive product issue. Despite the skills and qualifica-tions of its team, the company was having an enormously difficult time responding effectively; indeed, it appeared that the company's response was making the situation worse. Time was of the essence, so I caught the last flight out of New York on a Tuesday and arrived at their offices Wednesday morning.

From the time I entered the company's cavernous boardroom to a meeting already in progress, I could see what was wrong.

First, I couldn't find a seat. (You'll understand why that's important in a moment.) As a general premise, let me point out that, as a consultant, I've been amazed over the years by how you much you learn about an organization and its problems *not* from the facts and issues, but from the client itself—how the company is organized, how executives interact, the decision-making process, and the lines of authority. It's these little things that tell the story—particularly during a high-pressure event like a crisis—and if you are perceptive, these vignettes can show you exactly what's wrong with the organizational response and what to do about it.

This was one of those learning experiences.

As I entered the conference room—and a junior staffer scrambled to find me a chair—I noticed the following: The company had a large group assembled, a large room to work in, and a big white board to write stuff on. They were engaged in a wide-ranging discussion, with a host of divergent views on how to handle the issue, and had come up with a series of whiteboard "take-aways." But 90 minutes into the meeting, they still had no plan of action.

We didn't have a crisis communications team. We had a seminar.

More than this, what I heard over and over during the meeting was:

"Well, we'll need 17's buy-in on this."

"I don't think 17 is going to go for that."

"Tom and his team on 17 will need to think about this carefully . . . "

"17" meant the seventeenth floor, where the CEO and senior executives had their offices. It became apparent that no one with decision-making authority was actually in the room.

At the end of the meeting, the assistant General Counsel, who was more or less chairing the proceedings, stood up and said: "Okay, so we're going to need to get someone to write this up, to see if we have approval from 17 before proceeding."

All the while, the clock kept ticking.

Leadership and the Authority to Act Bring Good Results

You can see the problem. My new client didn't have a crisis communications team capable of action, nor a strong leader with the ability to execute.

This company did not need better messages, better training for its spokespeople, or advanced social media strategies; it needed a Chief Crisis Officer.

Throughout this chapter, we will examine the need for the skills of the Chief Crisis Officer, how you can identify these skills, and how you can put the structure in place to ensure success. We'll look at the various elements and characteristics that are important in the selection and development of the Chief Crisis Officer, as well as the types of people, characteristics and skills to avoid.

But let's begin with our thesis, one that answers the following questions: Who is this leader, the Chief Crisis Officer? What qualities does he or she need? What is the reporting structure and team needed? Who should have the authority to act when responding?

I summarize the principles I will discuss in this chapter as follows:

> *Your Chief Crisis Officer should be highly flexible and ready to respond at a moment's notice. He or she must be a decisive individual who can work across organizational lines and have the authority—and willingness—to act. This person must be an experienced communicator, with skills adaptable to communicating with sensitivity and nuance before a variety of audiences.*

This sounds simple, right? But it is remarkable to me how often organizations go astray in both the selection of the core crisis communications team and its leader.

Lines of Communication

Let's start with lines of communications. Your Chief Crisis Officer and his or her team should have the ability to communicate with key decision makers throughout the organization. In most cases, this will include the CEO, Chief Operating Officer (COO), the General Counsel, and other members of the so-called C-Suite.

The team needs to be small enough to make decisions rapidly and communicate with each other directly and decisively. In other words, you should aim for a small action team rather than (as in the example above) a large debating society. The problem with a large team is obvious: With large groups, you often have too many opinions coming at you from too many angles—some of which are very good, but some of which were voiced so that the attendee could show he or she was listening and contributing. I'm all for input, of course, but without a tight, well-oiled team at the top, you often wind up with an unwieldy hodge-podge of ideas and competing agendas, with no roadmap for an actual response.

Hence the need for a limited group of team members—the "core crisis communications team"—headed by a clearly identified leader who can turn analysis into action.

The Chief Crisis Officer

We will look more closely at the core crisis communications team toward the end of this chapter. Let's turn now, though, to the person who should lead them: the Chief Crisis Officer. At its most elemental, your organization will want a Chief Crisis Officer with the:

1. Authority to act;
2. Willingness to act; and
3. Background, experience, and communications skills to act effectively.

By examining each of these criteria, we can further flesh out the Chief Crisis Officer concept and the unique blend of skills, experience, and perspective needed to make such a leader a success.

The Authority to Act

An interesting aspect of the example that opened this chapter is that no one in the crisis "War Room" actually had the ability to make decisions on behalf of the corporation. All they could do was lay out the problem, discuss the various options for response (sometimes *ad nauseam*, given the size of the group), and "paper it up" for review by the CEO and her executive team. The higher-ups would have to review the summary prepared by the group, maybe ask a few of their own questions (which would need to be routed to the right person on the extended crisis team for response in some cases), then either approve or reject the proposed action, or send the summary back for further refinement. If the ideas were rejected, that big, unwieldy crisis team would have to reassemble, tailor their ideas to better meet the new parameters established by the C-suite (or come up with new ideas entirely), then run them up the flagpole again.

This sort of system may work in other areas of operations and organizational management—when planning new product strategy, for example, or a marketing or advertising campaign—but it can be deadly when responding in a crisis situation.

Why? Time is a big reason. In most crisis communications environments, you must act *now* to ensure that the crisis doesn't accelerate to the point that it is spinning out of control. Once a crisis is unfolding exponentially before you, it can be very hard to catch up. So if you are waiting for word from the CEO's office before executing each step in your response, you're almost guaranteeing failure. You don't have the time, and you can't get it back once the events have overtaken you.

More than just the time element, though, a flaw in this system is that the party with the ultimate authority to act isn't even in the room to fully consider the various options—and no two-page summary will accurately convey all the nuances and strategic thinking behind the development of an action plan. If a crisis team works in one part of the building, but approval for the response lies somewhere else (e.g., floors away or even in a headquarters location in another city), the situation ends up like a big game of "telephone," where one person whispers a message to another, which is then passed through a line of players until the last announces his or her version of the message to the entire group. Inevitably, the final message bears little resemblance to the original. In the context of crisis communications response, if an actual decision maker is not in the room when the crisis response team is meeting, the final strategy laid out in the two-page summary may be a mere shadow of the actual plan the team discussed.

Again, in operational decision making in other areas of corporate life—where there is at least some luxury of time—this may not be a problem, since summaries can be longer and more detailed, accompanied by in-person meetings to explain the thinking behind the plan, or sent back (as described above) for further delineation several times before a final course of action is determined. In most crisis communications response, the luxury of time just doesn't exist. This tends to be true whether the crisis is *exploding* or *unfolding* (as we've learned in Chapter 1). Although an unfolding crisis like an investigation or legal proceeding may happen over time, events along the way tend to be sudden, immediate, and often unexpected. Thus, they often require immediate response, even if the current issue is only a small element of broader crisis (e.g., a new legal filing in a court case, an unannounced visit to one of your local offices from SEC investigators, or a new series of protests from animal rights advocates over a certain issue). Certainly, "long-tail" crises occur in the life of every organization, to be sure, but each "event" in the unfolding drama is usually time-sensitive in its own right. Hence, the need for speed exists in all manner of crisis communications response.

Consequently, this is why having the authority to act is so important. It comes down to efficiency and effectiveness: Your decision-making processes during a crisis must be *efficient* so you can respond during the time allotted, and *effective* to have the desired impact.

Authority at the Right Level

Consider the concept of "command and control" in military parlance. While we tend to think of the military as the ultimate "top-down" organization, over time military science has engendered a highly developed system for ensuring that decision-making authority during military operations is as close to the battlefield as possible. This process developed historically to minimize time delays, limit misinformation and erroneous reporting, and otherwise mitigate the effect of the "fog of war" in the midst of contentious battles. This need to provide decision-making authority to the commanders actually on the field was particularly acute in the days before advance technologies, networked communications, real-time images of battlefields—a time when generals miles away from the action could only guess what was happening on the front lines. Within clearly established guidelines, military leaders delegated authority for leading the battle to the battlefield commanders who were on the front lines and could execute based on complete information.*

In crisis communications response, authority to act is key, just as it is in the military context. Thus authority is something your organization's Chief Crisis Officer desperately needs.

My CEO Won't Cede This Authority!

At this point, you may be thinking one of two things. First: "There's no way my CEO could be a participant in every crisis communications War Room meeting." Congratulations—you are correct. Second (and this is the more dangerous alternative): "There's no way my CEO would be willing to give up involvement in decisions that might have a huge impact on the company and its future."

This latter mindset is the one we're going to work on. The solution lies in proper buy-in beforehand of the well-constructed crisis plan and the execution of that plan from the "front lines" during the heat of the battle.

This is not to suggest that your CEO and other top leaders have no input or role in crisis communications response, but rather that an agreement should exist during the planning process as to the proper role of the CEO and the authority he or she is delegating to the Chief Crisis Officer.

---

* Interestingly, however, as in all areas, technological changes on the battlefield are not without their own challenges. Consider: New technologies certainly enabled a powerful revolution to occur in military capabilities, allowing senior commanders to see the battlefield up close though miles—or even continents—away. But these new technologies have also enabled old trends of command interference, even taking them to new extremes of micromanagement. Too frequently, apparently, generals at a distance use technology to insert themselves into matters formerly handled by those on the scene and at ranks several layers of command below them. "It's like crack [cocaine] for generals," says Chuck Kamps, a professor of joint warfare at the Air Command and Staff College speaking of battlefield-viewing technology. "It gives them an unprecedented ability to meddle in mission commanders' jobs." Peter Singer, "Tactical Generals: Leaders, Technology, and the Perils," *Air & Space Power Journal,* Summer 2009.

Work the Plan

For as you'll see in our next chapter, every organization should have a crisis plan in place well before the crisis hits. This plan, in broad strokes, lays out exactly who has the authority to act in various circumstances and what authority that person has in those situations. In other words, when a crisis occurs, you shouldn't have to think about what the plan is, and who should be in what meetings to make which decisions, after the battle has started. No one should be making the plan up out of whole cloth as the crisis is unfolding—that's like a football team making up the plays *after* they've taken the field! If you put together the right plan initially, there's less reason for the CEO or other senior executives to insert themselves right into the center of the action while the play is in progress.

In addition, in a well thought-out plan, the right person with authority to make individual decisions during a crisis will be in constant communications with the CEO and/or other senior leaders on "big picture" issues as appropriate. I've done this many times in crisis situations, where I am the person with the direct line to the CEO. If anything comes up that needs his or her direct input, I quickly hail the CEO via phone or email and get clarification—usually immediately and in real time while the crisis communications team is deliberating. If the Chief Crisis Officer or a member of the team has the proper relationship and lines of communication with the leader of the organization, a streamlined process for "command and control" can be maintained. As long as there is a clear understanding as to the authority of the Chief Crisis Officer—which decisions can be made at the crisis team level and which require input from the higher ups—the system tends to work pretty well. (Again, technology can greatly help with real-time communication and collaboration.)

One final point regarding the authority to act, serving as a word of caution to CEOs in particular: You must restrain from abandoning a well-conceived crisis communications plan and jumping into the battle as a "field general" the moment the going gets tough. Everyone on the team—from the CEO down—must understand that crises bring bad news. A crisis is an inherently negative situation. As we learned in the Introduction, it's a mess—the only question is: "How big?" So, my dear CEO, don't charge into the midst of a properly conceived crisis response after the first few bad stories or social media posts are written, thinking that you must take over the team to make things right—that is a recipe for disaster. There is no better way to undermine your Chief Crisis Officer and ensure chaos reigns as the crisis unfolds. I give you this advice from the heart, based on many years of experience: Stay the course, remain in communication with your crisis team, but don't try to take over if you've got a qualified leader executing a good plan. Instead, as the saying goes: Work the plan.

Willingness to Act

"I was going to get involved in this, but quite frankly it's not the type of thing I see any value in sticking my neck out for."
—Corporate lawyer with a media background, when asked why he didn't volunteer for the crisis communications "rapid response" team.

The Chief Crisis Officer, once imbued with the authority to make certain decisions in the heat of a smoldering (or raging) crisis, must be willing to put that authority to work. Sometimes, that's easier said than done.

Once you have the authority to act, you must be willing to use it. This sounds obvious, but often during a crisis, an individual with the authority to act won't—for reasons of temperament, culture, or simple self-preservation. If you don't act when you should during a crisis event, you can usually expect the situation to get worse.

Consider the quote that opens this section: A well-qualified company lawyer in the sports industry, during a particularly sensitive matter, was not willing to step up and be the lead in crisis communications response, because—let's face it—there was nothing in it for him. He had nothing to gain, from a career perspective by taking such a bold, difficult assignment and everything to lose. It is a cold, hard fact that in many corporate environments, it is not the person who sticks out his or her neck that gets ahead, but rather the person who keeps his or her head down. In my own cynical view, this type of career playbook looks like this:

- Reinforce the beliefs of the higher-ups at every turn;
- Echo conventional wisdom;
- Minimize personal and professional risk in the actions you take; and
- Don't suggest bold steps if there might be blowback.

Let me put it to you simply: This mindset is deadly when confronting a crisis. The right Chief Crisis Officer is never reckless or foolhardy. He or she doesn't make moves for the sake of making them. A good Chief Crisis Officer doesn't take action for action's sake. In most circumstances, the ideal Chief Crisis Officer works to mitigate the negative ramifications of a reputational crisis rather than throwing the ball downfield in a reckless hope for victory. *But* the right Chief Crisis Officer acts when it's important, whether it involves sticking his or her neck out on an issue or not.

Because here's the reality: Anyone who has been tasked to respond in a crisis situation is facing an inherently negative event where the best outcome is minimizing the damage. In other areas of corporate communication, this is often not the case. Engaged in a product launch or acquisition? That's an inherently positive event. Managing a crisis? In most cases, there's no way the organization is coming out of this well. This leaves anyone in that role open to criticism regardless of his or her efforts and the ultimate result. Your Chief Crisis Officer needs a thick skin, a confidence that what they are doing works, and a willingness to act in the face of second-guessing.*

The Impact of Training and Experience on Perspective

Beyond this, there are other reasons that particular executives, though qualified in their areas of expertise, might be ill-suited for the role of Chief Crisis Officer. For example, educational training and experience can often make an otherwise highly competent candidate exactly the wrong person for the role.

A lawyer's education is the most obvious example. Part of the mission of law schools is to teach students how to "think like a lawyer." Although there are enormous benefits to this training, negatives abound. A "lawyer-like" response can often cause more harm than good during crisis situations.

We'll come back to the legal profession in a moment, but I want to emphasize that educational and experiential biases are by no means limited to the legal profession. By examining other professions, you can see how the particular mindset of these professionals influences their approach to problem-solving and, as a result, crisis communications.

For example, when I was a young father, my son had a medical problem and was referred to a surgeon for consultation. I thought this was great until I mentioned it to a doctor friend of mine. He said: "Jim, when you are a surgeon, every solution involves surgery." In this case, it did: The surgeon recommended a complicated and, as it turned out, unnecessary procedure. Thankfully, we were prepared, sought other opinions, and decided against such an invasive solution. The problem went away.

Or this example, more specifically related to the field of crisis communications: A few years back, a medical device company we were working with was in the midst of a crisis involving—believe it or not—allegations of ties to organized crime. My team met with the institution's head of communications and the CEO. The CEO was a very prominent doctor who still maintained an active medical practice. He was every inch the doctor, right down to conducting our meeting in the cold, detached manner that is all too familiar in the doctor-patient relationship.

---

* I speak from experience: Even as I write these words, I'm sure there are a dozen or so executives, colleagues, and competitors second-guessing every decision I've made this week. *C'est la vie!*

In this particular meeting, I laid out a plan of response. My team knew this company was very conservative, so our advice was on the conservative side. We did not recommend anything too aggressive: no full-page ads, one-on-one interviews with the local newspaper, or heartfelt videos of the CEO on YouTube. Rather, we presented a measured, very basic plan that avoided escalating the crisis, avoided the "he said, she said" of a debate, and mitigated the risk of drawing more attention to the issues than was necessary.

We presented this outline to the doctor/CEO and his PR director. When we were finished, CEO asked: "But why treat this problem at all? Isn't it true that the more you engage, the more you're going to feed the disease? We don't want to overprescribe it if it's not necessary."

I pointed out that although you may *not* convince the company's detractors, they are a minority—a vocal minority, to be sure, but a minority nonetheless. That, I argued, is not who we're after.

"There is a vast middle of reasonable people," I said, "who haven't yet heard of your issue. Some won't care, but some will—and they'll make a decision either to believe you or not based upon the messages you are sending."

"You know how it is, Phil," I continued, gesturing toward the PR director, "if you don't frame these issues in the minds of the reasonable middle early on, they're going to believe the other side."

After a moment or two of silence, the CEO got up and said: "Thanks Jim, we'll take it under advisement," then quickly walked out the room. The consultation was over.

Later that afternoon, I got an email from the PR director:

Hi Jim,

We've decided to do nothing at the moment. Dr. Jones wants us to monitor the situation, and if spreads we'll consider taking a more aggressive route.

That was that . . . or so I thought.

Three months later, the crisis had spread, with several major media articles attacking the company. Moreover, the attacks seemed to be spreading to other areas, including the regulatory and political arenas. Metastasizing, I believe, is the medical term for it.

I was called back into the CEO's office and joined the PR director in a conference room. We waited there for a few moments, just the PR Director and me, making small talk. The then CEO burst in from a door in the rear of the room with a pad of paper and sat down. It was as if he'd grabbed the patient chart from outside the door and entered an examination room.

"Ok," he said, "We tried it my way, now let's try the Jim Haggerty course of treatment."

By this point, unfortunately, the patient was nearly gone.

Training and Temperament in Crisis Communications Response

As you can see from his example, the fact that the leader was a doctor had everything to do with the way he approached the issue and ultimately his decision not to respond. It wasn't that the doctor was not bright; in fact, he was brilliant. The issue is that the manner in which he trained for years to approach problems was not conducive for this particular type of crisis. If he'd been a lawyer, he would have taken another approach. An advertising executive? You can be sure advertising would be part of the solution.

That's my point: The way an individual responds during a crisis stems in large part from that individual's training and experience. We tend to think that people act and behave the same way in analyzing problems and coming up with solutions, but that is not the case, which greatly affects how they approach and react to problems.

More about Lawyers

At first glance, lawyers might be considered the ideal Chief Crisis Officers, and lawyers often have many positive attributes in crisis situations. They know how to state their case. They think well on their feet. Most lawyers have the ability to put positive window dressing on all manner of negative fact patterns or scenarios.

Unfortunately, lawyers look at problems . . . well, like lawyers (as a lawyer, this is something I know quite a bit about). Books have been written about the way lawyers approach problems, but I'll give you a few examples:

- **Lawyers learn through argument.** By attempting to dispute the central premise of any proposition, they prove or disprove its value. So be prepared for discussion (to put it mildly) and the testing (or is it demolition?) of ideas.

- **Lawyers thrive on precedent,** what has gone before. In a changing world, that's of limited value, but it doesn't stop them from thinking that way.

- **Lawyers are taught not to confront an issue until it's "ripe,"** that is, before the court for consideration. This may work in a relatively controlled environment like the courtroom, but (as you know by now) it can be devastating in the court of public opinion, where getting *ahead* of issues can often mean the difference between success and failure.

- **Lawyers think they're going to win any battle with the force of logic and reasoning.** But as we know, the world—and particularly the public—is highly emotional and usually irrational.

- **Lawyers will always try to make an argument in full.** A lawyer's motto can sometimes be stated thus: Never say in 1,000 words what you can say in 10,000. This is fine when you are at the courthouse and the judge (or his or her clerks) *have* to read your court filings. Less good when you have 10 words or less to tell your story or, in the Twittersphere, 140 characters!

- **Lawyers often try to intimidate others in the room.** They're lawyers after all, so everything they do is for negotiating advantage. They'll often force down contrary opinions through intimidation or sheer force of argument. In crisis communications, the best course of action shouldn't be determined based on who can shout the loudest.

So while lawyers can make excellent Chief Crisis Officers, the ones who succeed in this role tend to "see the whole playing field," and—while taking the best elements of their legal training with them—have learned to discard, or at least rise above, some of the rough edges you find in the legal profession.

And let me not just pick on lawyers (although I've been able to sell more than a few books that way over the years).* Other professions have their own ways of viewing the world and responding accordingly.

Take real estate executives and developers, for example. They've learned through the years that if opposition exists to an individual project, many times the solution is to just ignore it. They work behind the scenes, get the proper approvals, then build. When the project is completed and everyone is enjoying the building and its amenities, they'll forget all about the small minority (or, perhaps, majority) that were against the deal. Throw in a park, or a playground, maybe a library—just get the damn thing built.

This strategy works most of the time . . . when it's a real estate deal.

When it's not, however, such as when a developer has a labor dispute or lawsuit, a divorce, or has gone into other businesses where there is no

---

* For a deeper look at the difference between lawyers and PR people, two obvious pools where candidates for the role of Chief Crisis Officer might be found, check out Chapter 6 of my book, *In the Court of Public Opinion.*

beautiful new office building or senior community at the end of the road. You need a different set of skills when dealing with these sorts of crises.

You could also look at business executives who are trained as engineers. Engineers have their own mindset, their own way of looking at particular situations. Engineers tend to divorce the human element from the process of problem-solving altogether. It's all about process and finding the flaw in the mechanism that is causing the problem.

Consider the analysis by Malcom Gladwell in a 2015 *New Yorker* article on the problem with engineers in responding to the Toyota sudden acceleration crisis of 2009. The empirical evidence gathered by the engineers at Toyota seemed to indicate that the problem was not widespread and was often caused by the driver accidently depressing the gas pedal rather than the brake:

> *"The Toyota guy explained this to the [safety] panel," Martin went on. "He said, 'Here's our process.' So I said to him, 'What do you imagine the people are thinking? They're shaking like a leaf at the side of the road and after that whole experience they are told, "The car's fine. Chill out. Don't make mistakes anymore." Of course they are not going to be happy. These people are scared. What if instead you sent people out who could be genuinely empathetic? What if you said, "We're sorry this happened. What we're worried about is your comfort and your confidence and your safety. We're going to check your car. If you're just scared of this car, we'll take it back and give you another, because your feeling of confidence matters more than anything else." ' It was a sort of revelation. He wasn't a dumb guy. He was an engineer. He only thought about doing things from an engineer's standpoint. They changed what those teams did, and they started getting love letters from people."*[1]

What about Political Consultants?

For many people, perceptions related to crisis communications are often intertwined with the field of political and campaign communications. Consider the 2015 Sandra Bullock movie, *Our Brand Is Crisis*, which tells the story of mercenary political consultants running a political campaign in South America, or an article from the *Washington Post*, published around the same time that described "How Washington became the nation's busiest training ground for scandal PR."[2] To say nothing of the popular TV series *Scandal*, in which the crisis communications consultant, Olivia Pope, is in bed with the political world . . . quite literally.

It is true that some who tread the political minefield are well suited to crisis communications—including my good friend and colleague, Eric Rose, who will give you his opinions on the topic toward the end of this book.

Indeed, many of the top professionals in crisis communications have backgrounds in politics, but it is important for organizations and their advisers to realize that a crisis is not the same as political campaign. The skills and tactics of the political consultant, therefore, do not necessarily transfer well to crisis or litigation communication.

True, political campaigns experience crises every day—the mud is constantly being slung—and many, both inside and outside the field, might think: "What better training could there be for crisis response? Who better to know how to deal with make-or-break situations than a political person?" Consider the following:

- The audiences in a crisis are more targeted and segmented—customers, employees, vendors, neighbors, the investment community, and so forth—and therefore have specific, often differing, individual needs. And while the goal of campaign communications may be to win 51 percent of the vote, this is not so in crisis communications, where the goals are far more nuanced and there is no election-day "finish line."

- Although many politicos believe that every attack requires a response, this is often not true with crises. Decisions must be made about how serious the situation is and what level of response, if any, to make. Moreover, political and government communications often involve having a "message of the day." Demanding a constant flow of messaging in response to a crisis can often make things worse—you may attract more attention to an issue that, with the proper management, can be put behind you quietly. It is important to remember as well that while most political campaigns have a dedicated press corps that must report on something related to the campaign on a daily basis, the same is likely not true on the crisis communications front. If you respond to every attack or spin a "message of the day" related to the matter, you may be fanning the flames of a crisis that would otherwise die of its own accord.

- As mentioned above, while political campaigns build momentum to an end point (the election), crises can be much shorter-lived or can ebb and flow with outside events and with little real sense as to when the issue will ultimately simmer down.

All of this is not to say that an adept government or political professional can make the proper adjustments to go from political to crisis work, but this takes work and an understanding that the two disciplines are, in many ways, quite different.

Danger occurs when the political consultant approaches crisis communications as another political campaign—like the surgeon we discussed earlier who views every health issue as a problem to which surgery is the solution. (As the old saying goes: When you own a hammer, everything is a nail!) Executed improperly, campaign techniques are often exactly the type of "in your face" tactics that ensure a crisis gains momentum or receives more attention than it should.

There are many experienced political consultants who do an excellent job transitioning to the crisis communications field from the political realm. However, just like with the good lawyers, it takes the ability of the individual to step back and understand the particular intricacies of responding publicly to a crisis and how the response differs from that of a political campaign. This is something that organizations must be careful of when considering both the consultants involved in their crisis communications effort and the tactics undertaken when a negative event threatens the reputation and ultimately the business of your organization.

So Who, Jim . . . Who?

Now that I've described who the Chief Crisis Officer *isn't* . . . who *is* it? Is he or she a lawyer? A PR practitioner? Someone else within the organization—perhaps at the executive level or on the CEO's staff? There must be some generally accepted definition we can use.

If only it were that simple. The take-away is that the perfect Chief Crisis Officer is less evidenced by *title* than by *style*—the way the individual deals with others in the organization, the facts and issues, and a flurry of unexpected events.

True, in most cases the Chief Crisis Officer might be in the PR or public affairs department. These professionals are natural communicators after all (it is hoped, anyway); therefore, they are ideally suited for such a role. In other cases, the Chief Crisis Officer might be a lawyer—not usually the General Counsel, but rather an assistant General Counsel with experience in dealing with these types of public-facing issues, or a lawyer with a background in media, writing, communications, or some other relevant discipline. In still other cases, the Chief Crisis Officer might emerge from the executive offices of a corporate or nonprofit organization, such as a White House Chief of Staff. The selection of a Chief Crisis Officer often depends on the organization and structure with which you are dealing.

Let me give you a few examples.

Imagine you are a member of a three-person PR staff in a half-billion-dollar company in the real estate industry. Your PR department's days are spent dealing with issues related to real estate development openings, leases, amenities, and other announcements that might be of interest to potential tenants, development partners, or owners. You may spend some time writing speeches for the CEO, directing the development of website offerings, or managing social media. You spend your day handling public relations activities related to these areas. You are extremely good at a very sophisticated job, but it is a totally different set of skills than those needed for crisis communications.

Now imagine you are in the public affairs department of a government agency or working as a senior aide to a political figure. Each day brings a new issue that must be confronted. Many of these issues, or perhaps most, cannot be anticipated. They spring up when you least expect them. For example, a leading civic advocate hosts a press conference decrying some public action that your boss has taken, or a local rival is on the attack.

You deal with these issues, day in and day out, on behalf of your boss. It's about 50 percent of your job, in addition to writing speeches, announcing good news, and arranging media coverage of meetings in the community. Are you a good candidate for Chief Crisis Officer? More than likely, yes.

Let's go back to that real estate firm. You may not find the right candidate for Chief Crisis Officer in the three-person PR department that deals with events, the announcement of development milestones and the preparation of brochures and website copy. But let's now walk across the hall to the legal department. Who are your lawyers? Is there a lawyer on your team with a background in media or PR? Do your lawyers deal with complex and suddenly erupting permitting and regulatory issues? Adversaries filing lawsuits to fight the development of certain projects? Rival developers, making quick announcements that threaten a project or other business interests?

Or perhaps the ideal candidate is in the CEO's office. Let's check out the Chief of Staff for the head of the company. Is he or she the one who handles the tough stuff—the difficult and complex issues that need to be handled? Like Clint Eastwood's Dirty Harry, is he or she the person in the organization that handles "every dirty job that comes along"? If so, this person may be the right candidate at this particular company.

In sum: The person in your organization who is ideal for the role of Chief Crisis Officer should depend not on that person's title, but on a particular set of abilities, temperament, and experience.

Writing and Communication Skills

Let's now talk about writing and similar communications skills needed by your Chief Crisis Officer, particularly the skills of your PR people, who are naturally considered your front-row candidates for Chief Crisis Officer. Yes, they're communicators, but does your PR candidate only write in one style? Can she or he only do product announcements and events, or the arrangement of the latest satellite media tour? Is this the type of person who sees everything as a 6- to 12-month PR program rather than a distinct series of events requiring a rapid or nuanced response? Can this PR person work only with good news?

In other words, no matter how good a writer the individual is, you need to ask this question: What is this person's ability to deal with unexpected, complex, and explosive issues? Is her or she able to handle the curveball or—to torture a different sports metaphor—the situation that changes the playing field and requires a shift in the way the defense is laid out?

In many organizations, you find workers in fields that include public relations, legal, and even the executive ranks who just don't handle unexpected events well. They struggle. They start each day with a list of what they're going to accomplish, and, by God, they stick to it. There's no room for sudden improvisation, no room for change. I have a friend, for example, who is an extremely talented marketing executive, a great worker. Supremely organized. We joke that he has a binder for everything. Binders at work. Binders at home. Buying a new car? Binder. Outdoor grill? Binder. Family vacation? Big binder. He is the most diligent researcher you never want to meet, but if the problem doesn't fit into one of those binders, he doesn't want to hear it. Uncertainty can create a lot of problems in an otherwise superior professional such as this.

So despite his obvious skills, not a great candidate for the crisis communications field. A company's Chief Crisis Officer must be able to deal with the unexpected, because no matter the crisis—whether it is an event-driven crisis or a more drawn-out crisis like high-profile litigation or a government investigation—the unexpected has to be expected.

If your Chief Crisis Officer doesn't have the right set of skills, he or she may not be the right person regardless of their otherwise excellent traits.

Letting the World Know Who's in Charge

Having read the above, you may already know a person in your organization who fits the role of Chief Crisis Officer. In fact, perhaps there's already someone who, *de facto*, assumes the role of Chief Crisis Officer when issues arise, because he or she is so darn good at it. They are your go-to person. They have the skill set; they just haven't been given the title. Is this your Chief Crisis Officer? Yes.

But the fact is this: Unless the Chief Crisis Officer is clearly identified in an organization, he or she won't develop the skills, and the team, to be effective. An *ad hoc* system where one individual is identified . . . sometimes . . .

maybe . . . in certain situations . . . well, that's just not going to work. Situations where there are two, three, or more crisis leaders who a CEO or other senior executives turn to when a crisis hits can also be problematic—sometimes it's the Chief Financial Officer (CFO), other times the General Counsel, and other times the head of public relations. In each of these cases, no one person develops the skills and expertise, the authority, and team to do the job successfully. This is why clearly identifying a single Chief Crisis Officer for an organization is so important.

More Specific Skills

"I've missed more than 9000 shots in my career. I've lost almost 300 games. Twenty-six times, I've been trusted to take the game-winning shot and missed. I've failed over and over and over again in my life. And that is why I succeed."

—Michael Jordan

Getting even more specific, let's look at a few other characteristics that are vital in your Chief Crisis Officer. The ideal Chief Crisis Officer:

- **Doesn't mind getting the ball when the clock is running down.** Like Michael Jordan, your Chief Crisis Officer can't be afraid to be the one with the ball at the end of the game. In fact, they should relish the opportunity—not for the accolades that a successful resolution to the crisis will bring (which may be sparse, believe me), but because they want to be the best. They want to be tested; they want to see if they can tame the wild beast.

  As discussed, there are many good people out there who have gone far in life by specifically *not* wanting the ball when the game is on the line. In fact, they want nothing to do with it. As described earlier in this chapter, "keep your head down and stay out of trouble" is their credo. No matter how good they are at other aspects of their jobs and how long they've been with the company (and probably a long time, since they know how to play the game), they are never going to be good at this work. They'd rather pass the buck (or the ball to continue the analogy) and collect the paycheck. This is not someone who is ever going to be good at this sort of work.

- **They need to work fast and accurately under pressure.** One of my first jobs was as a cook for McDonald's. It was hard work, but it taug̲ me a thing or two about working under pressure. Back then, duri̲ rush you'd actually be cooking two dozen hamburgers at a time̲ lay the frozen patties on the grill, then as you flipped that fir̲ you'd lay another dozen next to it. (This was called cooking a "run on the turn" if I recall correctly.) As you pulled the first dozen, you'd lay another dozen, and so on until the rush was over. I remember one time one of my fellow cooks was a little slow in his delivery and made the mistake of asking the manager: "Well . . . do you want it fast, or do you want it done right?"

The manager's response was simple: "I want both."

Here's my point: for better or worse, the Chief Crisis Officer is often the McDonald's fry cook of the PR world. You're working under extremely tight time frames, and the customers are watching you all time. You've got your frozen patties, your timers, your procedures manual, and your training to help you to do things faster and more efficiently—and when the rush is on, you must deliver.

Chief Crisis Officer as "Point Guard"

Having opened this section with a quote from Michael Jordan, let's develop the basketball analogy a little further. In the context of the Chief Crisis Officer, you'll often hear people refer to having someone in place to "quarterback" the response effort when a crisis event or other sensitive issue confronts an organization, but I think the most apt analogy is that of a "point guard" in basketball. The skills that make a basketball player a good point guard are particularly applicable to those needed in the role of Chief Crisis Officer.

First, for those of you who have never played basketball or followed the sport closely, let me describe the role of a point guard. Simply, a point guard is the player who directs the offense on the court. The point guard's job is to know the playbook by heart, assess the situation before him or her, and look for opportunities. At times, this means taking the ball to the hoop themselves, and at other times, it means passing off to another player in the best position to score. Sometimes called the "on-court general," the point guard—while usually the smallest player on the court—is often the most important to success.

Point guards dictate the tempo of the game by how they bring the ball up the court and what they do with it when they get into the action. They have one
_____ another on the shot clock. They are thinking about where
_____ many time-outs both teams have, and the matchups
_____ guards need shooting skills certainly, but more impor-
_____ ng skills, ball-handling skills, decision-making ability
_____ hat is known as "court vision"—the ability to see the
_____ ling before making a decision on which play to run.

Sounds familiar, doesn't it? In many ways, the perfect Chief Crisis Officer is like a point guard. Consider the following:

- **A good point guard can make all the difference.** A point guard brings the ball up the court, directs the offense, and distributes the ball to other players on the team. Without such a leader, the team flounders. With such a leader in place, everyone is at the top of their game, and the team executes the fundamentals.

  This is also true in crisis matters, high-profile litigation, and other complex public perception events. The lack of a sure-handed leader—a skilled Chief Crisis Officer directing the action—can lead to failure. Public implications of developing crises are ignored until it is too late. No one is properly explaining what is happening: to investors, regulators, employees, and other influential audiences. Ill-conceived public statements, slapped together at the 11th hour, do little to help. Companies fall back on clichés that simply reinforce the sense that the event is spinning out of control.

  The ideal Chief Crisis Officer understands that it falls on him or her to be the point guard for your organization in the heat of a difficult corporate crisis. You've got to coordinate the right defense and run an effective offense—moving the ball down court, anticipating what's going to happen next, and passing at the right time to team members who can score.

- **You can play the game at their tempo . . . or you can play it at yours.** In basketball, you can play an "up-tempo" game (pushing the ball up the court at a breakneck pace), a "set" offense (taking time to execute defined plays, sometimes with several passes before every shot), or some combination in between. A good point guard dictates the tempo of the action and gets the other side playing his or her game, not theirs. If the other side is constantly on their heels, responding to the point guard's latest move rather than running their own offense, your team is probably winning.

  Let's translate this to crisis communications response: If you spend all of your time responding to chaotic events that seem to be spinning out of control—or commentators or opponents' characterization of issues and facts—you are probably losing. I advise clients confronting crises to start playing the game at *their* tempo: Make your arguments and explanations effectively—especially in adversarial situations—and force opponents to wrestle with your facts for a while, perhaps facing questions about their own motivation and characterization of the facts. Get them back on their heels. Bring in key third parties to reinforce your views. Rather than just responding, playing the game at your tempo opens new avenues of communication that begin to reshape the debate. When you start dictating the tempo, good things happen.

- **You aren't going to win every time you execute a play.** No matter how good your point guard is, you're still going to miss a few shots, even lose a few games. Yet smart organizations, like good sports teams, know that a "season" lasts a very long time. They don't dwell on today's loss, or take their ball and go home in the face of any particular setback.

A high-profile crisis will usually be a negative experience for everyone involved. You are going to take your hits. The only question is how hard, how long, and to what effect? Media coverage can ebb and flow over weeks and months—sometimes years for those crises with a "long tail." In more drawn-out crises like investigations and litigation, facts and evidence develop over time, and today's devastating news coverage can be overcome if the Chief Crisis Officer and his or her team remain steadfast in their messages, themes, and commitment to ensure that the public understands their side of the story. Organizations that give up after one bad story are playing for a single game and not for a winning season.

Groupthink Immunity

Let's throw in one final qualification that I feel is important to an effective Chief Crisis Officer: He or she must be attuned to, and push back against, any knee-jerk reliance on groupthink and "going through the motion" responses when confronting a crisis or other negative reputational situations. This is a theme we will come back to when discussing crisis communication messaging, but when considering who should be your Chief Crisis Officer, it's advice worth reinforcing.

So be wary of conventional wisdom, as it is often wrong. Test common suppositions you and your company have about the ways in which you operate in a crisis, including the planning and the execution. I've worked with organizations of all sizes for nearly 25 years, and I can tell you that one of the most common mistakes I see involves executives, in-house lawyers, and outside counsel who fall back on clichés, easy answers, and rote responses when confronting complex crisis matters. This road is easier in the short-term, but it is often *not* the road to success. I've seen too many smart people at too many large organizations go with what they think is the safe choice— the way things have always been done—without really thinking through the ramifications of *this* decision on *this* particular situation, and whether things can be done better. Learn from the past, of course, and replicate what has worked where you find it, but a knee-jerk, "because that's the way we've always done it . . . " is not a strategy.

The Core Crisis Communications Team

Okay. So now that we've identified the key qualifications for your Chief Crisis Officer, we will examine the experience and skills needed by the core crisis communications team that will work with the Chief Crisis Officer to ensure the best possible crisis response protocol for your organization.

You learned earlier in this chapter that this team should be small, but how small?

In my estimation, for most crises, the core crisis communications team should consist of a maximum of six to eight members from various disciplines throughout the company, all with the ability to reach across organizational barriers as needed to get the job done. In other words, the members of your core crisis team shouldn't be those who are beholden to a single division, department, function, or stakeholder group. In their role on the core crisis communications team, they are working for the team, not their own departmental interests.

Who are these people? Again, every organization is different.

Many members will have individual qualifications similar to those of the Chief Crisis Officer, particularly when it comes to character and temperament. Team members should not be afraid to take bold action, but they should be sensitive enough to know when and when not to take action. They should believe in the power of communication to alter the course of events during a crisis. They should also be willing to take the heat from others in the organization who may second-guess them at every step.

Like the Chief Crisis Officer, members of the core crisis communications team must understand how to play chess on a three-dimensional chessboard, across several different levels at the same time, while keeping their eyes on reaction to the crisis from media, employees, the investment community, customers, and more. As with the Chief Crisis Officer, it's a tall order.

Let's assume six to eight members. Depending on the particular type of company, I would lay out something similar to the following:

- Someone from the legal department, particularly a lawyer with skills in the communications/media arena;
- One or two people from public or government affairs who understand the various extra-organizational stakeholders (i.e., regulators, politicians, and government officials) and their needs;

- One or two members from the public relations team, including a social media specialist;

- Someone from the investor relations side (if your organization is public or otherwise exposed to the vagaries of the financial markets);

- If needed, a member of the executive team who can assist in facilitating direct communication with the CEO and other C-suite officials (but care must be taken so that this person does not usurp the leadership of the Chief Crisis Officer); and

- Someone from a key operational division if possible. For example, in a product company, this person could be a product or brand manager. In a nonprofit policy organization, this individual may be the leader of an issue group. In other words, someone who has the day-to-day responsibility of "pushing out product," whatever that product might be.

That's it. This is your core team. This is the team who should work together on both the creation of the crisis plan and on coordinating execution when a crisis occurs.

This doesn't mean they are the only people who will be involved during a crisis. Depending on the crisis, you will likely add ancillary members to this core team—this should be delineated in your crisis plan. For example, if it involves a product of the company, an adjunct member of the crisis communications team could be someone from that particular product division (but only one person, not six!). Similarly, if the crisis involves an employment lawsuit, someone from the human resources department and/or an internal or external employment lawyer might be added to the team.

In all instances, the core team remains the same. This is your SWAT team, your strike force, your Seal Team 6: the core six to eight people tasked with maintaining crisis response readiness in good times and bad.

And to maintain that readiness, you team should be meeting regularly— on a monthly basis, at least—to assess the crisis communications plan and various scenarios that may be on the horizon. They should also coordinate training for the entire organization once or twice a year. They should review the latest intelligence, examples, and best practices in crisis communications response, both in their industry and in others (because it's amazing how many examples you can find from other industries that apply to your own).

In addition, the team should continually update contacts and crisis response materials, as well as evaluate and update website assets and coordinate the social media team as needed.

It's a lot of work. Hence, the core team must meet on a regular basis, not just once a year or when the budget allows for an updated crisis communications plan—to ensure these things are not forgotten. It's just smart risk management.

And it's the Chief Crisis Officer's role to ensure that the team does meet on a regular basis, does stay abreast of the latest trends in crisis response, and does update the crisis plan regularly to ensure it's a living, usable document and not a stuffy binder sitting on a shelf. (We'll learn more about this particular problem in the next chapter.)

"But Jim," you say, "we have enough to do right now, and—let me tell you—budgets are already tight! Now you want to create a new team solely for the purpose of responding to crises that maybe will never occur? Seems like a luxury, and quite frankly, given all the changes in our industry and the economy, it sounds like a luxury my organization can't afford!"

Fair enough, but in the words of the old AAMCO transmission television commercial I grew up on: You can pay me now, or pay me later. (Beep, beep!)

On to the Plan!

Now that we have this great team together, we must get them to work. In the next chapter, we will look at crisis communications planning—the first task your Chief Crisis Officer and core crisis communications team should undertake—and how to perform this planning to ensure it adds value when the inevitable crisis occurs.

Action Points

- An effective crisis communications response protocol requires, first and foremost, leadership: This means a strong Chief Crisis Officer and a tight, well-oiled core crisis communications team to facilitate both planning and response.

- Your Chief Crisis Officer and his or her team must be highly flexible and ready to respond at a moment's notice, and contain decisive individuals who can work across organizational lines.

- Beware of large, unwieldy crisis communications teams without the authority to act. They will impede effective company response rather than facilitate it. We're executing an action plan, not conducting an academic seminar.

- In character and temperament, your Chief Crisis Officer must be willing and able to act. Some otherwise very talented individuals, by training or inclination, aren't predisposed to the type of decisive leadership needed to effectively respond to a crisis threatening an organization.

- Lawyers may seem like ideal candidates for Chief Crisis Officer, but beware. Many of the skills that make a good lawyer can be disastrous in crisis response situations. Similarly, some very talented public relations professionals working in other communications arenas can be equally ill-suited to the task.

- The perfect Chief Crisis Officer is like a good point guard in basketball: They know the playbook by heart; they execute on the fundamentals; and they have "court vision," which allows them to be flexible and take advantage of opportunities as they develop.

3

Preparing a Crisis Communications Plan That Actually Works

We now have a basic understanding of the need for effective crisis communications in companies and other organizations, and the critical interplay of legal, business, and perception issues when organizations face unexpected situations that threaten to have negative reputational ramifications. We've also looked at the role of the Chief Crisis Officer and the need for leadership and structure in the creation of your core crisis communications team.

But how do you actually translate these new skills and resources into practice? You create a crisis communications plan—an action plan that ensures the machinery works well when a crisis hits. Beware, though: As you'll learn in this chapter, true crisis communications planning is often absent in even the most forward-thinking organizations. When crisis communications planning does exist, it is often inadequate to address real needs. In this chapter, we'll discuss why that is and what you can do about it.

In other words: How you can create a "living" action plan for responding to crisis events, one that—perish the thought!—actually works.

> *"Indeed, many businesses are able to secure lower insurance premiums if they have written crisis management procedures in place . . . "*
> — *Crisis Management: Master the Skills to Prevent Disasters*, 2009[1]

> *We've got a crisis communications plan, alright. It's a piece of crap . . .*
>
> —PR director of a Fortune 500 manufacturer

I am in the offices of a major global retailer in Texas. The subject at hand is crisis communications planning. The Senior VP of Public Affairs for the company is lamenting the poor state of his crisis communications plan, his assistant nodding in agreement.

He points to the bookshelf in the corner of his office.

"There's our crisis plan right there," he says. He gets up from the conference table, pulls a thick binder off the shelf with a grunt, and slams it down on the table with a resounding thud. For a moment, I fear the table might collapse under its weight.

The binder has a well-designed, custom-made cover with the company logo emblazoned in white on the front. But from the dust now floating in a stream of light through his office window, I have a hunch what he's going to say next.

"$50,000 . . . three hundred pages . . . and nobody uses it," he says, sitting back down.

He flips a few pages. The assistant adds: "Half of these contacts aren't even here anymore."

A few more pages, then:

"This all also exists somewhere on our company's servers, but I have no idea where."

He looks across at the assistant: "The K drive?"

"N drive."

"N drive. Whatever. The point is: I wish we had a tool we actually used."

He stops talking and stares at me for a moment. I ask: "Well, what do you do when a crisis occurs?"

He laughs.

"I search my email to see what we did last time. Find some examples of statements, call a handful of people I consider 'go-tos' when a crisis occurs . . . see who's around."

A final pause.

" . . . basically, we just wing it."

How to Create a Plan Nobody Uses

I'd like to say the exchange above is unusual, but it's not. I've been to companies of all sizes over the years and I've had the same exchange time and time again.

The dirty little secret of crisis communications is this: Most crisis communications plans are thick, bloated tomes that no one ever uses—if they are created at all. In reality, most companies, including large companies that you think would know better, sometimes don't even bother to have a crisis communications plan. Those that do tend to create final documents that are not user-friendly; therefore, the communications plan is not used when the eventual crisis occurs.

At a Fortune 100 technology firm, I asked whether the resources in the crisis communications plan were ready and accessible.

"Well, sort of . . . we have same statements, templates, that sort of thing, both in the hard copy plan and somewhere on SharePoint* . . . but I've never quite learned how to use that system," the communications director told me.

"So when I need a statement, I just pull the binder down, flip the pages, and retype it by hand."

And this was a technology company. Clearly, across all industries, Corporate America has a real problem with crisis communications planning.

Research backs up this statement: According to a 2011 survey by the global PR firm Burson Marsteller, 46 percent of global business leaders say they do not have a crisis communications plan in place. A full one-half of those who do have a plan in place say that although it may assist in the handling of a crisis to some extent, it is inadequate for their needs.[2]

Why create a crisis communications plan at all if everyone hates them, and no one uses them? Like much of what happens in the corporate environment, crisis communications plans are created for reasons that sometimes have little to do with their actual utility during a crisis. In my experience, these reasons can include:

- **We heard we should have one.** It's PR 101. Every public relations trade publication I've read—and many business and insurance trade publications as well—say that you should have one. Besides, our agency of record recommended it (and then they sold it to us!).

- **The Board of Directors told us to create one.** The board is charged with being the strategic mind of our corporation, after all—they are all about mitigating risk and maximizing opportunity. If they tell the CEO to create a crisis communications plan, we're going to create a plan.

- **Our insurer likes to see things like this.** Insurance companies are the ultimate risk managers, and as part of their regular review of policies and practices, they recommended we create a crisis communications

---

* SharePoint is a web application platform in the Microsoft Office server suite and has been a popular, if complicated, part of the corporate landscape for more than a decade. Launched in 2001, it combines various functions which are traditionally separate applications: intranet, extranet, content management, document management, enterprise social networking, enterprise search, business intelligence, workflow management, web content management, and an enterprise application store (https://en.wikipedia.org/wiki/SharePoint). You'll learn more about these sorts of software applications in Chapter 7.

plan. I know it's reducing our overall insurance rates . . . or I've been told it is reducing our rates, anyway.

- **We had extra money in our budget line that we needed to spend before year-end.** If I don't use that budgeted money this year, I may lose it in next year's budget. (This happens more often that you'd think in the corporate environment.)

You'll notice that none of these reasons have anything to do with the actual improvement of the crisis communications response itself. Rather, it is about satisfying board or operational imperatives. And while it is entirely possible that, in the service of satisfying these imperatives, a company will create a useable plan, it tends to not be their goal. In other words, organizations create something they can *show*, not *use*.

To be fair, some might argue in favor of a larger crisis plan—particularly the PR firms that are selling it to you. They tell you that all of your relevant information must be in a single location—forms, templates, checklists, media lists, a list of organizational contacts, a statement of the company's approach to crises, its belief in being transparent to all of its stakeholders, and so forth. In my own cynical view, the reason for this is: *The outside PR firm believes they must produce a big document to justify the cost of the project.*

In other words, your PR firm needs "a deliverable" (usually a big one) to justify the cost of the product they just sold you. If a 30-page plan is worth $5,000, surely a 300-page plan is worth $50,000.

This is the reason why most organizations wind up with a "table-breaker" of a crisis communications plan—a weighty tome filled with position statements, philosophy, forms, and contact information (both internal and external). This information tends to be outdated before it even lands on your public affairs director's shelf; it is rarely used by anyone on the team when a crisis erupts.*

There must be a better way.

What Should Be in a Crisis Plan . . . Really

A better way exists. Crisis communications teams must keep the focus on what they *need*, rather than what they think they should *have*. Strip away all items that are tangential to the task at hand—you can always add them selectively at the end of the process if necessary (perhaps in a separate resource or as appendices to your main plan). Start with the express goal of *beating the*

---

* It's not just PR firms that have a problem with bulk. Corporate executives suffer from this problem as well. They also must justify the cost of the tool they're creating—what better way to justify such a cost than with a binder of a size that fits the price, especially when the higher-ups in the organization, who will approve the budget expenditure, will likely never have to use it.

bloat, and stick to it. Every decision on what to put into your crisis plan and what to leave out should begin with the premise that bigger is bad.

Put another way: As in most things—and all communications-related areas—think "digestibility." Work backward from the following goal: creating a crisis communications plan that can be digested easily in the heat of the battle. Keep your eyes on this prize and success will follow.

Technology can be a facilitator of this effort. In Chapter 7, we'll review technological solutions that can help streamline the process of both crisis communications planning and execution when a crisis or other sensitive communications matter occurs. Be warned though: Technology can also be the great enabler. In other words, if you can create a 500-page document thanks to the ease of content creation in this modern age, you will. And if your IT department can create a complexity-laden technological solution that's exciting to computer science folks but useless when a crisis erupts . . . well, you get the point.

As such, there needs to be cognizance at each step of the process of the fact that you are not creating a binder or a complicated set of folders on your company's intranet. You are creating an action plan. A roadmap.

In fact, let us stretch the map analogy even further. Ideally, in this technological age, you will create not just a map, but rather a Google Maps of crisis response. Not a static document, but a living document. One that can be changed as that new Interstate connector is added between Raleigh and Durham, or a new airport is added in Dubai.

And, like Google Maps, it should be simple. If you use simplicity and flexibility as your North Star, you won't go wrong.

You'd be surprised how heretical this approach can be in the hallways of many companies: Anyone who has been trained in crisis communications, in public relations, in general MBA-style courses in crisis management—not to mention as lawyers—likely feel that you need the "book," whether in hard copy or electronic form, to respond correctly during a crisis. But, as we have seen above, a thick binder is more likely to be the weight you use to prop the door open as you run from the building during a crisis than the tool you use to respond. Forget about what you've been told you should have and focus on what you need. Work backward from the goal.

The Essential Tool

Based on my experience in the crisis communications field, here are the elements of a crisis communications plan in its most basic form:

1. You need a **roadmap** for action for when a crisis occurs;
2. You need a way to **bring the crisis communications team together** quickly and efficiently in the early stages of a crisis; and

3. You need **pre-prepared tools and resources** at your fingertips and the proper methodology for distributing this communication to your various publics and stakeholders after the crisis occurs.

That's it. All else, as the rabbis say, is commentary. Crisis plan creation involves identifying potential future problems, which could range from technical glitches, product recalls, cyber-attacks, or facility fires to activist investor troubles or litigation. From there, assign clear responsibilities to each member of your crisis communications team and make sure each person can jump into action when the crisis hits. You also need templates for press releases, employee emails, and social media updates at-the-ready.

Finally, once you have all this together, you need to make sure the plan works. That's where training comes in. You must work the team through the crisis process, putting the plan into action in various scenarios based on the most likely crisis situations your organization might face. This is the only way to truly know whether the plan is effective and accessible.

If used well, technology can be key to this accessibility. We live in a world where technology is disrupting every industry. If your organization still has its crisis plan sitting in a binder on a shelf or buried somewhere on your server, it's never going to be used. Again, be forewarned: Technology is only helpful if it facilitates the process, frees the crisis plan from the static pages of a binder, and breathes life into the entire crisis communications response.

And this is key: a crisis plan should be a "living document"—without getting all *TED Talk* on you, it should be a verb, not a noun. *Action*, not prose, is what your crisis plan is all about.

How to Create a Crisis Plan That Actually Works? Just A.C.T.

I usually shy away from acronyms that spell out cutesy words when labeling the various communications processes I espouse, but in this case, I'm going to use one, as it fits so well with the *action* philosophy needed in crisis communications planning. When creating a crisis communications plan, my advice to companies of all sizes is to use the acronym A.C.T., which stands for Assess, Create, and Train:

- **Assess** potential crises and the team(s) who will handle them;
- **Create** a plan of action that includes the checklists, templates, and other resources you will need in the event of a crisis; and
- **Train** the core team, as well as the broader team where applicable, in tabletop or other virtual scenarios to ensure the plan is executed properly in a variety of situations.

Moreover, it's best to think of A.C.T. not as a one-time project, but as a cycle. Without getting too cute about it, you should constantly be in **ACT**ion. Crisis communications planning becomes a continual business process through which you develop the type of "living" approach to crisis response that will provide you with the highest level of value as you confront the inevitable. In other words, you are in a constant cycle of assessing the potential matters your organization may confront and the personnel best suited to handling such issues, creating the structure and resources needed to effectively respond, and training to ensure the plan works in the heat of a real-time crisis.

After training or in the wake of response in an actual crisis situation, you assess what worked and what didn't to help better create and execute your plan when a crisis occurs.

Figure 3.1 provides an illustration of the "living" A.C.T. system:

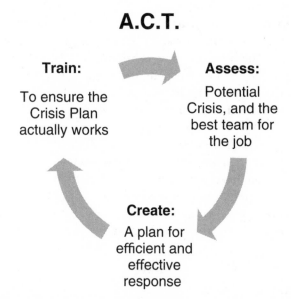

A.C.T.

Train:
To ensure the Crisis Plan actually works

Assess:
Potential Crisis, and the best team for the job

Create:
A plan for efficient and effective response

Figure 3.1: The continuous A.C.T. process during crisis communications planning

Without unduly burdening your organization, if you follow the A.C.T. cycle, a Chief Crisis Officer and his or her team will have a crisis plan that is accessible, actionable, and alive.

To further understand the A.C.T. system, let's look at each these elements and how they come into play during the creation of a crisis plan.

Assess

Simple but elemental, this is the first step of the process. The core crisis communications planning team—led by the Chief Crisis Officer—must identify the many potential crisis scenarios the company could face and come up with the teams, tools, and systems that will help them respond. These distinctive crisis events could be related to accidents, data breaches and other technological issues, product recalls, physical attacks on offices or employees, facility fires, and other matters.

I provide a more comprehensive list below, but here is an important point to remember: *Keep the list manageable.* Refine your scenarios to a select number of core situations that represent the types of events that are most likely to occur. For example, don't include every possible variation of a facility fire or cyber-attack (i.e., a fire in the materials intake facility versus a truck fire in your the loading dock). Although the situations are different in some ways, they likely have the same basic elements. You will drive yourself and everyone around you crazy if you think of every possible variation for every crisis scenario—so resist the temptation.

It does happen. Recently, I was at a meeting with a client and asked about scenario planning for a single product issue where the company was facing a potential crisis. The head of public relations proudly announced that with the assistance of the legal department, they prepared a list of potential scenarios the company might face in relation to the matter. She then pulled out a four-page spreadsheet with no less than 45 different potential crisis events and scenarios related to the product and 16 different columns of activities related to each potential scenario.

This spreadsheet was comprehensive, but ultimately unusable in the event of a real crisis. It contained too much information to digest and sort.

Based on my experience, a limited universe of actions and events can befall an organization with the potential for negative reputational ramifications. I often break these potential scenarios into the following general categories:

- An accident or physical event;
- A product or service issue (which might include anything from a product recall to a service complaint);
- A cyber or IT issue, including data breaches and the like;
- An employment-related issue, such as a firing, a labor action, or a discrimination claim;
- A financial issue with negative impacts on the company's reputation (as opposed to just the company's financial performance or some other non-reputational aspect of business operations);
- A governmental or political issue;

- A legal matter, including litigation, investigations, or adverse regulatory action; or

- A general reputational attack on your organization, its products or services, or personnel.

Each of these categories may have a few subcategories that could be added—these subcategories will depend on many factors, including the industry you are in and the size of your organization or number of locations. The key takeaway is as follows: You must review your company's business operations and come up with a *manageable* number of issues and events that your organization might confront. How many scenarios are right for your organizations is up to you, but keep in mind: Simplicity is the key to success.

One other note on assessment: As you assess the types of crises with which your company may be involved, you should also assess:

(a) Your personnel, that is, the crisis communications team ready to spring into action when a crisis occurs, along with a broader team that will be included in the process depending on the actual type of crisis or issue you are facing; and

(b) The logistical and technological tools that can be brought into service to facilitate the process of both preparing for crisis situations and responding when the inevitable crisis occurs.

We took a closer look at personnel in Chapter 2 when we examined the role of the Chief Crisis Officer in your organization and the core crisis communications team. Similarly, we'll examine logistics and technology more closely in Chapter 7.

Create

Okay. So you've done your assessment, and you know the types of crises and issues your organization might face and the team that will execute your crisis response protocol. Now you need to create. This is where we get to the nuts and bolts of your crisis communications plan.

Earlier in this chapter, we discussed the three basic items you need when creating a crisis plan: a *roadmap* for action for when a crisis occurs; a way to bring the crisis communications team together, quickly and efficiently, in the early stages of a crisis; and pre-prepared tools and resources at your fingertips. So let's look a bit more at these elements.

A Roadmap for Action

The word "roadmap," I suppose, is self-explanatory: It is a mixture of graphics and words that shows you where to go. The map should be as detailed as necessary for the audience and the mission at hand. A simple roadmap to get from my house to the Macy's in the mall might only show a few roads and have a few labels. A detailed Rand McNally of New York City is much more complex and detailed, with in-depth information and descriptions, but still (hopefully) instructive at a glance when trying to figure out how to get from Battery Park to the Macy's flagship store on 34th Street (although the extra detail, in some cases, might become a hindrance). Here lies the inherent tension there between information and simplicity. Done right, however, a proper roadmap should be perfectly designed to get you where you want to go.

So, too, with your crisis communications plan: Like a roadmap, it should be exactly as complex as needed to get the job done. It should clearly and simply tell you what to do and where to go when confronted by a crisis or other sensitive reputational situation. Your plan should guide you to your destination in an intuitive, user-friendly way.

In practice, your plan will require a series of guides and checklists to lead you through the response protocol for the various scenarios you identified during the assessment phase of the A.C.T. planning process.

For example:

- For an accident, fire, or other physical incident at one of your facilities, the crisis plan should immediately identify what type of communication response is needed, who should be notified as part of the core crisis communications team, who needs to be added to this team (e.g., a facilities manager, a director of security or fire safety, etc.), and what steps are recommended in the process for responding.

- For a data breach at one of your IT processing facilities, you will look for a different set of crisis responders, including an immediate meeting with IT staff and data security experts and the involvement of the company's legal department to determine the notification requirements in the various states in which you operate.

- For an employment discrimination complaint, the first step could be a request for relevant documentation (obviously with confidentiality laws in mind), a conversation with your company's outside employment lawyer, and a meeting with your director of Human Resources.

This roadmap can be in the form of a bulleted narrative, a graphic workflow chart with arrows and boxes, or a checklist (or series of checklists), depending on what will work best for your organization.

As an example, we often use the following checklist when confronting an accident or physical event at a company facility:

SAMPLE CHECKLIST
ACCIDENT OF PHYSICAL EVENT

In the event of an accident or other physical event at one of our facilities that will require a communications response, the crisis communications team should take the following steps to begin coordination of response:

- ❏ Identify the crisis site or location and nature of the incident.
- ❏ Identify the appropriate on-site manager who will serve as liaison to the crisis communications team.
- ❏ Speak to security about securing the facility, including procedures for restricting media access to the site.
- ❏ Open a Virtual WorkRoom on CrisisResponsePro.com and gather the core crisis communications team, including legal counsel and, if appropriate, outside crisis communications consultant.
- ❏ Decide whether to set up a media center onsite if needed.
- ❏ Coordinate with legal departments regarding preservation of the crisis scene and legal/regulatory restrictions
- ❏ Determine whether company's online crisis media center should go "live."
- ❏ Notify insurance carrier(s) and other third-party insurers/indemnitors as to accident.
- ❏ Beginning gathering information from managers and incident response personnel on-scene and formulate initial strategy regarding communications by the company.
- ❏ Crisis communication team should take the lead in drafting the initial statement regarding what is known. This includes a statement for the media, talking points, and email or other communications for employees. NOTE: StatementReady templates should be accessed and edited carefully. Limit statement to facts presently known.
- ❏ Spokesperson(s) should be identified and appropriately briefed.

External Communication

- ❏ Short standby statement and talking points for spokesperson(s) finalized.
- ❏ Twitter guidelines should be followed to compose initial Tweet.

❑ Online media center should go live (if appropriate), and a copy of standby statement should be posted to Facebook

❑ Key media identified, including the "lead steers" who will drive coverage.

❑ Crisis communications team should work closely with internal IR resources to determine how to continually update key members of the financial community as the crisis unfolds.

Internal Communication

❑ Email or other communication to employees finalized and disseminated.

❑ Talking points for managers and sales staff finalized and disseminated.

❑ "Public-facing" internal staff, including security guards, receptionists, and others, should be briefed, provided talking points, and reminded that no one should speak to the media.

❑ All questions should be forwarded to the crisis communications contact.

❈ ❈ ❈

Again, the actual content and structure of this roadmap for the various crises you may face are up to you, but it is important to remember that the roadmap must be accessible and intuitive. In all elements of crisis communications planning, the *thinking* should have been done well before the crisis hits. As a crisis unfolds, it is time for *doing*.

Bringing the Team Together

My wife was a social worker for many years at school for the physically and mentally impaired. When a snow day or other issue arose, the principal had a phone tree in place: She called the three top members of the team; they each called three more, who then called three teachers and so on.

Although rudimentary, the phone tree was nonetheless an effective way to alert the school's entire team that an unexpected event had occurred that would impact the schedule.

When preparing your crisis communications plan, ask yourself: What's your version of the phone tree?

At many organizations, even the notification process itself is ad hoc: Whomever learns about the issue calls their superior and so on as the news works its way up to the level deemed appropriate for the type of crisis the organization is facing (perhaps all the way to the CEO, COO, or General Counsel level). One of the individuals who has been called (sometimes the CEO's assistant) then attempts to convene an initial conference call to figure out the situation. Along the way, hopefully, someone remembers that the company already has a crisis communications plan in place for just such a situation, and this plan has already identified a team delegated with coordinating response. Hope springs eternal, but in reality, the crisis communications plan is often forgotten about entirely.

My point is this: If my wife's school can do it, so can you. Ensure that proper notification is baked into your crisis communications plan, including notification of the Chief Crisis Officer and members of the core crisis communications team. As discussed in the preceding chapter, every senior manager in the company should know who the Chief Crisis Officer for the organization is and have that person's name front-and-center on his or her Rolodex (or, in modern parlance, their Contacts). Make them post it on their wall; set it as the homepage on company smartphones; tattoo it on their foreheads if you have to. This initial notification of the Chief Crisis Officer and his or her team is where it all begins.

Technology can be a key driver of this process—particularly crisis communications software with a simple notification process that can be set in motion with a few clicks from the portal's homepage from any smartphone, tablet, desktop, or laptop. The core team can be supplemented depending on the exact nature of the crisis at hand.

Whatever technology you use—phone, text, email, 20th century, or 21st— make the protocol for notification a central part of your crisis communications plan to ensure that the team you worked so hard to identify, bring together, and train is immediately activated when a crisis erupts.

Tools and Resources

Finally, every crisis plan should contain tools and resources that the team can access in the event of a crisis to guide the process of communications response. In most cases, this will be a set of templates tailored to the various scenarios you identified as likely to occur.

Templates are amazingly effective—and *not because* you are going to use them word-for-word. Far from it, in fact: In most crises, the team will edit the initial template considerably before it is posted on the company website, Tweeted, emailed to employees, or sent out to media.

But the value is this: the proper templates give everyone on the crisis team a *starting point* for preparing the messages that will be distributed to various public audiences in the event of a crisis. So in providing such a starting point, you are *mechanizing* the process. There is no need for discussion or back and forth. The team, with buy-in from senior management, has already agreed on a set of messages and their application to the various crisis scenarios you developed.

Without preapproved templates, the entire process can be gummed up by that well-meaning wordsmith in the communications department who believes he or she has a better way of writing the statement or that traditional-bound lawyer who believes the company should say nothing at all lest they subject themselves to some miniscule risk of potential liability. These concerns were already considered and dispensed with when the plan was approved. The process is streamlined, and you can get your message into the hands of audiences that need it quick.

We'll examine the actual content of our templates in Chapter 5, which discusses proper messaging in crisis situations. In the meantime, I'll leave you with one last thought: *If you're going to create a comprehensive set of communications messages for various crisis scenarios, you must be able to find them.* As in all things crisis communications, accessibility is key. Too many times I've seen crisis communications managers look for the approved template somewhere in the crisis plan on the company server or in their email trail, fail to find it, give up, and start typing something new. Throughout your crisis plan, you need easy identifiers and visual clues to ensure this information is at your fingertips exactly when you need it.

The Use of Visual Elements

This brings me to the use of visual indicators like tabs, side-borders and color in crisis communications planning. As you know, one of the things I emphasize in this process is that a crisis plan should be simple and easy to use. To reiterate, it is a roadmap, and there are reasons roadmaps are in color, with visual indicators like symbols and keys.

Color, for example, can help lead the eye to the right places: on most maps, interstate highways are red, turnpikes and other toll roads are often green (as in you'll be shedding some green to use the road), bodies of water are blue, and so forth. The mind registers color more quickly and effectively than words. Thus, if you can create a tool using color, you will naturally encourage quicker and more efficient use of that tool.

Hence, when my firm has assisted in the creation of crisis plans using the traditional binder system, we have been very big on margin columns, borders, and color-coding sections and pages for easy use. After experimenting, we came to the conclusion that a right-margin color-coded bar works best to catch the eye as you page through the binder (in addition to the usual assortment of tabs and other section dividers you routinely find in any corporate binder). Figure 3.2 provides an example.*

Point to be made: like a roadmap, find ways to use colors, symbols, and other visual clues to get your crisis communications team where they need to go. In other words: If you have to use a binder, us it well.

---

* While e-book readers will see the Figures in this chapter in color, readers of the print edition of Chief Crisis Officer have to make due with black-and-white images. For full-color versions, visit www.prcg.com/chief-crisis-officer-color-images/.

EMPLOYEE ACCIDENT

Three probable accident scenarios involving company personnel would trigger the company crisis communications response:

- Employee(s) injury that impacts company operations,
- Multiple employee injuries from same or separate incidents simultaneously; and
- Employee(s) death on company campus

In all of these scenarios, the number of customers/stakeholder and employees that are impacted by the accident/ death and impact on overall company operations becomes a communications concern.

Key Audiences Include:

- Media
- Customers
- Employees and their families
- Local, state and federal officials
- Community leaders
- Investors
- Board of Directors
- Union representatives

Response Team

- CEO/COO
- Public Relations Director
- Security Director
- Attorney
- Facilities Supervisor
- Outside Crisis Communications Advisor

Goals of Effective Communications Response:

- To assure the community that the company is prepared for this type of situation and is doing everything they can to fulfill customer needs.
- The company open and is serving customers despite the incident.
- The company is conducting an investigation into the accident and reviewing all procedures.
- Redirecting customers for services to other areas of the facility if it must close for the investigation.

Figure 3.2: The use of visual indicators to attract the eye's attention to specific information in a crisis communications plan

The Crisis Flash Sheet

My company has experimented over and over with various tools and short-cuts that could help a crisis plan become more useable in the event of an actual crisis. In other words, we looked for ways to avoid relying solely on a traditional binder when preparing the plan.

We created a 10-page, spiral-bound hanging plan that could be kept on a hook on the factory floor and in administrative offices. We used color-coded sheets that identified the particular category of crisis along the out-side edge of the page for easy reference. We even created tri-fold wallet cards that could be carried by key executives and be pulled out in the event of a crisis.

My favorite, however, was what we called the "Crisis Flash Sheet"—an 8½-x-14-inch, laminated, two-page document similar to what is used by National Football League (NFL) coaches for play calling. The Crisis Flash Sheet is supported by a traditional binder that contains appropriate back-ground and factual information—the templates and checklists, contact sheets and media lists, and all other material necessary to make crisis communica-tions effective. It remains a staple of our crisis communications planning. Recently, we have combined this tool with a user-friendly, cloud-based "vir-tual war room" technology to allow companies to effectively call the types of plays that will help ensure a crisis response that reassures the public that your company is ready and able to meet the challenges at hand.

The Crisis Flash Sheet allows the executives in question to have the most basic information needed for crisis response at their fingertips, which is espe-cially useful in the wake of "explosive" crises, such as events related to acci-dents, violent acts, natural disasters, and other workplace incidents.

For those of you who are not familiar with the NFL's system, a brief description is in order. More than a decade ago, NFL coaches started to use laminated sheets of various sizes that contained every play the coach might call in various situations, a list of calls by referees and whether they can be challenged, and even a formula for when to call a field goal or two-point con-version. The placards, which look like a food menu, serve as useful "cheat sheets" for football coaches, who could be considered the ultimate crisis managers. In the heat of unpredictable events, the coaching team must make a series of high-pressure, real-time decisions with enormous ramifications for the organization. Some cards contain descriptions of more than 100 plays a coach might call in various situations, sorted by situation, strategy, and staffing.

Although all NFL teams have full playbooks, usually totaling hundreds of pages, it wouldn't be easy for a NFL coach to tote one of these suckers on the sideline during a game.

Sound familiar? We had this idea in mind when we created our Crisis Flash Sheet. Why 8½ × 14 inches? Simple, because you can see it. The Crisis Flash Sheet can sit on a bookshelf with other key corporate documents, but it is 3 inches taller than your typical 8½-×-11-inch corporate document, book, or magazine. Thus, it is easy to pluck off your shelf when the first news of a crisis reaches your desk.*

When we create these Flash Sheets, they are highly tailored to each particular client, with the exact information they need for their industry, size of company, number of facilities, and other criteria. In Figures 3.3 and 3.4, you see a generic version of an actual Crisis Flash Sheet that we created for a small hospital system client.

The Crisis Flash Sheet given in these figures is just one example—what you include on your Crisis Flash Sheet will vary based on the particulars of your business. That said, I think it is instructive to review the Crisis Flash Sheet in detail to give you the full flavor of what we created.

First, you'll notice that the Crisis Flash Sheet is color-coded for easy reference, with a quick key at the top front to direct you to the right section. All of this is by design, of course, and comes from our aforementioned experience in streamlining the crisis response system during the first critical minutes after notification. Color directs you to the right section of the flash card far quicker than a Table of Contents.†

In this case, we looked at the overall range of issues the hospital faced. Working with the CEO, public affairs executives, and the legal department, we determined exactly the information that would be needed in the event of a sudden, public-facing crisis. Again, it is critical to understand that this is not a cookie-cutter process. The team tasked with creating the crisis plan, as well as the Crisis Flash Sheet, should deeply understand exactly what information needs to be at the team's fingertips during the front end of a crisis to respond most effectively and efficiently when a crisis does, indeed, occur.

First, the hospital needed a listing of who was on the core team, with ready contact information. In this case, we identified the hospital's "Chief Crisis Officer" and an alternate, along with the institution's internal PR executive.

---

* In this "mobile" age, corporate executives aren't chained to their desk, cubicle, or office the way they used to be, and as such (as you'll see in Chapter 7), we have been moving recently to cloud- and mobile-based systems that serve the same purpose. The reality of the current business world, though, is this: Most executives at corporations above a certain size still spend most of their time in their office, at their cubicle, or in front of their desktop PC—and when on the road, with laptop in tow.

† Again, print edition readers should visit www.prcg.com/chief-crisis-officer-color-images/ for the full experience.

CRISIS COMMUNICATIONS FLASH SHEET

COLOR KEY CODE

	Crisis Communication Response Team		Establishing the Public Information Area
	HIPAA Regulations		Unannounced Media Visit
	Sample Media "Holding" Statement		Ready-Reference: Communications Templates

---

CRISIS COMMUNICATIONS RESPONSE TEAM – KEY CONTACTS

NOTE: In the event of a crisis communications event, team leader or alternate should be contacted immediately. Team leader(s) will decide which members of the crisis team are required for effective crisis response.

Administration: Jane Smith (team leader) Office (123) 456-7890; Cell (123) 456-7890; jsmith@abchosp.com
John Jones (alternate): Office (123) 456-7890; Cell (123) 456-7890; jsmith@abchosp.com
Pat Adams (public relations): Office (123) 456-7890; Cell (123) 456-7890; padams@abchosp.com

Legal: Clarence Darrow: Office (123) 456-7890; Cell (123) 456-7890; cdarrow@biglaw.com
PR Firm: Ann Apple: Office (212) 683-81XX; Cell (917) 555-XXXX; prteam@prcg.com
Bob Cobb: Office: (212) 683-81XX; Cell: (917) 555-XXXX; Email prteam@prcg.com

---

ESTABLISHING THE PUBLIC INFORMATION AREA

In the event of a natural disaster, major accident or similar crisis situation, ABC Hospital's Crisis Management Plan requires the creation of a public information area for media and other public audiences. The Public Information area will be located in the hospital administration building across Main Street from the main hospital building.
  - Depending upon the severity of the event and the number of media representatives (and potentially others) looking for information, media should be directed to either the large Second Floor conference facility (Room XXX), or the small first floor Conference Room directly across from the entrance to the building.
  - Public Information Areas should be pre-stocked with the following equipment and supplies:
    - 3-5 operable phone lines
    - An operable fax machine
    - Wifi, Ethernet cables and adequate ports for Internet communications
    - Appropriate tables and chairs
    - A podium or lectern for disseminating important information.
    - Easel and whiteboard to display information
    - 3-5 surge protectors for plugging in additional electrical equipment
    - Pens, pencils and notepads
  - Media should be properly monitored by hospital public relations or security personnel.
  - ABC Hospital's Crisis Communications Team should be stationed in a nearby office for confidential communications, exchange of information and the preparation of media statements, press releases and other background materials.

FOR MORE INFORMATION, Consult **Section XX** of the *Crisis Communication Handbook*: "Public Information Area"

HIPAA REGULATIONS

The Health Insurance Portability and Accountability Act (HIPAA) greatly restricts the information that can be made public regarding a hospital patient, condition or admission.

  - Hospitals that maintain a patient directory can tell those who ask about specific individuals whether the individual is at the facility, their location in the facility, and a one-word description of general condition:
    - Undetermined
    - Good
    - Fair
    - Serious
    - Critical
    This information can be made available only if the caller asks about the person by name. **NOTE: "Stable" is never an appropriate description of condition.** The hospital may also disclose that a patient has been "treated and released," or that a patient has died. Patients have the right to restrict such information and how it is disclosed.
  - In the event of an accident or other emergency or crisis situation with multiple injuries or patients, the hospital can disclose, in general terms, information about the number of patients, age group, gender and condition.
  - The hospital can share patient information with anyone, including media, to prevent or lessen a serious and imminent threat to the health and safety of a person or the public.
  - The hospital can also share patient information, including through the media, to identify, locate, and notify family members, guardians, or anyone else responsible for an individual's care.

FOR MORE INFORMATION, Consult **Section XX** of the *Crisis Communication Handbook*: "HIPAA Privacy Laws"

Figure 3.3: Crisis Flash Sheet, Front

UNANNOUNCED MEDIA VISIT

NOTE: In the event of an unannounced media visit – particularly a television news crew – it is important to do everything possible to avoid confrontation, including physically ejecting a news crew or otherwise causing a scene. This is exactly the type of response the "ambush" interviewer is looking to incite.

Checklist

- ☐ Hospital PR representative should meet the media as close to the front entrance of the facility as possible.
- ☐ Politely inform video crew that it is a violation of federal privacy law to shoot interior video of hospital.
- ☐ Explain that it is hospital policy not to grant interviews without an appointment. If the reporter or crew would like to arrange an appointment, you can take their information and make the proper arrangements.

Depending upon the nature of the pending crisis, the media representative may demand an interview immediately. In this case:

- ☐ Most importantly, be polite and understanding as to media needs.
- ☐ Suggest the reporter or news crew move to the Public Information Area in the hospital administration building (see green section).
- ☐ Walk with the crew to the hospital administration building.
- ☐ Explain that given the lack of notice, it might take some time to arrange an appropriate response. Ask the reporter's deadline and if a written statement from the hospital will suffice.
- ☐ Offer coffee, water or soft drinks and ask the crew to make themselves comfortable.
- ☐ From the Public Information Area, arrange that the news crew be monitored, by security if necessary.
- ☐ Take appropriate time to arrange a statement or interview by a hospital spokesperson, using templates contained in the Crisis Communications CD-ROM.
- ☐ For in-person interviews, spokesperson should take some time to memorize their statement or talking points before entering the interview room.

SAMPLE MEDIA "HOLDING' STATEMENT (Crisis Handbook, Section XX)

Statement of [Hospital Spokesperson]
[Title]

DATE -- [Optional Paragraph: Express sympathy, if appropriate, for loss].

[Paragraph 1: A short factual statement of what has happened – as much information as is known. Do not speculate, and remind media that you are still collecting relevant information].

[Paragraph 2: Explain as much as is known about what will happen next, e.g. "As we learn more, we will immediately..."]

[Paragraph 3: Reiterate ABC Hospital's commitment to the community and to safety/security/best practices]

###

NOTE: The above is designed for dissemination to media. Communication can be adapted for other constituencies – through email, memo, letter, or in-person using talking points.

Ready Reference: Communication Templates

Your Crisis Communications Handbook and accompanying CD-ROM contains numerous communication templates for the following crisis situations. Time permitting, please consult the crisis communications handbook for specific responses to various crisis situations, along with detailed strategies for managing media, employees, public officials and other important public audiences:

Medical Error/Negligence Allegation	Section XX	Accident With Multiple Injuries	Section XX
Patient Abuse Allegation	Section XX	Biological Spill/Contamination	Section XX
Escaped Patient	Section XX	Hospital Facilities Failure/Accident	Section XX
Workplace Violence	Section XX	Dangerous Person on property	Section XX
Labor/Employment Claim	Section XX	IT Breach	Section XX
Natural Disaster	Section XX	Medical Records Problem	Section XX
Terrorism	Section XX	Stolen Narcotics/Other Medications	Section XX
Epidemic/Pandemic	Section XX	John or Jane Doe Admission	Section XX
Employee Injury/Death	Section XX	Demonstration or Protest	Section XX

Figure 3.4: Crisis Flash Sheet, Back

We then identified a lawyer for the team and two outside crisis communications specialists (in this case, from my firm).

That's it. The core team can and would be supplemented by others depending on the particulars of the crisis situation in question, but this was the immediate group—the SWAT team (as you saw in Chapter 2) trained and ready to be engaged in the early stages of a crisis to put the plan into action.

Next, we thought about the types of crisis events that were most likely to befall a healthcare institution like a hospital. For example, many events—like an accident, fire, police emergency, outbreak, or patient issue—send media directly to the hospital for information. After all, if a multi-fatality accident, terrorist incident, or disease outbreak occurs in your city, media don't just lob polite calls to the PR department of the institution. They show up. As such, you need an area to put them—a room or rooms to provide them with the support they need to report on the crisis event.

With that in mind, the second section of this Crisis Flash Sheet contained an "Establishing the Public Information Area" to bring the media together and provide them with the information they need to report accurately and fairly on what was happening. This section provided the building and room number for the media to use, their phone line and Wi-Fi information, and all the other logistical support needed to ensure the room allowed journalists to work and report as a crisis unfolds.

The third section of the Crisis Flash Sheet contained information particular to healthcare institutions. One of the first concerns brought up whenever a health-related organization faces a crisis issue is what can and cannot be said under the restrictions of what are commonly known as HIPAA laws.* This knowledge is critical for hospitals and other healthcare facilities. Often, in the opening stages of a crisis, there just won't be time to remind front-line public relations and other executives as to the nuances of what information can be shared. This has two implications. First, during a time of crisis, the institution might say too much and run afoul of HIPAA guidelines. Secondly—and this is just as important—they may say too little and create more controversy, unanswered questions, rumors, or skepticism, because they assumed they were unable to say anything due to the HIPAA laws. Thus, we created a simple description that could be prominently displayed on the front of the

---

* HIPAA is the acronym for the Health Insurance Portability and Accountability Act passed by Congress in 1996. The purpose of HIPAA includes providing for the ability to transfer and continue health insurance coverage when individuals change or lose their jobs, reducing healthcare fraud and abuse, and mandating standards for healthcare information. For the purpose of this discussion, HIPAA also requires certain protections and confidential handling of health information (see http://www.dhcs.ca.gov/formsandpubs/laws/hipaa/Pages/1.00Whatis HIPAA.aspx).

Crisis Flash Sheet that immediately told the institution's crisis team what they needed to know about HIPAA when distributing information in the initial stages of a crisis.

On the other side of the Flash Sheet, we prepared a section for the "Unannounced Media Visit." In our discussion with this particular client, one of the problems they faced on a regular basis was reporters and news crews showing up at the medical center unannounced for one investigative report or another. It was a real issue for this hospital.

We used this section of the Crisis Flash Sheet (which used a fair amount of the sheet's "real estate") to detail, step-by-step, what to do if media showed up unannounced at their door. This section helped the hospital avoid scenes like the hand-over-the-camera-lens response that is sure to generate a media story or escorting media out of the reception area where they might cause a scene in front of your employees, customers, or other important parties (which is usually what reporters want). This section also recommended using a written statement to avoid an on-camera interview and using security only as a last resort. All of these items are critically important and exactly the information needed for this institution.

The next section was also critically important to this hospital, as it could be to a variety companies in different industries. This section contained a sample statement template that could be used to respond to a physical event, such as an accident, or an unintended event that causes casualties. The client needed a simple a template that could be used as a starting point to write a statement to the media in the first moments after a crisis occurs.

On this particular Crisis Flash Sheet, we provided a statement template that encompassed the following:

- The optional opening is designed to express sympathy for any loss, where appropriate;

- The first full paragraph is a short factual statement about what happened, providing as much information as is known at that moment (as we'll discuss in Chapter 5, when preparing a public statement, it is vitally important not to speculate or assume facts but rather, where appropriate, remind audiences that you are in the process of gathering relevant facts);

- The second paragraph explains as much as is known about what happens next; and

- The third paragraph reiterates the institution's commitment to safety, health, and the community (it never hurts to remind your audience of this fact).

Again, our goal with this generic statement on the Crisis Flash Sheet was to provide the basic structure for an initial statement, specifically tailored to the scenario the hospital felt they needed if it was necessary to come up with a statement quickly. In other words, it gave them a place to start.

Simple, you say. Yes, but here's the underlying truth: To respond effectively, you must have certain information at your fingertips even as a crisis is unfolding in front of you. Not buried in a binder or deep within a computer server somewhere, but right in front of you. Or, in the alternative, a signpost to take you there immediately.

In that vein, the final section (in yellow) was critical and served as an extension of the sample media holding statement in the section above. Here we listed 18 additional template statements for various situations that the hospital could face and where such information could be found in the crisis handbook, on the computer server, and, in days gone by, on CD-ROM. These statements were specific to the particular types of crises this hospital faced, including (to name a few):

- An escaped patient;
- Stolen narcotics or other medications;
- Medical errors or an allegation of negligence; and
- A "John or Jane Doe" admission—that is, the admission of a patient without identification who has not been identified at the time of the media inquiry.

As in the Sample Holding Statement, the goal was to make the right template easy to find as the crisis is unfolding, which is the next best thing to having the full text of the template on the Crisis Flash Sheet. Again, our goal was to take the guessing, questioning, arguing, and thinking out of the process as much as possible, so that when a crisis event hits, everyone knows exactly where to go, exactly what to do, and in what order to minimize the potential for negative reputational impact, even as a difficult, sensitive situation is occurring. So we took what was most important to this client in this situation and made sure it was available in a format that could be used at a moment's notice.

But That Wouldn't Work for Me! My Company Is Too Big/Not Big Enough/in Another Industry

If you're thinking now: "Yeah, Jim, that's great, but that wouldn't work for my company . . . " Well, you're wrong.

Let me explain why.

You may think: "We're way too big for a tool like this; I've got a dozen divisions and 20 locations around the globe. This ain't no dinky hospital, Jim, this is a multinational. That Crisis Flash Sheet isn't going to work for me!"

And you're right: *That* Crisis Flash Sheet isn't going to work for you, but a Crisis Flash Sheet (or similar tool that puts critical information before your eyes) tailored to your particular company and its needs probably will.

Here is my point: The description above is not an attempt to persuade you to use this particular tool but rather to get you to look for ways to streamline the content and materials you use to respond to crises by developing your own version of a Crisis Flash Sheet—for your company, its divisions, and its locations. Just as Bill Belichick (coach of the New England Patriots) has a different NFL play-calling sheet than Rex Ryan (most recently with the Buffalo Bills), General Motors will have a different tool than Apple, Apple will have a different tool than a three-location manufacturing company in the Southwest, and this company will have a slightly different tool than a hospital in a mid-sized U.S. city. I've work with companies of all sizes—from the Fortune 500 to small firms, across an array of industries. They all do some things well; they all do a lot of things poorly. Big, complex organizations tend to think they need big, complex solutions in the event of a crisis. They don't.

The Role of Technology

When you think about it, the Crisis Flash Sheet is just another way we use technology in its broadest sense to provide the Chief Crisis Officer and his or her team with a solution. This is the way crisis communications has developed and should continue to develop: with a mixture of complex technology and simple signs to make it all more intuitive. Look at it this way: Even in this age of technology, of Google Maps, we still use street signs. Why? Because they catch your attention and are still pretty good at pointing you in the right direction. In the same way, simple, intuitive tools like the Crisis Flash Sheet uses brevity, size, and color to point you in the right direction as a crisis hits.

Historically, crisis communications started with the crisis plan in a binder or book—the most low-tech of all communications vehicles. Over the years, we introduced new iterations, including the Crisis Flash Sheet, CD-ROMs with templates, and sections of servers cordoned off for communications response. We then moved on to SharePoint and similar portals within the servers of companies.

What is the next frontier? I believe it is cloud-based technology that allows the crisis plan and materials to be available from any computer, tablet, smartphone, or other device. We'll discuss this topic with more detail in Chapter 7, when we look at technology's role in crisis response and specific tools that are intuitive and efficient in helping the crisis team come together and provide the right response to the right audiences at the right time.

Train

The final element of our A.C.T. system is training, the importance of which should be obvious. As in most things worth doing in life, if you haven't practiced, you probably won't execute well. Or put another way: if you haven't cracked the books before being tested, don't expect an "A" performance. And this is especially true in a crisis environment, where the action is fast and furious, and there's a little time to learn as you go.

Now in truth, I could fill a whole book with the proper elements of designing training programs for crisis communications response, but for the purposes of *Chief Crisis Officer*, let's just lay out some basic elements to consider as you look to train your core crisis communications team for effective implementation of the plan.

Most importantly, it is imperative that your crisis communications response training be a *simulation*, not simply classroom instruction. Too often in the corporate environment, crisis communications training becomes a seminar—perhaps with some case studies woven in, but a seminar nonetheless. As you look to plan and execute crisis simulation training, avoiding the "seminarization" of the exercise is key. Sure, there will be a review and an instructional component at the outset of any training, but keeping your simulations as close as possible to a real-life crisis experience can mean the difference between a training simulation that's succeeds, and one that is, well . . . just another corporate meeting.

A few other points worth considering:

- **Don't be too clever by half.** Yes, you want your crisis simulations to be as realistic as possible, but don't sacrifice learning and then effort to simply put on a good show. I've heard of workplace violence simulations, for example, where during a presentation an armed gunman explodes into the seminar room and begin shooting at the presentee. Dramatic, yes; but I'm not sure how much at the end of the day that teaches the audience (and you'd better hope, I suppose, that no one in the audience is packing!).

- **Get out of the conference room.** Meetings are ubiquitous in Corporate America, of course, but there's nothing that says you have to hold your crisis simulation in a conference room. In my experience, most crises don't occur when you are sitting around in a room together. A simulation might take place in several locations, with some of your crisis team members at your offices, and others on the road. Anything to help simulate an actual crisis as it unfolds. Indeed, if you have incorporated crisis communications technology into your overall crisis response process, training programs can be created to manage simulated crises virtually—just as they would be handled in real life.

- **Create a schedule of crisis training you can keep.** Quarterly? Twice-yearly? Annually? It all depends on your organization. But I can give you two bits of advice: first, it must be often enough so that skills are developed and maintained, lessons learned and actionable results obtained on a continuing basis. In other words, if you have to spend the first half of the program reminding everyone why the hell you are there, you are probably not scheduling trainings often enough. Second, and this is, perhaps, *contra* to my first point: you should endeavor to create a training schedule you can keep. Nothing kills a training regimen more quickly than a schedule that, quite obviously, will never be kept.

In the end, the goal of any training program for crisis communications response is two-fold: first, if you want to get ready; and second, you want to learn—what works, what doesn't, and why, so that you can fine-tune your crisis plan and the activity of the Chief Crisis Officer and his of her team for maximum efficiency and effectiveness.

After-Action Review and Crisis Communications Measurement

Finally, a key element of any crisis communications response plan is measuring the results of your efforts and preparing an after-action report to better understand what worked well and what didn't in the heat of the battle. Indeed, this after-action assessment is one of the more important tasks to accomplish when a crisis abates (in addition to correctly maintaining all documents used for future reference), or in the wake of a training exercise. Your goal should be to gauge the success of your crisis communications plan, which allows you to make changes as needed to make the plan better and more effective going forward—which brings us full-circle, back to the assessment part of the A.C.T. system we learned about earlier in this chapter.

The key to this assessment is an understanding of what to measure during "after-action" analysis. The subject of measurement will differ depending on your organization, including how big you are, whether you are a for-profit business, nonprofit, or governmental agency and whether you are consumer-facing or operate in a business-to-business environment. Regardless, one rule applies: Measure the results and not the work product. For companies, this premise can be stated often as follows: Business goals are more important than communications goals. Let me explain.

Often in the public relations context, we look at things like the number of articles written on a topic or the number of media and social media impressions we've garnered as a means of measuring success. This is not to say the "hits" (as we say in the business) themselves aren't important, just that they are the tool through which you achieve success in crisis communications (or in any communications endeavor) and not an end in themselves. If you are only measuring "press-by-the-pound" (or, in modern parlance, by the pixel), you are not getting a full view as to whether your crisis communications response had (or is having) the requisite impact.

To put it more practically, a single story in *The New York Times* on a particularly thorny regulatory crisis, with the right tone and message, one that influences key stakeholders in Washington, DC, may have more impact than 20 different pieces in *Business Insider* or the *Huffington Post*. If you only measure media impressions rather than their impact, in the case of *The New York Times*, you only have one story. If you focus on the tools you use to manage public perception during a crisis rather than the results of your management efforts, you will skew your measurement and as a result your entire after-action assessment.

For the same reason, it's best to avoid what is known as "Advertising Value Equivalents" or A.V.E., which is the concept of using the value of advertising to determine the value of news stories that have been generated as a result of an organization's communications efforts. PR companies usually love to throw these statistics at clients when putting together media clipping reports as a way to justify the value of the public relations retainer you are paying them—that is, "That story on CNN would have cost you $24,000 if you had paid for advertising during that time slot."

Such comparisons tend to be wrong-headed in any circumstance,* but they are particularly bad during a crisis event. In a crisis, most of the stories written about the event and your organization's response will be bad. Quite frankly, your concern should be how bad the coverage is and how much of the right message is getting in there to ensure that the crisis is eased rather than accelerated. This is nearly impossible to measure using an advertising equivalent. For example, consider how much airtime BP received in the wake

---

* Three quick reasons they don't make sense in any form of PR measurement: (1) They don't take into account the tone of the coverage, whether any competitive products are mentioned in the coverage, or whether the entire story dealt with the company or product in question; (2) they don't take into account negotiated discounts on advertising—if you are buying that time on CNN, you're likely not buying a single ad but have negotiated discounts for multiple placements; and (3) they don't consider the impact of social media and the sharing of key stories.

of its 2010 oil spill in the Gulf of Mexico—that was billions in free advertising to be sure, just not the type of advertising any organization would want!

As such, focus on results, rather than tools. In this regard, I am reminded of this old aphorism: In home improvement, no one ever buys a drill bit because they want a drill bit. They buy a drill bit because they want a hole.

So what are these business goals? If you are a public company, you may decide that one week (or one month or one year) after a crisis, your stock price should be down by only a certain percentage (or, ideally, have recovered entirely). You may decide net sales staying flat rather than plummeting is an acceptable goal. If the crisis is severe enough, this could be considered a job well done.

As a reference, review the "Barcelona Declaration of Measurement Principles," which was originally adopted by the public relations industry in 2010 and updated in September 2015.[3] These principles start with the notion that, in all PR measurement practices, "the effect on organizational performance can and should be measured where possible." Another key principle from that report: "Measuring communication outcomes is recommended, versus only measuring outputs." In other words, it's better to focus on areas like purchases, donations, membership loss, corporate reputation, and/or brand equity (both of which can be measured by appropriate surveys or other methods), rather than the work product of your public relations effort, such as news clips, social media mentions, and public utterances in response to a crisis.

Your organization may also have its own set of goals for different types of crises. For example, the goals for a facility fire may focus on revenue, whereas those for a product issue may concern brand equity. Your approach may also differ by region location and product line. The point is this: Find a business-related metric through which to measure success, identify it before a crisis occurs, then measure it after the crisis passes.

Now let me add that this focus on results rather than work product does not eliminate the measurement of direct communication goals where appropriate. For example, you may want a certain percentage of stories generated to include your message points, or you may decide to evaluate the tone of the stories as the crisis unfolds to assess the accuracy of facts over time or whether your message is, in fact, changing the media and social media coverage during a crisis. In addition, a post-crisis survey could ask the public what it understands about the crisis' facts to see if your side of the story got through. However, you must ensure that all data is properly related to business goals.

To repeat, business goals should predominate your after-action assessment. After all, that's why you have a crisis plan and engage in crisis communications in the first place. This plan does not serve as an end in itself, but rather ensures that the reputational damage inflicted by a crisis doesn't permanently impact profits, practices, and organizational goals.

Action Points

- Many existing crisis communications plans are thick, bloated tomes that were created for reasons other than serving as effective tools for responding to crisis and other negative events that threaten the reputation, business, or goals of an organizations.

- Many large companies don't have a crisis communications plan; of those companies that do have a plan, most find them inadequate.

- For effective crisis communications planning, you must "beat the bloat," stripping away anything that is not absolutely essential in the crisis communications process.

- To create a crisis plan that is actually used, just A.C.T.: Assess, Create, and Train.

- The best crisis communications plans provide a *roadmap for action*, a way to *bring the team together*, and the *tools and resources* to give the entire team a starting point for effective communications response.

- The use of color and other visual identifiers can greatly enhance a crisis communications plan.

- Use tools like a Crisis Flash Sheet to ensure that basic crisis communications information is at your fingertips.

- The proper "after-action" assessment measures business goals rather than media impressions.

4

Rapid Response: Where BP and Target Went Wrong . . . and Where You Can Go Right

So far in this book, I have purposely avoided in-depth analysis of some of the "name-brand," front-page crises of the past several years. This is intentional, to better make the point that proper crisis communications planning, execution, and leadership is not just the realm of the largest multinationals with the biggest problems, but every organization that might face an event that threatens to have an undesirable or negative impact on their reputation, business, or goals. In other words, I wanted to keep this book relevant to all audiences, regardless of the size of your organization and the particular types of crises you may face.

But let's shift gears a little bit and take a closer look at two of the largest crises of the past several years—the BP oil spill in 2010 and the Target data breach in 2013—to show that big crises can also provide lessons for organizations all sizes. Particularly, we will discuss how our trademarked Control, Information, Response® (CIR) protocol can provide your organization with a key framework for response—no matter the type or size of crisis you face.

> *"The rig was tilting as much as 10 degrees after the blast, but earlier fears that it might topple over appeared unfounded. Officials said the damage to the environment appeared minimal so far."*
> — First in-depth AP story on the BP oil spill, two days
> after the initial explosion occurred.[1]

On April 22, 2010, less than 12 hours after the story above crossed the AP newswire, the Transocean Deepwater Horizon oil rig, now burning for nearly two days, collapsed and sank to the bottom of the Gulf of Mexico. Thus began the worst environmental crisis ever faced by a major corporation, and what is surely one of the worst PR responses the world has ever seen.

Although I argue in other parts of this book that smaller, day-to-day crises offer the best lessons for organizations of all sizes when preparing for and dealing with their own events, we will open this chapter with a look at two of the bigger, brand-name crises of the past several years, as they highlight key themes of this book:

- You need to have a plan in place, a playbook, for "rapid response" in the event of crisis event; and

- You need the proper leader executing the plan to ensure that the public elements at the heart of the crisis are managed efficiently and expertly.

The "officials" quoted in AP the story above are most likely BP personnel themselves (probably from the internal PR team), who clearly didn't have accurate information about what was going on, or perhaps—intentionally or unintentionally—downplayed the incident before a major media reporter covering the story. Either way, this was just the first in a series of missteps in the public response to the crisis, which will forever serve as a case study in what not to do and how not to do it when managing crisis communications.

Let's back up and recall the facts: On April 20, 2010, at approximately 9:45 p.m. local time, a mixture of natural gas, mud, oil, and concrete erupted from approximately 5,000 feet below sea level, exploding onto the deck of the Transocean Deepwater Horizon oil rig stationed in the Gulf of Mexico. The explosion killed 11 platform workers and injured 17 others. The fire burned for a total of 36 hours before the oil rig sunk into the sea.

Due to a malfunction with the blowout preventer's emergency function, the oil well was unable to be sealed for nearly three months. In the meantime, approximately 4.9 million barrels of crude oil leaked into the ocean before the well was capped. Although disagreements persist over the final scope of the oil discharged and the damage done, the BP disaster is universally considered to be the largest oil spill in U.S. history.[2]

That BP's executives, advisors, and the company as a whole were unprepared from a crisis communications standpoint is as undeniable as it is inconceivable. Nearly everyone knows, in general terms, of the PR blunders that occurred in the wake of the spill, and the fumbled public response has been analyzed in nearly every way imaginable. The BP oil spill is among the most covered events of the past several decades, up to and including a real-time video feed of the oil rushing out of the pipe at the bottom of the Gulf of Mexico—about 62,000 barrels a day, in fact.[3] Indeed, Amazon sells close to 20 books on its website analyzing the disaster and BP's response—nearly all of them focused on the public response by BP and the public outrage over the environmental damage it spawned. A quick Nexis search of the terms "BP oil spill" and "public relations" reveals close to 2,300 individual articles from the date of the spill until present.

So our challenge is to find a way to add something to this discussion—a new perspective, a new way of thinking about crisis management and crisis communications in this case. In a book about crisis communications, you certainly cannot ignore the BP oil spill, but it doesn't help anyone to rehash what has been said previously.

With that in mind, I believe a good way to think about the spill, keeping with the theme of this book, is to examine the way structure and leadership during and after the initial events in the Gulf conspired to turn a horrible event into one of the world's greatest crises. The way to do this, I believe, is by analyzing the crisis through the lens of the CIR system—Control, Information, Response®, which we first discussed in Chapter 1. CIR, you'll recall, is the trademarked system for managing crises that serves as the foundation of my firm's approach to communications response.

For the fault, as I see it, lies not in the weak, fumbling messages that BP put out in the initial phases of the crisis—including the famously tone-deaf utterances by then-BP CEO Tony Hayward—but rather the lack of an adequate, *executable* plan that led directly to those fumbled responses. A review of the BP disaster shows how a lack of planning led to a lack of *understanding* of what was happening during the initial stages of the event, which subsequently led to a skewed sense of how BP's public responses would be perceived by public audiences in the days, weeks, and months that followed.

As you can see from the quote that opens this chapter, confusion reigned in the initial stages as to both the extent of the damage and its ultimate potential impact on the Gulf of Mexico. Subsequent media reports and analysis indicate that no actionable crisis communications response plan existed at the time of the accident, and there was no effective conduit of information flowing to a qualified team to help ensure the public knew what was happening, and what the company was doing about it. As we've learned throughout this book, confusion reigns at the onset of any crisis, and in a crisis as big as the BP disaster, it reigned supreme.

As you know by now, the goal of the Chief Crisis Officer and his or her team is to gain control over information and execute a response plan that minimizes damage from the crisis and restores public confidence in both the organization and its ability to control what is happening. BP, by all accounts, had no plan. It had no control. And its Chief Crisis Officer? None other than the CEO himself, Tony Hayward.

They Want Their Lives Back

"We're sorry for the massive disruption it's caused to their lives," *[BP CEO] Hayward said. "There's no one who wants this thing over more than I do, I'd like my life back."*[4]

—Tony Hayward, BP CEO

One of the more infamous elements of the crisis occurred when then-CEO Tony Hayward's made this statement to the media in an interview that was broadcast on the *Today* Show and rebroadcast around the world. This was only one in a series of missteps by the BP CEO, including:

- Declaring in the initial stages of the crisis that the explosion and fire "wasn't our accident . . . " but Transocean's (the ultimate owner of the rig). This became a running theme throughout BP's initial crisis response, which served to further enrage, rather than ameliorate, the public.

- The CEO walking along the beach in the Gulf of Mexico in an expensive-looking, freshly pressed, pristine white dress shirt, looking more *bon vivant* than competent, compassionate CEO.

- After declaring he would remain in the Gulf until the crisis abated, Hayward was photographed on his sailboat in the south of France, even as images of a rapidly growing oil slick and impoverished fishermen flooded the airwaves, cable channels, and Internet across the United States and around the world.

- Hayward testifying before Congress in a vague and evasive manner that further fanned the flames of disgust from the general public and U.S. government officials.

Clearly, Hayward, trained as an engineer, approached the BP oil spill the way an engineer would, rather than as a leader and communicator concerned about his company's public perception. He viewed the accident in the Gulf of Mexico as an engineering problem to be solved, not a crisis to be managed. (As we learned in Chapter 2, in the engineer's mindset, there are no crises, only problems.) By contrast, his lawyers approached the crisis from a liability standpoint—that is, who ultimately owned the oil platform and therefore was responsible from a legal standpoint for the spill. No one, it seems, approached the crisis from a public perception standpoint; therein, I believe, lay a large part of the problem. The engineer/lawyer mindsets were a deadly mix.

In fact, if you look at BP's statements from the beginning, you can see how the company's initial responses were not intended to address public concern over the crisis, nor to reassure the public that the crisis was under control. Rather, the initial statements were designed solely to shift liability from BP to Transocean.

Indeed—and quite remarkably—BP's first communication was *not* a statement from the company itself, but rather a republication of a statement from Transocean. It even began: "BP confirms that Transocean Ltd. issued the following statement today: 'Transocean Ltd. Reports Fire on Semisubmersible Drilling Rig Deepwater Horizon . . . '" Without further comment, BP republished the statement from Transocean.[5]

In fact, the first "official" statement from BP wasn't released until the next day. This statement was even more blatant in its attempt to shift the focus from BP to Transocean:

BP Offers Full Support to Transocean After Drilling Rig Fire

April 21, 2010—BP today offered its full support to drilling contractor Transocean Ltd. and its employees after fire caused Transocean's semisubmersible drilling rig Deepwater Horizon to be evacuated overnight, saying it stood ready to assist in any way in responding to the incident.

Group Chief Executive Tony Hayward said: "Our concern and thoughts are with the rig personnel and their families. We are also very focused on providing every possible assistance in the effort to deal with the consequences of the incident."

BP, which operates the licence on which Transocean's rig was drilling an exploration well, said it was working closely with Transocean and the U.S. Coast Guard, which is leading the emergency response, and had been offering its help - including logistical support.

Transocean reported the fire earlier today on the rig, located approximately 41 miles offshore Louisiana on Mississippi Canyon block 252, saying that a "substantial majority" of the 126 personnel on board were safe, but some crew members remained unaccounted for. A number of personnel were reported to be injured.[6]

Obviously, those first two statements from BP are as defensive as you can get (despite the expression of concern for Transocean employees— but even that seems subtly designed to point out it is Transocean's concern, not BP's). Indeed, is only on April 23—three days after the initial incident—that BP issues a statement that does anything other than shift the focus:

> ### BP Offers Sympathy to the Families of Those Lost in the US Oil Rig Fire
>
> *April 23, 2010—BP today offered its deepest sympathy and condolences to the families, friends and colleagues of those who have been lost following the fire on the Deepwater Horizon oil rig in the Gulf of Mexico this week.*
>
> *Group Chief Executive Tony Hayward said: "We owe a lot to everyone who works on offshore facilities around the world and no words can express the sorrow and pain when such a tragic incident happens."*
>
> *"On behalf of all of us at BP, my deepest sympathies go out to the families and friends who have suffered such a terrible loss. Our thoughts also go out to their colleagues, especially those who are recovering from their injuries," he said.*
>
> *He added: "BP will be working closely with Transocean and the authorities to find out exactly what happened so lessons can be learnt to prevent something like this from happening anywhere again."[7]*

Structurally, it is clear that BP had no idea how to respond to the crisis, from coordinating an efficient communications response team to otherwise taking control of the public perceptions of what was happening. So they fell back on lawyer-like statements that deflected liability to another party.

Why did this happen? The answer is simple: As Hayward admitted in an interview on BBC weeks later, BP just wasn't prepared for the intense media scrutiny in the wake of the Gulf oil disaster, so they were "making it up day to day."[8] This statement is, in and of itself, quite remarkable. One would think that if you are an oil company and your main task is drilling for oil, you might have given some thought as to how you would react and what you might say if an accident ever occurred. Yet, this was exactly what BP neglected during the opening stages of its crisis response to the Deepwater Horizon oil spill. By their executives' own admissions, they simply had no plan in place. There was no leader ready to bring a team together and nothing to execute.

In my experience, this is something you'll find throughout Corporate America, regardless of the size of the company or their sophistication. Much of the time, they really don't have their act together when it comes to crisis communications. As we saw in the last chapter, in many organizations, crisis plans are either nonexistent or withering on a shelf somewhere. In the BP case, when you put aside the foolish statements by the CEO, his evasive testimony on Capitol Hill, and all of the other embarrassing individual elements of the crisis response, what you find at the core of the crisis is a large multinational company that had no plan to control a crisis, gather and utilize the right information, and respond in a manner that provided the public with any sense that the crisis was manageable.

Loss of Control

Indeed, if you look at recent crises like the BP oil spill, you see how, in the absence of proper planning, loss of control and lack of accurate information happen very quickly. In BP's case, not only did they lose control of the spill itself, but they also lost control over images of the spill and the way the public was perceiving those images. This loss was aggravated by the fact that the public stopped believing what the company was saying early on, due to the company's fumbled response during the crisis's initial stages.

The company had no ability to see the horizon (if you'll pardon the pun), to get a clear view of what was happening so that they could be prepared for what might happen next. Ultimately from a communications standpoint, this was the emergency function that failed.*

Come on, Jim, you say, I don't care if BP had a crisis response structure to rival NORADs, there's no way they could have properly addressed the Deepwater Horizon spill. Crises are going to happen, you say, so the best way to handle it is to suck it up, put your head down, and get through it!

This is exactly the kind of thinking that gets companies into trouble in the first place. And may well be what BP thought before the Gulf oil spill. And what General Motors thought as they scurried to cover up their ignition issues. And Volkswagen. And Toyota. And (as we'll see) Target.

The point is this: How many times does Corporate America have to be wrong before they start getting religious about these things? When will they understand that preparation for communication and having the right leadership in place for crisis communication is the solution?

Consider this example, which further drives home my point: I'm currently working with a company in the media arena that faced an enormous crisis in early 2012. By the time we were called, considerable harm had already been done. My company spent the next six months sharpening the response mechanism, the leadership (including working with the Chief Crisis Officer) and messages. They were lean, mean, and ready for rapid response. By the end of 2012, the crisis was in control and the damage ameliorated.

---

* In the interest of full disclosure, in spring 2010, several weeks into the crisis, we were contacted by a third party to see if we were interested working with BP on this matter. Given certain conflicts, we were unavailable.

But here's the interesting part: They contacted me again in late 2015, and after a short conversation, it became clear that once the initial crisis abated, the infrastructure we created for effective crisis communications response was dismantled. The company went back right back the way it'd been doing things before—and now they were in the midst of another crisis—with no Chief Crisis Officer at the helm, no core team, no workable plan. Things were once again spinning out of control. And with no rapid response system in place, company executives ignored the developing crisis until it was too late. Then they started making public statements and arguments that mattered more internally than externally, issuing bland statements that were not compelling in the slightest, but instead seem designed to say as little as possible, as quickly as possible, and hope for the best.

All of the things I preach against throughout this book . . . and all of the things that got the company into trouble in the first place!

There must be an *institutionalization* of crisis communications response structure. Too many companies treat crisis communication the way a new father treats a dirty diaper—gloves on, fingers over the nose, arms extended as far away from the body as possible. The Chief Crisis Officer and his or her team are designed to specifically avoid this posture.

The Virtual Crisis: The Target Data Breach

The lack of an effective crisis communications response mechanism is not just an issue during a physical crisis but virtual crises as well. Another name-brand crisis, the 2013 Target data breach, provides an excellent example.

Just after Thanksgiving 2013, IT personnel at Target—considered one of the darlings of the retail world at the time—were notified by federal investigators of some unusual activity related to their payment card data. The department store chain had just come off of a fantastic holiday weekend, and executives were looking forward to the Christmas season with anticipation.

Unfortunately, the Feds dropped a lump of coal in Target's holiday stocking—specifically the theft of tens of millions of customers' credit and debit card information. Target's notification and response to the crisis provides another prime example of a company whose fumbled initial reaction to a crisis led directly to a burgeoning, rather than controllable, pubic firestorm.

According to *The Wall Street Journal*, Target CEO Gregg Steinhafel was informed of the breach by CFO John Mulligan while at a Friday evening dinner with his wife and another couple.

"It's probably nothing," *The Wall Street Journal* quoted Mr. Mulligan as stating. "We're checking it out."[9]

By Sunday, Target confirmed that hackers infiltrated Target's network and installed malware to capture credit card numbers—62,000 stores were affected, with up to 70 million credit card numbers stolen.[10]

Target spent the next two days notifying credit card processors and preparing store and call centers for the storm to come. It was later that week when Target board members were informed of the breach and a press release was drafted. According to *The Wall Street Journal:*

> *When they distributed a final draft to executives around the conference table, Mr. Steinhafel complained that it read like a lawyer wrote it. The group reworked the release until 3 a.m.*[11]

The last minute hustling didn't help, as the initial press release didn't reveal much:

> *Target today confirmed it is aware of unauthorized access to payment card data that may have impacted certain guests making credit and debit card purchases in its U.S. stores. Target is working closely with law enforcement and financial institutions, and has identified and resolved the issue.*
>
> *"Target's first priority is preserving the trust of our guests and we have moved swiftly to address this issue, so guests can shop with confidence. We regret any inconvenience this may cause," said Gregg Steinhafel, chairman, president and chief executive officer, Target. "We take this matter very seriously and are working with law enforcement to bring those responsible to justice.*
>
> *Approximately 40 million credit and debit card accounts may have been impacted between Nov. 27 and Dec. 15, 2013. Target alerted authorities and financial institutions immediately after it was made aware of the unauthorized access, and is putting all appropriate resources behind these efforts. Among other actions, Target is partnering with a leading third-party forensics firm to conduct a thorough investigation of the incident.*[12]

What did Target do wrong in this initial release? Among other missteps, the company failed to mention that the breach didn't mean payment cards were fraudulently used, nor did the release mention that customers wouldn't be responsible for paying for fraudulent charges. Indeed, the initial statement was so weak that the company was forced to put out an update the next day to make exactly these points. This subsequent statement read in part:

> *It is very important for our guests to understand that receiving an email from us or a letter from their financial institution is <u>absolutely not</u> an*

indication that there has been, or will be, fraud on their card . . . [t]o date, we are hearing very few reports of actual fraud, but are closely monitoring the situation. We want to reassure guests that they will not be held financially responsible for any credit card or debit card fraud.[13]

You can see four key elements in this fumbled response that will, by now, seem familiar:

1. There was no preparation beforehand for confronting such a crisis—even though collecting and processing credit card transactions is a big part of what Target does on a daily basis.
2. No Chief Crisis Officer appears to be coordinating the communications response to the crisis. As in the BP example, the task was left to the CEO of the company—Mr. Steinhafel, who has a master of business administration (MBA) degree and is a lifelong retail executive.
3. Lawyers had taken the lead in drafting the initial statement in response.
4. Perhaps most concerning, the press release was being worked on at 3 a.m. *the morning before it was to be released.*

We will now examine these points in more detail.

Preparation

A constant theme throughout this book is that preparation is key when confronting the inevitable crisis that could cause damage to your company and its reputation. Most companies know this, at least on some level, and pay lip service to the concept of creating a crisis plan. Yet, as we learned in the last chapter, very few actually have a plan, and fewer still do it well. So in the heat of battle, is it any surprise that no one looks at the crisis communications plan very closely?

In the Target example, it is clear that although there may have been some sort of crisis communications plan in place, the folks at Target were "winging it" when the data breach crisis reared its ugly head. As in the BP example, the Chief Crisis Officer seems to have been, *de facto,* the CEO. As far as I can tell from public sources, no one else was designated to take the lead and execute a well-defined and tested plan.

Instead, it appears that the CFO, in an *ad hoc* manner, informed the CEO in the early stages of the discovery of the data breach that a breach had taken place, and ultimately CEO Gregg Steinhafel became the Chief Crisis Officer himself. But there was no plan to execute and no way to take control of the unexpected event in a manner that would ensure a positive outcome. In the end, the Target crisis appears not to have been about the severity of the crisis itself—in other words, about the substance of the crisis unfolding around them—but rather the structure, logistics, and systems in place for crisis response. Target appears to have had little, if anything, of value by way of a playbook or protocol to follow. Indeed, the more you read about the Target data breach example, the more you truly get the sense that, like BP in their oil spill, Target was "making it up on a day-to-day basis."

What Do Crisis Communications and Heart Attacks Have in Common?

> *"With no new medical discoveries, no new technologies, no payment incentives—and little public notice—hospitals in recent years have slashed the time it takes to clear a blockage in a patient's arteries and get blood flowing again to the heart."*
> —Gina Kolata, The *New York Times,* June 19, 2015[14]

Shift gears for a moment and let's approach this problem from another direction by asking a seemingly unrelated question: What can cardiac intervention teach us about effective crisis communications response?

As it turns out, plenty.

A fascinating story in *The New York Times* in 2015 detailed how hospitals have been working to reduce the time it takes to open arteries and get the blood flowing to the heart again. Hospitals across the country have adopted common-sense steps that include having paramedics transmit electrocardiogram readings directly from ambulances to emergency rooms, and summoning medical teams with a single call that sets off all beepers simultaneously.

Using this system, one community hospital in West Virginia reduced cardiac response time from nearly three hours to under an hour. This growing trend in our nation's hospital systems has contributed to a remarkable 38 percent drop in deaths from coronary heart disease in the United States from 2003 to 2013.

Among the innovations (as described by my colleague, Thom Weidlich, in a CrisisResponsePro blog post):

- Instead of waiting for the patient to arrive at the hospital to conduct the electrocardiogram, paramedics do it as soon as they reach the patient and electronically send the results to the emergency room. A phone in the emergency room is dedicated to paramedic calls. The idea is to streamline the system to make the response faster.

- Instead of multiple calls to summon doctors, nurses, and other personnel to the emergency room, a single call beeps all of them at once.
- Instead of having far-flung employees, on-call staff are required to be within 30 minutes of the hospital.
- Instead of discovering at the last minute whether necessary supplies are at hand, a room is designated for heart-attack patients, stocked with all needed supplies.
- Instead of having long consent forms filled out before the surgery, only very basic information (name, date of birth, Social Security number) is required.
- Instead of requiring a specialist called an "interventional cardiologist" to decide whether the patient is having a heart attack (and another cardiologist to determine whether to call that specialist), emergency room doctors are given the authority to decide whether the specialist is needed.[15]

Interestingly, those last two specialists have to consent to give up control to emergency room doctors in order for the system to work—not the normal course of affairs for presumably head-strong cardiac practitioners, I'm sure. This can be hard in any organization, but it is critical to an efficient response. Indeed, the *Times* article quotes one of the doctors involved as stating: "It is very rare for a group to give up power and get nothing in return. You are saying, 'You can call me at 3 in the morning and I am not going to question you.'"

Another doctor summed up the way the right approach, the right way of looking at the problem, can have an enormous impact on its resolution: "What I feel about this, what is really meaningful to me, is when we finally stopped saying, 'You know, this stuff happens,' and started taking control and saying, 'This is not acceptable.'"

What is particularly interesting from the perspective of crisis communications—particularly in light of our review of the fumbled responses from BP and Target—is the fact that it was *not* the substance of the response that led to the improvement but rather the *mechanics* of the response. In other words, no new medicines or procedures for operating and clearing clogged arteries were developed and no new understanding was formed of the basic physiology of the heart and its function that led to this improvement in treatment. Rather, it was simply fixing the system for response when a heart emergency occurs.

Substitute the word "crisis" for "heart emergency" in that last sentence and you arrive at exactly what we're trying to do in *Chief Crisis Officer*. In the success of hospitals in reducing the time it takes to clear a blockage in a cardiac emergency, we find a useful guide to building a better crisis communications response protocol for any organization.

What is that better response protocol? It is the CIR system that we first looked at briefly in Chapter 1.

Rapid Response: The Control, Information, Response System®

I just finished up a particularly sensitive writing assignment for a client, hit "send" on my email, and turned my attention to other tasks. It was mid-afternoon on a Friday, and I was looking forward to tying up some administrative loose ends for my company before heading out to watch my fourth-grade son play the saxophone at his annual holiday concert. ("Hot Cross Buns," anyone?)

An Excel spreadsheet was open on my desktop when a co-worker burst into the office.

"We've had a plane crash!" she said, "and there are fatalities! Susan is freaking out!"

Let me explain.

A client of ours runs a posh resort in the western United States, one with its own airstrip. Susan was their internal PR representative, and she was currently rushing back to the resort after a meeting nearby. She'd just learned that a plane had crashed just off the property.

Susan was the only PR professional for the entire resort and was more attuned to travel bloggers and promotional announcements than crises with fatalities. She had no real training in the discipline and little practical experience.

She was about to get both. Over the course of the next day, we executed all of the systems you've been learning throughout this book, including:

- From our crisis plan, we assembled the core crisis communications team, made up of both members on the ground at the resort and our team in New York. Using technology, we were able to communicate quickly and seamlessly to collaborate, exchange information, and prepare and approve messages;

- We established clear and objective streams of information from the site of the accident, so we weren't running on rumor or speculation;

- We set up a local command center so that media and other members of the public could get information on-site;

- We prepared messages from preapproved templates in our crisis plan that struck exactly the right tone by explaining what we knew about the accident so far, expressing compassion for the victims, and assuring the public that they would be updated as more information became available;

- We coordinated with local first responders and regulatory bodies to ensure we were saying nothing that would contradict other public statements (and actions) from our audiences; and

- We activated the appropriate media and social media monitoring to help ensure we were monitoring events in real time.

The public response was contained very quickly, with few negatives being raised (including related to the safety of the airstrip) that could have hurt the resort's reputation and impacted business for months.

This is a quick example to be sure, but I use it to make two points germane to our discussion:

1. This was not the BP oil spill or Target data breach, but it was a big deal to the resort in question. Therefore, it was every bit as critical from an organizational sense. If they had gotten their crisis response wrong, raising questions about their overall response or the safety of their airstrip, it could have impacted the resort's business for some time.

2. We succeeded because we had (a) a plan in place; (b) a leader and team to execute the plan; and (c) methodology that neither BP nor Target had at their disposal: Control, Information, Response®.

Control, Information, Response®

As we've discussed, at my firm, we use a trademarked initial response protocol we call Control, Information, Response® (CIR). Like all the processes in this book, this system is designed to guide you through the critical initial phase of a crisis event, to better allow you to gain a measure of control over your crisis site and the various elements of the event unfolding before you, then collect the information you need to correctly formulate a response.

In the example above, as soon as we received the phone call from our client, our thoughts turned to control. We had to get an accurate read on exactly what was going on before the situation began to spin out of control.

As you've seen in the BP and Target scenarios (and all of the other examples laid out in this book), crisis situations are inherently uncontrollable, as are the actions of the media and other "filters" that communicate the crisis to others. As such, absolute control is not the goal. Rather, the goal is to exert as much control as possible over the particular event before us to help ensure that we are minimizing the negative reputational ramifications of the crisis event to the fullest extent possible.

As we've described at various points throughout the book, you must begin putting the CIR process into effect at the earliest moment. Usually, this means as soon as your organization receives its first notification of the crisis, whether it is a hurried phone call or email from the site of a physical crisis or, in the case of lawsuit or similar issue, when the company first gets notice of a legal issue that has the potential to be litigated in the court of public opinion.*

Throughout the course of this book, we have given you examples from a variety of crises that give you a pretty good idea of when and how the CIR system was put into effect (or not), and the consequences. A description of each of these areas and the practical application of each to your particular crisis follows in the sections below.

Part One: Control

Control is key. It is why you:

- Decided to set up a structure for responding in times of crisis in the first place;
- Selected a Chief Crisis Officer to lead your company's response during crisis situations;
- Surrounded your Chief Crisis Officer with the best possible core crisis communication team, ready to respond as events unfold; and
- Prepared a crisis plan (and templated messages) to give you a playbook to work from when a crisis occurs.

Now, control can take many forms, but "control" during crisis response means: (1) control over the site of the events and the "points of contact" with the crisis; and (2) control over who is saying what to whom and when at various points in the action.

For example, as we saw from the BP oil spill, loss of control happened very quickly. BP not only lost control of the spill itself but also over the images of

---

* For many crises, the role of social media in exerting the proper level of control is key. Consider social media to be the **great pulse machine**: Careful monitoring of social media can give you a sense for what is potentially coming (such as a product issue, discrimination complaint, or even threats of violence directed at a person or facility), whether it is *really* coming (e.g., whether activists on social media are speaking primarily to themselves or their movement is gaining steam) and what you might expect next (such as a petition drive or a protest outside your facility). We'll examine social media monitoring more specifically in Chapter 7 (which deals with the use of technology in crisis communciations). Further along in this chapter, we'll also consider the role of social media in triggering a crisis communications response (including, sometimes, precisely the *wrong* response).

the spill and the way the public perceived those images. This loss was aggravated by the fact that the general public seems to stop believing what BP and other "official" sources were saying about the spill very early on in the crisis.

Therefore, the first step in managing a crisis is to get control. You must ensure that you have secured all points of contact—the locations and actors that will influence the course of events during a crisis. I don't mean this in an inappropriate manner by the way; I am not advocating hiding information, covering up, lawyering up, or otherwise restricting access to legitimate and important information about the crisis. Rather, it is about exerting some measure of control over the way the events are unfolding and the manner in which those events are described to the public and other key audiences. As we learned in Chapter 1, for example, the wrong images can turn a controllable fire into a raging inferno. Without the right control, the entire perception of a crisis can be radically altered.

Now some may say a company in crisis should just let information flow freely, confident in the fact that the truth will come out. Isn't this true?

Unfortunately, in many—if not most—cases, the answer is a resounding "No." Particularly in this age of social media, where facts are doled out 140 characters at a time, half a story is the *wrong* story. In any crisis, be it a simple facility fire or the most complex regulatory investigation, an interested party speaking to the wrong person—for example, a person caught up in the emotions of the moment, or one who has been given inaccurate or false information—isn't getting the full picture. Moreover, various actors may have their own issues or concerns that they want to address, or they may not be particularly good at explaining such events in the first place. As we'll discuss in the next chapter, a consistent, comprehensible message is key, and the wrong message can send a crisis spiraling off in the wrong direction. The result is a crisis that spins out of control along with it.

In a physical crisis like the BP oil spill or the plane crash that opened this section, control literally means physical control over the site of the incident. You must first secure the location of the incident to ensure that no one enters the site before you can correctly ascertain exactly what happened. As detailed in the opening to this chapter, if the crisis team and others who are working on a crisis don't obtain such information at the outset, you will start to lose control of the public perception element of your crisis with stunning speed.

Again, I want to emphasize that I am not talking cover-up: Control is not about hiding anything, but rather making sure that communication about an incident conveys a complete picture of what happened.

The control concept holds in virtual crises as well, such as data breaches, litigation and investigations, or attacks on reputation. These crises exist solely in lines of code, the documents of a lawsuit, the recollections of those privy to the facts, or on social media, websites, and other platforms. The first step here is to exercise whatever control you can over the flow of this information to ensure the right message is getting out.

Moving back to the physical realm: Think about our example in Chapter 1, where the industrial fire shrouded the Statue of Liberty in smoke. There were many ways we could have lost control over communications regarding the situation—and almost did. We could have failed to correct the AP reporter who published the first, highly distorted, photos of the fire. We could have allowed others onto the site of the accident to Tweet and otherwise report their own unintentionally skewed viewpoint.

Instead, we were able to correct the AP story and give the subsequent news crew what they needed to file a story while, as importantly, also conveying to the news crews the sense that we were being as cooperative as possible given the circumstances. Our "controlled openness" helped minimize the chance that media would pursue different avenues of coverage, like waiting around until employees left the building to see if their perception of events differed from the "official" storyline.

Does this work all the time? No, of course not. Sometimes you'll try to control the situation and you'll fail. For example, media may interview employees outside the plant anyway—whether or not you've provided them with a steady feed of "official" information as events unfold. But remember, it is all about increasing the likelihood of a positive result: In the "Control" phase of the CIR process, you are making sure that the message being sent from the scene of a crisis is a correct and accurate one, in a manner that frames the entire way in which a story is presented to public audiences.

Identifying the Points of Contact

Who are these "points of contact"? Whether your crisis is physical or virtual, exploding or unfolding, these contacts could include:

- Employees at the site;
- Employees in the customers service department of your organization, who are at the frontlines of customer calls;
- Senior executives with knowledge of the facts;
- Pundits, consultants, and other third parties in a position to comment on your issue;
- Internal and external PR personnel who have their own contacts;
- Attorneys privy to the legal elements of the crisis;
- Shareholders and other investors; and
- Bloggers and social media personnel connected with the organization.

Your ability to control these audiences is, of course, limited to a great degree: In this age of social media, people may comment before or after they speak to you. It's therefore all the more important to reach these audiences, directly or indirectly, to maximize your ability to control what is said about the crisis or other sensitive communications events. If you provide the right information to these audiences early on (i.e., get the "first bite of the apple"), you are more likely to control what is being said, by whom, about what is happening . . . and what it means.

Obviously, your content and method of contact will be slightly different depending on your audience: For example, shareholders will want to know more about the effect of the crisis on stock price; customers will want information on product safety and quality; and employees will want to know what the crisis means for their jobs. The key is to make the *right* information available to these audiences. The more these groups know about the event, the less likely you'll see speculation and rumor. This is a constant refrain in the work I do: Misinformation thrives in a vacuum. As such, in the initial stages of a crisis, it is important to fill that vacuum, even if you have limited verifiable information in the initial stages of the event. In other words, don't fall prey to this type of thinking: "I'll speak to employees when I have something to say" or "I'll notify the Board when it rises to the level of Board action."

The great paradox in communicating during a crisis is that *transparency brings control.*

Give Your Points of Contact a Place to Send Media and Other Inquiries

Finally, if you provide a mechanism for these points of contact to refer media and other inquiries, you provide an alternative to responding themselves. For example, if the audiences mentioned above have the right contact information, they'll be more likely to say: "You know who you should call . . . " and less likely to engage in speculation, gossip, or worse. Therefore, the interested party—a reporter, investigator, or otherwise—will feel less compelled to start asking questions on the spot.

As just one example, we advise clients to prepare an internal email or other communications for employees regarding the crisis at hand. It might say something like:

> *There has been an accident at our facility is Phoenix. We are currently gathering relevant information and will report back to you as soon as we know more.*
>
> *Given the nature of these events, there is a possibility that Acme employees may be approached by representatives of the media and asked*

to discuss the incident. If you are contacted by a representative of the media, please respond as follows:

- *Very politely take their name, who they are working for, and their contact information.*
- *Indicate that this information will be forwarded to the appropriate ACME representative for response.*
- *Contact information should then be forwarded to [NAMES AND INFO HERE].*

Again, it is very important that all personnel be polite and helpful, but without trying to answer questions themselves, since we are still gathering information about what has happened.

If the caller persists, just say: "I cannot answer any questions myself, but I will forward your request to our representatives who will be happy to assist you in any way they can."

So, in a few short paragraphs, we've: (1) described the situation to the employees; (2) explained that they might be approached by media or other parties at some point; and (3) gave clear instructions for what to do if they receive such contacts. The first element is critical, by the way, as it fills that "information vacuum." If you just say: "You may get called . . . don't ask questions, just refer the caller to . . . " without any context, the rumors and conjecture begin.

Part Two: Information

On Sept. 13, 2013, 12 people were killed in an attack at the Washington Navy Yard in Southeast Washington, DC. An entire neighborhood in downtown DC was put under lockdown after initial reports indicated a shooter was still at large. Indeed, later that day at a press conference, DC Chief of Police, Cathy Lanier, announced that police were actually looking for two shooters: a white man in military fatigues and a beret and an African American man with a "long gun."[16]

None of this information was true. The perpetrator was still in the building and already dead.

Where was this erroneous information coming from? Not from some irresponsible blogger or social media savvy bystander, but directly from Tweets put out by the Navy's public affairs personnel.

It is the crisis communications equivalent of the "fog of war": Initial reports vary significantly from the actual battle taking place. The same is true in crisis response: Often the first reports you receive from the scene of a crisis will vary significantly from what is actually happening. Indeed, in the Navy Yard example, the official "sanctioned" reports from the Navy itself facilitated the false information. This information was then parroted by other "authorities," adding further credence to initial reports that subsequently turned out to be wrong. It's easy to see how, without proper information, a crisis can very quickly spin in a very wrong direction.

In another example, Dr. Craig Spencer, a New York doctor who had been in Liberia working with Doctors Without Borders, was infected with Ebola during that crisis in 2014. After a few days back in New York, he checked into a local hospital with a temperature of 100.3 degrees Fahrenheit. However, initial media reports mistakenly stated his temperature as *103* degrees, because health officials relied on information from a single nurse who recorded the temperature incorrectly.[17]

What is the significance of this error? An Ebola sufferer with a slightly elevated temperature riding the New York City subway system (as Dr. Spencer did before he went to the hospital) likely wouldn't infect other passengers. A patient with a life-threatening 103 degree fever might infect thousands. It was more than a day before the inaccuracy was cleared up—a day of fear, hyperbole, and contradictory pronouncements between the mayor of New York City and the governors of New York and New Jersey.

These episodes reinforce the fact that accurate information is crucial in the initial moments after a crisis occurs. Even as the frenzy of a fresh crisis unfolds before you, members of the crisis communications team must gather accurate facts to decide how to correctly inform key audiences about what's happening and what might happen next. This highlights the delicate balance between accuracy and speed.

Consider another example from a matter my team worked on last year. An industrial company received word of an accident involving one of its trucks. The driver of the truck, which crashed on a busy stretch of interstate about 20 miles from the location, was killed. As outside crisis communications consultants to the company, we were called immediately. A panicked voicemail from the company's facilities manager indicated that they were being overwhelmed with media calls and that three passengers in the other vehicle were also dead.

We could have overreacted, drafted a statement, posted it on the company website, and boosted it on social media and to every major media outlet we could think of. In the process, we would have turned the accident into an even bigger story. But what would be the harm in that? After all, a bunch of people were dead and the media already knew about the accident, since the calls were coming nonstop. Shouldn't we be ahead of the crisis by getting something out there?

Yes, if that is what had happened. But it wasn't. In fact, there had been just one fatality: The driver of the company truck, a long-time employee of the company. The truth was that the driver had been killed while swerving to avoid another small accident that blocked the road. He steered his rig into a retaining wall to avoid injuring anyone. The driver was a hero.

What about the media calls deluging the office? Ten minutes later we learned that these calls were actually from concerned employees at the driver's destination, calling to inquire about the whereabouts of their longtime colleague. Media had not yet learned about the accident or who was involved; in fact, the accident occurred on a relatively deserted stretch of road. As such, it would be some time before any media would be aware.

Suffice to say, once the real facts of the accident were confirmed, our strategy and communications response changed dramatically—all because we waited to learn what *actually* happened, rather than relying on inconsistent initial reports.

The problem is obvious: In the early stages of a crisis, critical information about what is happening can be difficult to obtain. In the midst of hurried phone calls, emails, Facebook posts, and Tweets, how can you be sure that the information you receive is accurate and you are receiving unfiltered and unbiased reports from the front lines? Who should you trust to give you the best, most accurate story about what's going on?

Every crisis is different and the answer to these questions depends not only on the specifics of your company but of your industry (i.e., how regulated you are) and geography, as well.

However, there are a few general guidelines and best practices to keep in mind:

1. **Ensure information is flowing "unfiltered" from the crisis site to the crisis response team:** It is nearly always the case that the number of levels between you and what is happening during a crisis is proportional to the accuracy of the information you're getting. Therefore, it is critical to start receiving information unfiltered by levels of management, who may have their own agendas or perceptions subtly biasing their reports. It's not that these folks are explicitly lying; rather, they may be subconsciously describing things to you in a manner that is a little more self-serving than an independent evaluation would be.

2. **Don't assume the first information you receive is accurate. In fact, assume it is wrong:** It is better to assume that the first information you receive about a crisis event is completely wrong. This is why we create "holding" or "standby" statements in the first hours after a crisis that contain very few facts but a clear message: We are on the scene, establishing control, and will update you when more of the facts are known. (You'll learn more about creating messages for crisis communications in our next chapter.) In the initial moments of a crisis, avoid

making any factual statements that you will later have to "walk back" (as the politicians say) because they were based on false or inaccurate information.

Finally, a great way to get unfiltered information is to have a member of the crisis communications team at the site of the crisis immediately when possible. This allows the entire crisis communications team to begin receiving unfiltered information from the front lines. Technology can also be a facilitator of this effort (as you'll see in Chapter 7).

Whatever method you use, the key point is to establish the flow of information early to ensure the facts you are getting and subsequently conveying to media, employees, investors, and other stakeholders are accurate. This is the best way to avoid errors and inconsistencies in your initial public communications regarding a crisis event, which is key to instilling confidence that the crisis is under control, rather than spinning out of control.

One last point: Ensuring information is accurate is not just what you do when facing an immediate, event-driven crisis like an accident, a shooting, or Ebola outbreak. You must obtain proper information in all situations, including longer-term or slower-unfolding issues like data breaches, lawsuits, and investigations. In these situations, initial information is often sketchy or inaccurate, as the inside and outside legal team—or in the case of an issue like a data breach, the IT team—comb through the relevant information and begin to understand the facts of the case or matter before them. In this situation, there may be an urge to comment on what you think you know, rather than on what actually is happening. Despite the press of modern communication outlets like Twitter and Facebook, resist the urge to comment on facts that haven't been confirmed yet, until you know for sure.

Put another way, consider this comment from famed attorney Ted Wells of the New York law firm Paul Weiss, Rifkind, Wharton & Garrison, who was interviewed in my prior book, *In the Court of Public Opinion*, on the subject of communicating during litigation: "I often say to the PR people: 'Look, I'm interested in getting our side of the story out there in the press as well, but I don't know what the facts are yet.'" The problem with most complex areas, Wells says, is that it takes time before even the lawyers begin to fully understand the case. Wells states that "facts are framed by documents: what the documents say, what's out there. The legal business is about trying to get access to the facts, to understand and control the flow of information. All of that takes a while." Therefore, Wells's goal is not to respond too quickly with facts and admissions that may be used against his clients as more information becomes available.[18]

So just like an accident, explosion, fire, or any other type of sudden crisis, even in a crisis that unfolds at the speed of an investigation, lawsuit, or cyber-attack, you need to be nuanced and careful about the exact content of your communications until you know the full extent of the crisis you are facing. Again, I want to emphasize that I do not mean that you shouldn't comment at all; rather, you should restrict your comments to what you know—no matter how little you may know at the time.

Part Three: Response

The third part of the CIR process is Response, which is an element that runs through much of the rest of our discussion in this book. So I will leave you with only one thought in this chapter, and that relates to the *intensity* of response. Many types of crisis exist where the public needs to know everything immediately, including events like a natural disaster, an active shooter incident, or an oil spill or other environmental disaster (particularly one that might warrant an emergency response). In these situations, it is wise to press full-throttle on the public notification engine to ensure that the public knows exactly what they need to know, as quickly as possible, to ensure safety and security.

There are many other situations, though, where one of the first decisions relates to intensity: At what level should an organization respond, and to whom, to ensure a crisis isn't made bigger? Sometimes you will use a hammer, sometimes a feather duster, and sometimes a combination of the two.

Hitting the right notes with your crisis communications message is key. As such, in our next chapter, we will look more closely at proper messaging in the crisis communications context to ensure that you create messages that resonate with the right audiences at the right time and, ultimately, messages that help properly manage the crisis event to an optimal conclusion.

Action Points

- As much as the events themselves, what really caused the BP oil spill and the Target data breach to become among the best known crises of the past several years was: (1) the lack of a plan for dealing with an event that involved one of the core functions of the organizations; and (2) the lack of a leader to execute that plan.

- Effective crisis response is often not about the substance; rather, it is about the structure and systems you have in place. If you put the right structure and systems in place beforehand, an organization can handle virtually any crisis that comes its way.

- Lessons from "big," name-brand crises, such as the Target data breach and the BP oil spill, can offer key lessons for organizational crises of all kinds—events that are critical to your company regardless of size.

- Processes like the Control, Information, Response® (CIR) system are designed to provide a framework around the process of rapid response during a crisis, so that organizations of all sizes can exert control over the crisis site, collect information on what is happening, and respond effectively.

Sending the Right Message: Strategy, Words, and Actions

"Everyone thinks in terms of tactics . . . no one thinks in terms of message,"
lamented the CEO of a company I was consulting with recently. He was in the
midst of a crisis where everyone on his team was thinking about social media
presence, cable news appearances, full-page newspaper ads, and posting a video
message, but no one was thinking about what the hell to say.

Thus far in Chief Crisis Officer, *we've examined the structure, systems, and*
leadership an organization needs for effective crisis communications response. Let
us assume that you now have all of that in place. What's your message?

In this chapter, we take a look at why the message itself is important when
responding to various audiences during a crisis. We'll show how a company's
ability to effectively minimize the negative reputational impacts of a crisis can be
greatly affected by its ability to create a message that is compelling, straightfor-
ward, and—above all—succinct. Do it right, you will survive the crisis and per-
haps even improve your reputation when the issue subsides. Do it wrong, you'll
bury your point, muddy the perception you want to create, and risk long-term
reputational damage to your organization.

"What do you think of our statement?" I was asked.

"I think if your goal was to create something that ensures that no one will
ever understand your company's point of view . . . you've succeeded."

Our prior chapters have been about structure, systems, and leadership.
This is a chapter is about message—sending the *right* message to the *right*
audience at the *right* time during a crisis or other high-profile, sensitive situation that threatens negative reputational consequences. We examine why, in

the so-called information age, it's sometimes hard to do well, particularly in the organizational context.

In the example above, it was clear that someone in the organization—probably a lawyer—drafted a statement quickly and without much thought as to its intended audience. It was dense, layered with legalese and industry jargon, and otherwise indecipherable. I had to read it three times to understand what the company was talking about . . . and I was deeply involved in the crisis already! Not a good sign if you are trying to put the public's mind at ease regarding your company's response.

Yet these were smart people, very smart. And they were all over this crisis early—the company had a plan in place, a strong leader in charge, and already established the proper structure for action. Why didn't they make an effort to create a message that would be heard?

In this chapter, we're going to look more closely at the roadblocks to creating effective messages in this information age and the preparation, tools, and perspective your Chief Crisis Officer and his or her team need in order to create messages during a crisis that change the game.

Can You Hear Me Now?

The goal of communicating is to be heard, but in a society built on knowledge, information, and technology, sometimes the complexity of the task at hand can become so stifling that we lose sight of . . . well, the task at hand. When asked to explain, we fall back on jargon, legalese, and other confusing rhetorical tripe—usually because we don't have a clear idea of what we're trying to say. As Albert Einstein is said to have remarked: "If you cannot explain an idea to a six-year-old, you probably don't understand it well enough."

Here's just one example: Several years ago, I consulted on a project with a close colleague of mine from Washington. John is a fantastic public affairs professional—advising a wide range of companies and nonprofits on all manner of communications and public policy issues. In a few short years, his company has become one of the most respected in his region. But even though he's in the communication business, at times his language is so laden with industry jargon that it prevents others from understanding him, undermining the impact of his excellent work.

Our client was one of the world's largest companies, and John and I decided to discuss the project over coffee at a Starbucks near my office. I knew little about the project or what we were trying to achieve—only that it had something to do with media in the nation's capital—so John was going to explain it to me. Unfortunately, after 15 minutes of conversation over latte and crumb cake, I was even more confused than when I'd arrived.

"John," I finally interrupted, "What is the assignment?"

He thought for a moment, looking down at his notes. "The sense I get," he said, carefully measuring his words, "is that we need to do an environmental scan, then blue-sky some recommendations on DC-functionality."

I said, "John, I have no idea what you just said to me. I mean, I recognize all the words, but they just don't mean anything in the order you've arranged them."

The two of us just stared at each other in silence for a moment. Finally, I asked again: "What, John, *exactly*, are we supposed to be doing here?"

John looked dejected. He sank into his overstuffed easy chair, took a sip of coffee, and smiled at me. "That's the problem," he admitted. "I don't know!"

Eventually we figured it out, of course, and John went on to create exactly the kind of research presentation the client was looking for. Yet it is a remarkable fact in this complex, knowledge-driven world that even the most expert communicators can get bogged-down in the type of bureaucratic, jargon-laden language that makes effective delivery of a message all but impossible.

These days we are all *experts*, hip-deep in the details of the various aspects of our jobs. Thus, when it comes time to communicate what is important about what we are doing, we often falter—primarily due to our inability to explain our work to those who aren't as intimately acquainted with it.

In a business memoir written a number of years ago called *Who Says Elephants Can't Dance?*,[1] former IBM Chairman Louis Gerstner gave an excellent example of the way experts can "complexify" their messages. Gerstner was a brilliant communicator who credited much of his success at reviving IBM in the mid-1990s to his ability to cut through the corporate chatter that paralyzed one of the world's premier companies. Indeed, much of his book describes his efforts to change the ingrained culture of an organization that was the expert in its field but had enormous difficulties communicating that expertise to its many audiences. The key, Gerstner found, was creating smart, sensible messages—statements that would convince IBM's employees and customers, the financial markets, and others that IBM was still relevant in an era of web startups and open-source computing.

He accomplished this after discovering that complicated, bureaucratic language had tied IBM in knots. The jargon had become part of the culture (and beauracracy, it seems was rampant—the company's organizational chart at that point was apparently five pages long!) Moreover, IBM managers struggled with communicating even the most basic messages. Soon after being appointed chairman of the struggling technology giant, Gerstner discovered that his managers relied on overhead transparencies called "foils" at every business meeting—the precursor to the ubiquitous PowerPoint deck so prevalent in corporate America today. Rather than discuss what needed to be done, executives instead dimmed the lights and worked through the stifling detail of a stack of complex foils.

Finally, Gerstner had enough. As one of his executives began shuffling his foils for a presentation, Gerstner switched off the overhead projector, telling the startled underling: "Let's just talk about your business."

So they did, and as Gerstner reports in his book, the executive turned out to be "the godfather of the technology that would end up saving the IBM mainframe" computer.

"We had a great meeting," Gerstner wrote, adding that there was a "straight line" between that newly liberated presentation and this breakthrough for his company. If Gerstner hadn't turned off the overhead projector that day, the critical decision to cut the price of one of IBM's major products might have gotten buried beneath a pile of overhead slides.

The Message Paradox in the Information Age

I actually think this inability to create a succinct, compelling message—free of jargon, free of confusion—is one of the great paradoxes of our time: We live in a world awash in communication technology, where the ability to send messages across the street or around the world lies at our fingertips. Yet, in business, nonprofits, government, and our everyday lives, we have enormous difficulties being heard. Surveys have shown that the average American receives thousands of messages each day through a variety of mobile, email, computer, and other technologies. If you add in waves of mass media advertising and other messages, it's easy to understand why, even as communication has become as easy as breathing, we're all drowning beneath a sea of competing, yet often indistinguishable, messages.

This begs the question: With so many conflicting messages competing for our audiences' attention, is it still possible to get your voice heard? This chapter will show you how to avoid common mistakes and create messages that *resonate* with your audience during a crisis and, how the Chief Crisis Officer and his or her team can overcome the inherent obstacles of modern communication to deliver effective, convincing, and winning messages that will make people listen and understand.

We'll examine simple tools that can be utilized to create messages that rise above the clutter, complexity, and conflicting signals of the information age. Across a spectrum of business, professional, and even social situations, we'll examine concrete examples of effective message creation that serve as the core of great communication.

A Modern Problem for the Modern Age

We all send messages virtually all of the time—whenever we pick up a pen; hold a conversation; type an email message; give a speech; post to Facebook, Twitter, Instagram or Snapchat; address our employees or colleagues; answer questions from the media; or set out to market our products and services. Yet, most of us are far better at *generating* messages than we are at *crafting* them. I see the results of this imbalance every day in crisis communications. In an age rife with technology, specialization, and expertise, we forget the basic elements that lie at the heart of communication—the words and images that form the foundation of an effective message.

Indeed, an amazing byproduct of the ease with which we can send messages in this modern era is the following: Everyone pays lip service to the fact that the right message is vitally important to the overall success of the communication objective they are trying to achieve, but no one wants to work to get it done. In my view, it is the simplicity of modern communication itself that has fostered this laziness.

Yet some professionals and organizations are getting it right in highly charged, stressful, bet-the-company-style situations. They are the true leaders in responding to difficult situations—whether it be in business, politics and government, nonprofits, or the professions. If you look behind the success of these crisis responders, inevitably you'll find considerable attention to the creation of effective messages—usually well in advance of the onset of the actual crisis event. They know it matters.

Even in this era of limited attention spans and a multitude of media and social media exposures, the problem is not just that there are too many messages. Based on our research and experience, we've uncovered four basic reasons why we are losing our ability to communicate effectively in a crisis to those we wish to inform, instruct, and influence, and why this is such an intrinsically modern problem:

1. In a world of vast technological advances, we have become so enamored with the *logistics* of communication (i.e., the Facebook page and Twitter post, the YouTube video, the "dark" webpage, or direct communications via text message or other means) that we've forgotten about *substance*—the message that forms the foundation of proper communication.

2. In a world where *words are cheap and easy* to create, they've lost all value as a currency of communication.

3. As we've seen, in a world of information, we are all *experts*, knee-deep in the complexities of our particular discipline and unable to effectively communicate our message to those who don't wade in similar streams.

4. In a world that is stunning for its complexity and nuance, there is constant pressure on all of us to equivocate, to footnote, to qualify, rather than just stating what we mean, clearly and succinctly, to the appropriate audience in a manner they can truly understand.

Throughout this chapter, we'll look at companies that have fallen into these traps during a corporate crisis and consider ways to overcome the obstacles to give you a true understanding of what's preventing your message from being heard. In the midst of a crisis or other negative reputational event, this will allow you to rise above the competing voices and information static of our modern business and social lives, so that you can deliver a message to all audiences and stakeholders during your crisis that *resonates*—whether through media, social media, or direct or electronic communication with customers, vendors, investors, employees, or other stakeholders in your organization's success.

Saving the Words for Last

Too often, like the Target executives we met in Chapter 4, we focus on every element *except* the proper message when attempting to communicate with the outside world. We exquisitely plan the medium of message delivery while leaving the actual message behind. The result is a message that is muddled, vague, or just plain uninteresting to the audiences we are trying to reach.

Marshall McLuhan famously declared: "The medium is the message." For me, though, during a crisis, *the message is the message*, first and foremost. Hit the right tone, you are effectively managing the message; hit the wrong tone, your crisis will start spinning out of control.

This is why, in prior chapters of this book, I've harped on the necessity to have a "core" message prepared early, which can then be "tailored" to whatever audience and medium you are using to communicate. Ideally, as you are preparing your company's crisis plan (as we discussed in Chapter 3), you are also carefully laying out the various scenarios that may confront your company and creating templates that can be used as the starting point for creating effective messages. Further along in this chapter, we will examine exactly how this is done, using actual templates from my firm's crisis communications software portal.

Why It's Important

No matter who you are, communicating your message effectively can mean the difference between success and failure. A bad message can take a situation that is just beginning to brew, a crisis-in-the-making that is not yet a full-blown crisis event, and turn it into one quickly and completely.

For example, we were involved in communications counseling with a client many years ago. Our strategy was thus: don't mince words, state your case clearly, back it up with a few simple facts, and believe in what you say. We also counseled the client to avoid falling into "ostrich syndrome," where we pretend a crisis isn't gaining steam and hope it all goes away.

This client in question, a large multi-national based on the West Coast, knew our approach, our advice, and our skills. Despite this knowledge, as the crisis grew, the chairman of the company decided our approach wouldn't work in the current situation, that sharp message should be avoided, and that the company was better off "gumming up the works" (as their PR director put it). The company hoped that by being obtuse the issue would seem less interesting to the media, then maybe the whole crisis would go away.

Just after rendering our advice, I received an email back from the PR director:

Hi Jim,

Just want to let you know that the Chairman and the CEO have decided that they'll be handling this one personally going forward.

" . . . personally going forward?" What the hell did that mean? They didn't have a deep PR staff for this type of work, and they sure didn't have the skills needed to make the right kind of statements in this particular situation.

I asked exactly these questions, figuring my powers of persuasion would convince the organization that they were making a mistake. I must have been having a bad day, because I received this response:

Yeah, the thing is the Chairman and the CEO feel that the lower the profile they take in this, the better the result is going to be. So they're going to keep their response pretty bland for now. They'd like you to stand down at the moment. They'll activate you as an asset should the time come.

Part of me was flattered, I suppose, to be considered an "asset" that could be activated if need be, like a CIA agent from Showtime's *Homeland*. But "bland" was going to win the day? Based on nearly a quarter century of doing this work, I can tell you that "bland" rarely works when confronting a negative reputational situation.

To flesh out the whole picture, let me tell you more about this particular crisis. This wasn't the type of crisis that would go away quickly. It was a burgeoning scandal involving insider trading. Not only that, the insider trading involved two very prominent figures—among the best known in their particular field.

Needless to say, bland didn't work. The company's response to the first Bloomberg News inquiry regarding the insider trading issue was so full of holes that it left more questions than it answered. This led to a second inquiry from the *Los Angeles Times*, which led to a third inquiry from a major newsweekly, and so on.

Finally, two weeks later, I got another email from the head of PR for the client:

> Hi Jim,
>
> Just to keep this interesting I want to pose a question: If we were to tell our story in a more robust manner, what would that story be? If we wanted to present our side of the story to put us in a positive light and correct all the wrong information, what would that look like?
>
> I asked the CEO this morning and he said, "Write it up". Can we draft what this could look like, where we would place it, how we could execute, etc."
>
> Thanks,

Wow. I guess "bland" didn't work. In response, I explained to the PR head that they'd dug themselves such a hole trying to fly below the radar that a simple "story" would not work; they needed an all-out, full-court press to turn this thing around. After two weeks of negative media coverage, it was going to take time to begin cementing a new set of messages in the public's mind.

Message versus "On Message"

A disclaimer: You'll often hear PR consultants talk about the importance of repetition, of "message discipline," and of choosing the proper message and sticking with it. This is important, of course, but this chapter is not about "Staying on Message"—that contemporary cliché of the political and intellectual elite, often expressed as follows:

> Q: How'd the meeting [conversation, sales call, media interview] go?
>
> A: Very well! I really was "on message"!

Congratulations, I say. What was the message? Did it resonate with your audience? Was it concise, compelling, and substantive? Or was it obtuse, qualified, and filled with industrial jargon and bureaucratic doubletalk? Did it only provide half the information needed for a response, leaving the media and the public with a slew of follow-up questions?

In other words, it doesn't matter how "on-message" you are if your message is crap.

To effectively communicate your desired message to your target audience, these questions regarding the content of your message are as important as being "on message." In other words, content over delivery.

So heed this rule:

> *The right message delivered once is always more effective than the wrong message delivered over and over again.*

This is true regardless of your skills in "message discipline" and your ability to stay on message, and it in large part runs *contra* to much of the conventional thinking—particularly for those who come out of a political arena.

Indeed, the clichéd, conventional wisdom regarding staying "on message" can spell doom for almost anyone dealing with a crisis unless they have the right message behind them. More often than not, a communicator forcing "on message" responses with a bad message comes off as a blow-dried, robotic parrot rather than a compelling, caring individual with a story to tell.

In a way, politics has ruined this understanding—we are exposed to "staying on message" in its worst forms. Consider presidential debates (putting aside the most recent presidential debates in the 2016 election, which—with their vitriol and name-calling were—it is hoped—an anomaly): The moderator asks a question about healthcare, and they get an answer about education or national defense. The audience groans ever so perceptibly, and we all wonder why the moderator doesn't hop in and say: "Well, wait a minute, I didn't ask you about education, I asked you about healthcare!"

This is not what we're talking about; for some reason, we accept this contrived silliness from our political candidates. Rest assured, if you try it this way in a "real life" crisis, you'll fail.

Relentless adherence to the "on message" Kool-Aid is the best way to damage your credibility and the effectiveness of your communication. You come off as shallow, forced and rehearsed. In other words, the message is all style and no substance; all sizzle, no steak. This message will ultimately fail—and with it (usually, anyway) the leader trying to communicate the message.

Infamy

Now I'm going to give you a history lesson.

Specifically, I want to contrast the ideas above with famous messages from a bygone era, spoken during times of crisis, which demonstrate the different ways we construct messages in this modern age, and the point where, perhaps, the battle for resonance is lost.

First, let's consider what might be the most effective communication of the 20th century: President Franklin Delano Roosevelt's speech to Congress and the American people in the wake of the attack on Pearl Harbor.

Even those whose knowledge of American history is weak are likely familiar with the opening of Roosevelt's speech: "Yesterday, December 7, 1941—a date which will live in infamy—the United States of America was suddenly and deliberately attacked by naval and air forces of the Empire of Japan."

In Roosevelt's speech, the word *infamy* anchors the entire first sentence. Academic researchers have told me that the word "infamy" is so connected with that famous line that it rarely is used in other contexts today. To give you an idea of exactly how strong the word "infamy" was in that context, consider this: Although Roosevelt's speech is likely the most famous made by an American in the 20th century, many don't remember the second half of the sentence—everything that comes after that pivotal word "infamy."

Even more interesting is the fact that the word "infamy" almost wasn't used in that famous utterance.

A remarkable document exists in the FDR Museum in Hyde Park, New York—the original, typed first draft of Roosevelt's Day of Infamy speech. It has Roosevelt's handwritten notes. As Figure 5.1 shows, the original draft of the opening sentence to his famous speech, which read as follows: "Today, December 7, 1941, a date which will live in world history, the United States of America was simultaneously attacked by naval and air forces of the Empire of Japan."

Roosevelt had the foresight to alter two key words. He replaced "world history" with "infamy" and "simultaneously" with "suddenly and deliberately." This is more than mere wordsmithing. These are the edits of a man with a keen instinct for language that resonates with his audience and carries weight.

"Infamy" is a word with substance and baggage that brings forth all kinds of emotional responses. It makes us think of treachery, deceit, and the ignoble nature of the attack.

"World history," by contrast, is a dry pair of words, an academic phrase. It makes no value judgment. It is a "just-the-facts-ma'am" construction.

Similarly, "simultaneously" might have been accurate, but like "world history," the word is dry. It merely describes the coordinated nature of the

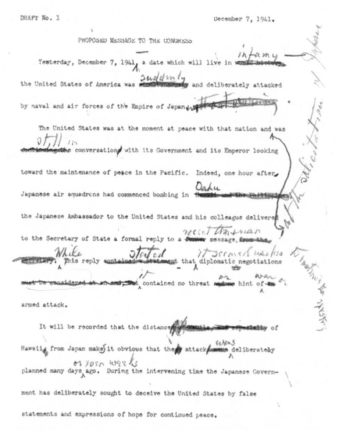

Figure 5.1: A draft of Roosevelt's Day of Infamy speech

attack. By contrast, "suddenly and deliberately" are *action* words—words that give voice to the unexpected nature of the attack, the intentionality, and the sneakiness.

Suddenly! Deliberately! Infamy! These were no reckless substitutions—they were clearly designed to create a message that more fully resonated with outrage, shock, and disgust. They did just that.

If Roosevelt had not made those fateful edits that afternoon, we might not even remember his speech—any more than we remember Woodrow Wilson's speech after the sinking of the Lusitania, an event that helped lead the United States into World War I. Although more than 2,400 Americans died on December 7, 1941, the date (not the event itself) might have faded from memory. Instead, we just commemorated the 75th anniversary of that event, and December 7, 1941, has become far more than just another day in world history. And Roosevelt is remembered as one of the greatest orators of his day.

Roosevelt clearly understood the value of choosing the perfect words for the right message; he knew that this was the foundation of effectively communicating with his target audience. How did he know? Why did Roosevelt value words so highly in a way our current political leaders rarely do? Was he a more gifted writer? There's nothing in the record to indicate that Roosevelt was more or less gifted than politicians today. But clearly he had a way with words: He also coined the famous phrase, "We have nothing to fear but fear itself," to inspire a nation suffering through the early years of the Great Depression. But his skill in crafting speeches doesn't explain the power his words still hold for modern readers, which begs the question: What other factors served him as he created such memorable messages?

Here's my theory: In the past, the process of creating messages was *hard*. Words were scarce; therefore, they had value. Take another look at the draft of Roosevelt's "Day of Infamy" speech. Note the typewritten paper with handwritten edits scrawled in pencil—even the process of getting these words on paper was hard.

To get his speech into the form you see in Figure 5.1, Roosevelt had to dictate the message to his assistant, Missy LeHand. He then sat at his desk for more than an hour working at other things, but also pondering the important message he just dictated and putting critical distance between himself and his words. His assistant then brought back the typewritten text. Roosevelt looked at his words again, considered them closely, and made the fateful changes that turned that draft into a history-changing message. The draft went back to his assistant, who made the changes, and the president considered it again before putting it in final form. This hard work led to an appreciation of the content of the message itself and the individual words that were the foundation of that message. In other words, it was the studied nature of the process itself that made this message what it was.

Compare this to the way we create messages today: Type, type, type, type, type, type, type, type . . . send!

The message is then sent immediately via email, Facebook post, Twitter, website, or other media commonplace to our modern existence. From the time the message leaves our minds and becomes words on our computer screen to the time it arrives at its final destination, we never think about that message again. We never reflect on it, asking ourselves:

- Is this communication accomplishing what it set out to achieve?
- Am I capturing the attention of my audience in the proper manner? In a way that considers who the audience is and exactly how much time I have to get my message across?

- Are the words I chose—in each sentence, on each line—exactly the words that will effectively communicate the message to the target audience?

As such, it is no surprise that our message, orphaned from moment of conception, falls flat or gets ignored entirely when it arrives at its destination—an inbox or social media feed that already contains hundreds of other messages, be they words, memes, emoticons, or gifs. This problem has nothing to do with your intelligence, and probably little to do with your ability as a communicator. The problem is the process by which the words are put together.

Even 20 or 30 years ago, communication was harder than it is today, and words were more valuable. Consider another critical crisis communication of the 20th century: Ronald Reagan's speech to the American people on the night of the Challenger disaster in 1986. Addressing the families of the Challenger astronauts, Reagan said:

> *Your loved ones were daring and brave and they had that special grace, that special spirit that says, "Give me a challenge and I'll meet it with joy." The future doesn't belong to the fainthearted. It belongs to the brave. The Challenger crew was pulling us into the future, and we will continue to follow them.*

He ended with the now famous line, quoting from a sonnet by John Gillespie Magee, a young airman who was killed in World War II: "We will never forget them, nor the last time we saw them this morning as they prepared for their journey and waved goodbye and 'slipped the surly bonds of earth' to 'touch the face of God.'"

Thirty years later, I can still remember those words, still hear Reagan's voice, and still see the president delivering that speech and, in television footage, the astronauts waving goodbye as they entered the Space Shuttle's cockpit.

Here's my point: These communications were effective *not* because they were easy but specifically because they were *hard*. The words were labored over; the process of creating them was more difficult than it is today, when anyone with a smartphone can broadcast a message over Twitter or Facebook. It is the difference between a handcrafted Sam Maloof rocker and one you might pick up outside of Cracker Barrel. When the ability to communicate was scarce, more value was placed on words as a commodity. Words were crafted with care, and the result was messages that resonate more effectively with target audiences.

I'll give you two more examples to further make this point. The first involves one of the greatest orators of the 20th century, Winston Churchill. Surely, there was no one more natural than he?

Remarkably, although Churchill often seemed extemporaneous and unrehearsed, this façade was the product of extensive preparation. "In Parliament," Churchill biographer William Manchester wrote, "his wit will flash and sting, but members who know him are aware that he has honed these barbs in advance, and only visitors in the Stranger's Gallery are under the impression that his great perorations are extemporaneous."[2] On average, for a 40-minute Parliamentary speech, Churchill spent six to eight hours in preparation.

Churchill was so interested in giving the impression of spontaneity that he prepared exhaustively for it. During a speech to Parliament, he would hold in his hand not notes but the entire text of what he was going to say, including stage direction ("pause; grope for word" or "stammer; correct self").[3]

Fast-forward a half century later and consider the example of Steve Jobs. He was also considered a great orator, a man who many claimed could create a "reality distortion field" that convinced himself and others around him, with mix of charm, charisma, bravado, hyperbole, and persistence, that almost anything was possible.

A true natural, right? Surely he didn't have to work hard to achieve his messaging goals?

Consider this passage from the 2015 book *Becoming Steve Jobs,* by Brent Schlender & Rick Tetzeli:

> *Working with a team of marketers and PR execs, Steve would rehearse endlessly and fastidiously. Bill Gates made appearances at a couple of these events, and remembers being backstage with Steve. "I was never in his league," he remembers, talking about Steve's presentations. "I mean, it was just amazing to see how precisely he would rehearse. And if he's about to go onstage, and his support people don't have the things right, you know, he is really, really tough on them. He's even a bit nervous because it's a big performance. But then he's on, and it's quite an amazing thing.*
>
> *"I mean, his whole thing of knowing exactly what he's going to say, but up on stage saying it in such a way that he is trying to make you think he's thinking it up right then . . . " Gates just laughs.[4]*

Churchillian, right? Here's my point: Those who are creating great messages, be it for a crisis situation or any other critical communications situation, are working damn hard to make sure they get the message right.

This is not a mere history lesson or philosophical debate. I want everyone to understand the real issue we have in this modern world, one that comes up time and time again when responding during a crisis. Leaders from the past weren't born better at communication. They worked hard at this part of their professional lives to communicate effectively.

Working equally as hard when planning and responding in a crisis or other sensitive situation is just as important.

What Crisis Communications Messages Should Do

"But Jim," you ask, "you've already stated that, in the heat of a crisis, time is the most critical factor in ensuring proper response. That's why we're appointing a Chief Crisis Officer and a core crisis communications team, after all—so that they can move quickly in the initial stages of a crisis to ensure the event is managed properly. Now you're telling me to take a deep breath, pull out the manual typewriter or Dictaphone, like FDR or Winston Churchill, and carefully hew every message. That's impractical!"

Indeed, it is, but this is exactly why you have a Chief Crisis Officer and team dedicated to crisis communications response in the first place, and why you created a crisis plan that anticipates a variety of potential crises. As we learned in Chapter 3, you want the playbook down and your messages largely written before you get into a crisis. Ideally, like Churchill, you've chosen these words carefully—you just laid the framework for those words before you needed them. The effect is the same.

The alternative, as we learned in the previous chapter, is to have nothing ready, have no plan, and start "making it up as you go along." As we've seen with BP and Target, this tends to result in messages that are weak and confusing, doing little to express an understanding of:

1. The gravity of the problem;
2. What the public is going through;
3. How this could have happened;
4. What the company is doing to respond; and
5. How the company is going to take steps to make sure this doesn't happen again.

In the BP case, you'll recall, it took three days to express any of these sentiments at all. As we learned in our last chapter, the statements were all designed to shift the blame to Transocean—the operator of the well. Indeed, contrast the message issued just after the event:

> *BP today offered its full support to drilling contractor Transocean Ltd. and its employees after fire caused Transocean's semisubmersible drilling rig Deepwater Horizon to be evacuated overnight, saying it stood ready to assist in any way in responding to the incident.*

> *Group Chief Executive Tony Hayward said: "Our concern and thoughts are with the rig personnel and their families. We are also very focused on providing every possible assistance in the effort to deal with the consequences of the incident."*

with the statement issued two days later, after the public frenzy over the incident had already reached critical mass:

> *BP today offered its deepest sympathy and condolences to the families, friends and colleagues of those who have been lost following the fire on the Deepwater Horizon oil rig in the Gulf of Mexico this week.*
>
> *Group Chief Executive Tony Hayward said: "We owe a lot to everyone who works on offshore facilities around the world and no words can express the sorrow and pain when such a tragic incident happens.*

Note the clichéd, detached language in the first statement (" . . . our concerns and thoughts are with . . . ") and contrast that with the statement made several days later (" . . . no words can express the sorrow and pain when such a tragic incident happens . . . ").

As we discussed, this is not the only reason why BP had such trouble responding in the initial phases of the crisis, but it certainly didn't help. If they had thought fully and carefully prepared some language for this type of incident before it happened (since it was clearly foreseeable), they might not have fallen back on initial statements that clearly did little to reassure the public that BP cared about what was happening.

Volkswagen's Weak Statements in the Initial Phases of Its Emission Scandal

Consider another one of the largest crises to erupt over the past several years: The Volkswagen AG vehicle emissions scandal, which leapt onto the front pages in 2015. Volkswagen's handling of reports of falsified emissions data over the course of half a decade quickly became one of the biggest crisis communications stories in recent years.

The background: On Friday, Sept. 18, 2015, the U.S. Environmental Protection Agency (EPA) accused Volkswagen of cheating by installing software in 500,000 diesel cars that allowed the vehicles to show low emissions of nitrogen oxides when tested. When these cars were actually on the road, they spewed as much as 40 times the U.S. legal limit.[5]

The software was installed in cars starting in 2009, and the company knew about potential issues for three years before the news broke. Volkswagen, in discussions with regulators, apparently chalked up the disparity between laboratory and road to technical glitches.[6]

Indeed, a fascinating element of the Volkswagen story is often overlooked: Researchers at the University West Virginia started testing Volkswagen vehicles in 2012. West Virginia regulators and the federal EPA knew about these tests (which were public knowledge) in 2013, and began their own investigations shortly thereafter. Yet, the company was completely flat-footed when it came to crisis communications response.[7]

In response to the EPA's announcement, Volkswagen issued a statement that is another prime example of weakness in messaging:

VOLKSWAGEN STATEMENT REGARDING EPA INVESTIGATION

September 19, 2015—Volkswagen Group of America, Inc., Volkswagen AG and Audi AG received today notice from the U.S. Environmental Protection Agency, U.S. Department of Justice and the California Air Resources Board of an investigation related to certain emissions compliance matters. As environmental protection and sustainability are among Volkswagen's strategic corporate objectives, the company takes this matter very seriously and is cooperating with the investigation.

Volkswagen is committed to fixing this issue as soon as possible. We want to assure customers and owners of these models that their automobiles are safe to drive, and we are working to develop a remedy that meets emissions standards and satisfies our loyal and valued customers. Owners of these vehicles do not need to take any action at this time.[8]

Volkswagen's response is a masterwork of cold, confusing, detached corporate speak. It is no wonder the story only began to grow as the crisis took off.

Indeed, you see this "bad statement/better statement" dynamic over and over again in each one of the crisis communications examples we cover. Like BP and Target before it, Volkswagen issued a new statement several days later, taking a more "human" approach to the crisis. This time, the statement came directly from Volkswagen's CEO, Dr. Martin Winterkorn, and addressed some of the key elements of an appropriate crisis communications message that we outlined above:

I personally am deeply sorry that we have broken the trust of our customers and the public. We will cooperate fully with the responsible agencies, with transparency and urgency, to clearly, openly, and completely establish all of the facts of this case. Volkswagen has ordered an external investigation of this matter. We do not and will not tolerate violations of any kind of our internal rules or of the law.

The trust of our customers and the public is and continues to be our most important asset. We at Volkswagen will do everything that must be done in order to re-establish the trust that so many people have placed in us, and we will do everything necessary in order to reverse the damage this has caused. This matter has first priority for me, personally, and for our entire Board of Management.[9]

Five days later, Winterkorn resigned.

In fact, Volkswagen's crisis communications miscues throughout its emissions scandal (which is still ongoing as of this writing) are almost too numerous to mention. One prime example revolved around the December 2015 release of the preliminary findings of an internal inquiry by the chairman of the company, which stated without equivocation that the cheating scandal was *not* a one-time error, that it was deliberate, and that the decision by employees to cheat on emissions tests and lie about the results was made more than a decade ago. However, just a month later, during an interview with National Public Radio (NPR) at the North American International Auto Show in Detroit, the Volkswagen's new CEO, Matthias Müller, stated that the company "didn't lie" to American regulators before the scandal came to light, instead chalking up the failed tests to a technical problem. After the segment aired, Mr. Müller called NPR to do another interview and retract this comment.

Again, Volkswagen knew this scandal was coming for two years—plenty of time to get your ducks in a row, message-wise. Yet, as is the case with so many major corporations, they did nothing and wound up with bland, cold corporate emissions (if you'll pardon the pun) that did little to reassure a questioning public, and in fact, raised as many questions as they answered.

Wal-Mart in Mexico

Or consider a different crisis response, one that—while full of tactics (and words)—was missing a coherent message and strategy as well: Wal-Mart's slow and ineffective reaction to 2012 Mexican bribery allegations against the company.

Indeed this case has a twist at the end that reinforces everything we've been learning about in *Chief Crisis Officer*.

In April 2012, published reports alleged that Wal-Mart was involved in a brazen pattern of bribery in Mexico, with the goal of reaching "market dominance" in that country. The first news report, detailed in a page one story in

The New York Times, stated that when confronted with evidence of this bribery campaign and a recommendation to expand an internal investigation,
"Wal-Mart's leaders shut it down."[10] The initial *Times* story dominated legal
and business news for more than a week, with each day bringing new allegations, information, and analysis. This reporting eventually won the Pulitzer
Prize for Investigative Reporting.

After the story broke, Wal-Mart began feeling pain not only to their reputation but financially as well, in ways that far outstripped the actual potential liability. The company's shares were hammered: At one point, Wal-Mart
stock was down more than 8 percent in two days. To put this drop in context:
According to Reuters, those two days of losses wiped out more than $10 bil-
lion in market value. In the meantime, there was a 12 percent loss in shares
of "Wal-Mart de Mexico," a separate company stock that trades on Mexico's
IPC index.[11]

Indeed, the damage to their reputation and finances appears to have
been far greater than any punishment contemplated under the worst cases
of the Foreign Corrupt Practices Act (FCPA), which bars U.S. companies
from paying bribes overseas. Consider this analysis from *The Wall Street
Journal*:

> "In the U.S., legal experts said Wal-Mart could face years of stepped-up
> regulatory scrutiny, hundreds of millions of dollars in fines, and the
> appointment of an outside monitor to oversee compliance with foreign
> bribery laws, if the Department of Justice determines the bribery allega-
> tions are true."[12]

This is tough stuff, but by no means in the $10 billion range, which high-
lights the importance of a crisis communications response. As in the examples of BP, Target, Volkswagen, and other companies, an effective response
just wasn't there.

In the wake of the initial revelations, Wal-Mart issued a long and incredi-
bly defensive statement:

> We take compliance with the U.S. Foreign Corrupt Practices Act (FCPA)
> very seriously and are committed to having a strong and effective global
> anti-corruption program in every country in which we operate.
>
> We will not tolerate noncompliance with FCPA anywhere or at any
> level of the company.
>
> Many of the alleged activities in The New York Times article are
> more than six years old. If these allegations are true, it is not a reflec-
> tion of who we are or what we stand for. We are deeply concerned
> by these allegations and are working aggressively to determine what
> happened.

In the fall of last year, the Company, through the Audit Committee of the Board of Directors, began an extensive investigation related to compliance with the FCPA. That investigation is being conducted by outside legal counsel and forensic accountants, who are experts in FCPA compliance, and they are reporting regularly to the Audit Committee.

We have met voluntarily with the U.S. Department of Justice (DOJ) and the Securities and Exchange Commission (SEC) to self-disclose the ongoing investigation on this matter. We also filed a 10-Q in December to inform our shareholders of the investigation. The Company's outside advisors have and will continue to meet with the DOJ and SEC to report on the progress of the investigation.

We are committed to getting to the bottom of this matter. The audit committee and the outside advisors have at their disposal all the resources they may need to pursue a comprehensive and thorough investigation.

We have taken a number of actions in Mexico to establish stronger FCPA compliance.

We have implemented enhanced FCPA compliance measures including:

- *Robust policies and procedures;*
- *Internal controls;*
- *Training;*
- *Enhanced auditing procedures; and*
- *Issue escalation and remediation protocols.*

In addition, we have established a dedicated FCPA compliance director in Mexico that reports directly to our Home Office in Bentonville.

The investigation is ongoing and we don't have a full explanation of what happened. It would be inappropriate for us to comment further on the specific allegations until we have finished the investigation.

We are working hard to understand what occurred in Bentonville more than six years ago and are committed to conducting a complete investigation before forming conclusions.

We don't want to speculate or weave stories from incomplete inquiries and limited recollections, as others might do.

Unfortunately, we realize that, at this point, there are some unanswered questions. We wish we could say more but we will not jeopardize the integrity of the investigation.

We are confident we are conducting a comprehensive investigation and if violations of our policies occurred here, we will take appropriate action.

Over the last several years, Walmart has focused diligently on FCPA compliance and implemented a series of changes to our FCPA compliance program to further strengthen them. This work is ongoing and continues today.

As part of that effort, in the spring of 2011, we initiated a world-wide review of our anti-corruption program. We are taking a deep look at our policies and procedures in every country in which we operate. This includes developing and implementing recommendations for FCPA training, anti-corruption safeguards, and internal controls.

Acting with integrity is the essence of our corporate culture. We have the same high standards of integrity for every associate— regardless of his or her position—and everyone is held accountable for those standards.

In a large global enterprise such as Walmart, sometimes issues arise despite our best efforts and intentions. When they do, we take them seriously and act as quickly as possible to understand what happened. We take action and work to implement changes so the issue doesn't happen again. That's what we're doing today.

Walmart is committed to doing the right thing and we are working hard every day to become an even better company.[13]

Wow—this statement is 630 words long. Wal-Mart also posted a video on their corporate website that refuted the charges and announced the creation of a new global compliance officer position that will oversee five regional compliance directors. The company said it would add "new protocols" to make sure FCPA investigations are managed "consistently and independently."

As you already know, the number one rule in responding to a crisis such as this one is: *Be Prepared*. In the message context, preparation is important when putting together statements, press releases, message points, and other documents that will help you convey proper information to the public in a timely manner, explain your company's position, or express the appropriate compassion or concern over injuries or other negative consequences. As we've seen, a tendency exists among corporations to respond in a muted manner to these crises in the hopes of downplaying the media coverage and minimizing its impact. Perhaps this works sometimes, but in Wal-Mart's case, the original reporting by *The New York Times* had obviously been under way for quite some time; Wal-Mart knew about it, and it was clearly going to be big news. This is especially the case considering the executives who were implicated (including the company's current and former CEO), as well as the detail and depth of the evidence presented (indeed, the article included actual links to memos and emails concerning the alleged bribery.) There was no way this crisis was going to go quietly.

And although I have no direct link into the minds and hearts of the Wal-Mart executives handling the matter at the time, I suspect "ignore and hope it goes away" was central to the initial game plan (followed, it would seem, by "panic and issue a long, ineffective statement"). In any case, the parallels to the other major crises we've discussed in this book is stunning. Consider this: After issuing a statement when the article was posted on *The New York Times* website on Saturday night, Wal-Mart felt the need to issue an "Updated Wal-Mart Statement" Tuesday morning, detailing the actions it was taking in more concrete terms. As we've seen, whenever a company has to issue a second press release a day later—not to update the public on latest developments but rather to explain the first—it's a pretty clear sign they weren't ready.

A second piece of evidence highlighting the slap-dash nature of the response: Although (as noted above) a senior corporate compliance position was created, no one was appointed to the post. Yet, according to the *Times* article, Wal-Mart knew about the investigation for at least six months. Again, I am speculating, but it is not unreasonable to suspect that this corporate compliance idea was hatched *after* the company and its advisors realized the crisis wasn't going to blow over.

What could Wal-Mart have done differently? Well, they had months to get their story straight and prepare proper messages to respond when the story inevitably hit the pages of *The New York Times.* If properly prepared, these messages wouldn't have read like a lawyer's screed (as above) and would have succinctly and compellingly communicated what is buried in that 630-word tome—that these are complicated matters, Wal-Mart is investigating the issue thoroughly (working closely with authorities), and the company doesn't tolerate bribery of any kind.

Personally—and now I'm getting very tactical—I wouldn't have let *The New York Times* get the first bite of the apple if I saw a negative story about my company's businesses' practices in the works. I might have considered getting the story out on the right terms, in the right context, and in a "friendlier" media outlet—acknowledging mistakes where appropriate and providing a complete description of the steps being taken to ensure a zero-tolerance policy for such practices—long before *The New York Times* could sink their teeth into the story. From my experience working on these sorts of stories, Wal-Mart should have known that the *Times* story was headed in a negative direction—the company (according to their statement) had been working with regulators on investigating these issues for months. I'd have advised Wal-Mart to get ahead of the story to frame it properly in the public's mind long before the *Times* piece went to press.

In addition, I would have had the right person in mind for that corporate compliance post: a "new sheriff in town" with a reputation that reassures the public, the financial community, and the media that there is a real commitment to change. I may have advised Wal-Mart to use this opportunity to start a real debate over the FCPA, its many "gray" areas, and whether the statute handcuffs corporations trying to compete globally. Although no one condones bribery, real issues exist that should be aired publicly as the United States rebuilds its economic muscle. Engendering such a debate in advance of the *Times* story might have put the allegations into the proper context.

I am Monday-morning quarterbacking, I know, but I think these very simple strategic and messaging practices are sometimes lost unless a company has prepared for them.

An interesting postscript exists to this Wal-Mart story. In October 2015, *The Wall Street Journal* published a story that indicated that more than three years *after* the initial allegations surfaced in *The New York Times*, "a high-level federal probe" of the allegations found "little in the way of major offenses, and is likely to result in a much smaller case than investigators first expected, according to people familiar with the probe."[14] While the investigation wasn't over, *The Wall Street Journal* story revealed that it was likely that the case might be resolved with just a fine and no criminal charges against any Wal-Mart executives. So, the initial stunning revelations in the pages of *The New York Times* may have had far less truth to them than had been realized at the time.

So—in another bout of Monday-morning quarterbacking—this suggests that the lack of crisis communications preparation, including getting the right messages together to combat what may have been a grossly exaggerated story, cost the nation's largest retailer more than $10 billion in market value, despite the apparent lack of fire to accompany the initial smoke.

Formulating Template Messages in the Crisis Plan

Hopefully, I've convinced you that if you have a strategy and the proper crisis communications plan in place (using the procedures we outlined in Chapter 3), you can avoid some of the pitfalls that we've looked at in this chapter and ensure you are creating messages that resonate with the proper public audiences in a manner that doesn't allow your crisis to spin out of control. But can you realistically anticipate every possible crisis scenario that might possibly face your company, and create template messages beforehand to respond?

Of course not. You cannot anticipate everything, but you don't have to. You only have to prepare scenarios for the most common crises your organization might face. It's really not that hard either—10, 20, 30, or whatever the number might be for your particular size, industry, and risk profile. If you're Wal-Mart, you might have more; a small Mom-and-Pop retailer with less than a dozen locations will have less. My point is that the Chief Crisis Officer and his or her team should have thought long and hard about these crisis scenarios and the messages that would work under a variety of circumstances well before the accident occurs, the data breach is discovered, or *The New York Times* investigative reporter calls.

Moreover, if your crisis plan is a "living document," you are constantly updating your templates for various crisis scenarios based on what works and what doesn't, as well as new potential crises that weren't on your radar when the crisis plan was first created.

I know there are skeptics out there: "Sorry, no, there's no way. Our business is just too big, too complex, the issues we face too often *sui generis*. It wouldn't work for us."

Respectfully, you are wrong. Just as BP could have anticipated an oil leak in the Gulf of Mexico, Target a credit card data breach, and Volkswagen rigged test data given to regulators, your organization's crisis communications team can sit down and anticipate the top crisis scenarios that might confront your company. After all, Wal-Mart, for example, surely could have anticipated potential FCPA investigations and media interest. They operate in 28 countries on five continents: Issues involving potential bribery in one of those countries is clearly within Wal-Mart's risk profile.

Technology can play a role here as well. Effective crisis communications software, which can bring the crisis team together virtually and provide tools and a collaborative platform for effective crisis response, can host a range of templates, talking points, employee emails, and other messages for your Chief Crisis Officer to use as a starting point for a range of crisis situations, everything from anonymous social media posts disparaging a product, to investigations and litigation or the sudden death of a key employee (the software my company created, in fact, even has a catalog of Tweets that can be employed in various scenarios when a crisis breaks.) The point is: A basic template that contains sample language and messaging serves as a starting point for the crisis communications team and will lead to the creation of better public messages (even if, in many cases, the final statement issued barely resembles the initial template).

We took a brief look at a "Sample Media 'Holding' Statement" in Chapter 3, as part of the Crisis Flash Sheet we created in our crisis communications plan. A more detailed template for a crisis scenario might look like this:

Accident: Facility Fire (Detailed)[15]

STATEMENT OF [Spokesperson]
[Company]

[LOCATION] (DATE)—On [DATE], at approximately [TIME], a fire was reported in [location of facility and area of fire]. Our personnel promptly notified [AUTHORITIES], while other employees [STEPS TAKEN, IF ANY, TO CONTROL FIRE IN INITIAL STAGES].

Fire crews arrived at approximately [TIME]. The fire was contained and controlled by [TIME].

[DESCRIBE INJURIES AND/OR PROPERTY DAMAGE AND EVACUATION MEASURES]. Local authorities tested [ENVIRON-MENTAL ISSUES, IF ANY, THAT HAVE BEEN DISCOVERED].

The cause of the fire is under investigation and is not yet known [ALTERNATE: DESCRIBE WHAT IS KNOWN ABOUT THE CAUSE].

We want to assure everyone in our local community that our company takes this incident, and all issues related to fire safety, very seriously. We work closely with fire officials and other authorities to provide the most effective fire response system possible. Our facility is regularly inspected by authorities, and we quickly responds to recommended corrective measures. We also engage in regular fire prevention training and inspect our facilities on an ongoing basis and implement corrective measures resulting from those inspections [CONFIRM ACCURACY].

We want to thank local fire crews and officials and [OTHER OFFI-CIALS] for their quick response and hard work. We will continue to take every possible measure to ensure that incidents of this type are infrequent, and handled with the highest level of professionalism when they do occur.

This is a basic "core" message that we will use to communicate to various audiences about this particular crisis, containing the necessary information, using a heartfelt tone, and short on legalese or jargon. Moreover, the message above can be adapted below as talking points for those communicating via telephone or in person to key stakeholders:

TALKING POINTS[16]

- At approximately [TIME], a fire was reported in [location of facility and area of fire]. Our personnel promptly notified [AUTHORITIES], while other employees [STEPS TAKEN, IF ANY, TO CONTROL FIRE IN INITIAL STAGES].

- Fire crews arrived at approximately [TIME]. The fire was contained and controlled by [TIME]. [DESCRIBE INJURIES AND/OR PROPERTY DAMAGE AND EVACUATION MEASURES]. The cause of the fire is under investigation and is not yet known [ALTERNATE: DESCRIBE WHAT IS KNOWN ABOUT THE CAUSE].

- We want to thank local fire crews and officials and [OTHER OFFICIALS] for their quick response and hard work. We want to assure everyone in our local community that our company takes this incident, and all issues related to fire safety, very seriously. We will continue to take every possible measure to ensure that incidents of this type are infrequent, and handled with the highest level of professionalism when they do occur.

MESSAGE TO EMPLOYEES

This text can also be adapted as a message to employees:

To [COMPANY] Employees,

At approximately [TIME], a fire was reported in [location of facility and area of fire]. Our personnel promptly notified [AUTHORITIES], while other employees [STEPS TAKEN, IF ANY, TO CONTROL FIRE IN INITIAL STAGES].

Fire crews arrived at approximately [TIME]. The fire was contained and controlled by [TIME]. The cause of the fire is under investigation and is not yet known [ALTERNATE: DESCRIBE WHAT IS KNOWN ABOUT THE CAUSE].

We have assured the community, and want to assure you, that our company takes this incident, and all issues related to fire safety, very seriously. We work closely with fire officials and other authorities to provide the most effective fire response system possible.

As many of you know, our facility is regularly inspected by authorities, and we quickly respond to recommended corrective measures. We will continue to take every possible measure to ensure that incidents of this type are infrequent, and handled with the highest level of professionalism when they do occur.

It is critically important to remember that if you are contacted by media or any other outside parties to discuss this incident, you refer such inquiries to [CRISIS RESPONSE CONTACT]. If you have any questions, please contact [EMPLOYEE CONTACT].[17]

TWITTER TEMPLATE

This information can even be given in a Tweet, linking to a more detailed statement:

There is a fire at #[COMPANY HASHTAG] facility at [LOCATION]. Fire crews are on the scene. More information: [LINK TO STATEMENT ON WEBSITE OR FACEBOOK].[18]

You get the point. The immediacy of crisis communications response means we don't have much time to compose messages after the crisis has begun. If you already have detailed templates, you are more prepared to deliver messages during a crisis that—while perhaps not Churchillian in their effect—fulfill their mission to help stop the crisis from spinning out of control.

Action Points

- Companies facing a crisis too often focus on the tool of message delivery—social media, YouTube videos, advertisements, or media appearances—and too little on the messages an organization is trying to convey to its stakeholders and other key target audiences.

- Complexity is often the greatest impediment to effective messaging. Since we are all experts, we create messages with the assumption that our audience will be experts too.

- Modern communications technology have created a world where messages are *commoditized*. For some of history's greatest communicators—Roosevelt, Reagan, Churchill—messages were to be labored over. They worked hard, and the results showed.

- Give the immediacy of modern crisis communications, creating messages that *resonate* after a negative event has occurred is nearly impossible. The pitfalls encountered by such "name-brand" companies as BP, Target, Volkswagen, and Wal-Mart have shown this, which is why organizations must create effective messages for a range of potential crisis scenarios as part of their overall crisis communications effort.

6

Litigation Communications: Managing the Legal Crisis

Traditionally, the public relations and legal functions of Corporate America grew up quite separately, with very little natural opportunity to interact. Public relations dealt mostly with product publicity and the overall reputation of the organization, whereas legal departments tended to work on risk management, contracts, acquisitions and other transactions, and the resolution of specific legal disputes, with little attention to broader public perception concerns.

My, how times have changed.

In this information age, it has become harder to see where issues of legal concern end and issues of public concern begin. This is also true in crisis communications, where legal action is often a central element of the crisis, or lurking slightly off-stage, waiting to make a grand entrance. Notably, the seminal "cyanide-in-the-Tylenol" crisis communications case of the early 1980s, while instructive on many levels, was missing this key element of the modern crisis. In the 30 years since that crisis, regulators, public prosecutors, and plaintiff lawyers have taken center stage in the midst of what had been solely public-facing crisis matters. Thus, the distinct discipline of litigation communications was born.

In this chapter, we will look at litigation communications and consider the subtle differences in handling the legal aspects of crises. We'll then discuss some recent cases in the legal realm that have become full-blown crises. We'll also examine that peculiarly publicity-hungry lawyer—the public prosecutor—who often gets the "first bite of the apple" when dealing with high-profile legal matters.

In October 2009 at 12:30 a.m., an explosion and fire occurred at a fuel storage facility in Puerto Rico. It was initially unclear whether anyone was injured in the explosion as the fire raged throughout the day, sending a cloud of smoke and ash into the sky.

By early afternoon, the first class action lawsuit was filed, naming the oil company and its insurer as defendants.

When the plaintiffs' lawyer was asked how he could file a lawsuit so quickly, without any sense as to the cause or potential damages, and before the debris from the explosion had even returned to earth, he simply stated:

"It's simple . . . what goes up, must come down."

This is the brave new world of crisis communications, where legal issues are intertwined with the actual physical event at the heart of what is traditionally considered a "crisis." Particularly in the United States, the modern crisis plays out in a world where law, regulation, and, yes, plaintiffs' lawyers now infiltrate all aspects of our business and personal lives. Just as this fact has changed the face of the modern crisis (and business operations in general), modern crisis communications must also change to confront these newly pervasive elements.

In other words, virtually all crises are now legal crises. Legal action—from the filing of a particularly scandalous complaint at the courthouse, through hearings and discovery, to the final disposition of the case—have become highly public events. With that in mind, in this chapter, we're going to take a closer look at handling the particular elements of the "legal crisis"—either the central event that triggers the crisis communications response or its offshoot—and how crisis communications can, and must, change in an era where all the world's your courtroom and every crisis has a legal issues baked into it.

The Confluence of Crisis and Litigation Communications

Now here's an interesting point: When I wrote the first edition of my book *In the Court of Public Opinion* in 2003, I made an argument that might seem contradictory to some of the discussion in this chapter. In my earlier book, I argued quite forcefully that litigation communications was a separate and distinct discipline from crisis communications, and those who treat litigation communications as just another crisis communications event are doing a disservice to their client, their case and their cause.

I pointed out that, traditionally, crisis communications is about having an *immediate* response ready (a main focus of this book, of course)—having a crisis plan and a crisis communications team in place long before a crisis occurs, alerting the crisis team at the earliest possible moment, securing the site or crisis location, and having a spokesperson trained and ready to respond within the critical first hours. By contrast, litigation communications may contain crisis elements (e.g., that first moment after a lawsuit is filed), but it doesn't unfold over 24, 48, or 72 hours. Rather, it ebbs and flows with the rhythms of the litigation itself. Moreover, the issues in litigation are often stupefying in their complexity, and the action takes place in a series of papers filed in court rather than in the real world. Finally, in a legal crisis, the company's CEO or other top executive is often may not be the company's best spokesperson—in many cases the company's lawyer is usually more suited to delivering the communications message.

All of this is still true, but what I have noticed more and more is the fact that while not all litigation communications matters are crises, nearly all crisis communications situations now involve a legal component that must be considered when responding. Thus, modern crisis communications necessarily includes considerations of legal ramifications when preparing a response during those first 24 to 72 hours—the "textbook" time frame for crisis communication response since, at least, the "cyanide-in-the-Tylenol" case of the early 1980s.

What has changed? Isn't the Tylenol case the gold standard for crisis response? Why start changing crisis protocols now?

The answer lies in the fact that, over the past 30 years, we have seen a build-up of factors that have altered the landscape of business and communication:

- **Increased law and regulation:** Consider the fact that in just the past several years in the United States, we've had Dodd-Frank Wall Street Reform and Consumer Protect Act, the Affordable Care Act, and a host of new laws in all 50 states aimed at protecting consumers, employees, and the environment. Whether you believe our society is better or worse off as a result of these new laws and regulations is irrelevant. These laws now exist and every business step—and misstep—has legal and regulatory reverberations that must be considered before action is taken. One example can be found in the 2013 Target data breach (which we examined in Chapter 5), where in addition to responding to the media and key stakeholders, the company faced the prospect of complying with 47 separate state laws related to public and regulatory notification during a data breach involving customers' personal information. This is a daunting challenge indeed, and one that simply wasn't on the landscape in the "cyanide-in-the-Tylenol" days.

- **Aggressive prosecutors and regulators:** Local prosecutors have always seen their position as a stepping-stone to bigger things (consider Thomas Dewey, Rudy Giuliani or Chris Christie), but in our media- and social media-saturated world, publicity in the pursuit of career advancement sometimes seems as if it has become as much a focus of local prosecutors' work as the pursuit of justice. If they're not thinking about Congress or the governorship, they're thinking about that lucrative job with a private law firm or a financial firm once their term is over. Hence, prosecutors and regulators can be every bit as aggressive as the most ambulance-chasing plaintiff's lawyer when engaging the media in the aftermath of a crisis or related corporate misstep.

- **The rise of the plaintiff's bar and class-action lawsuits:** Class action lawsuits may bring great social benefits to our society as a whole, righting wrongs and holding Corporate America accountable for all manner of misdeeds. Regardless, there is no doubt that from the late 1980s to the present, the class action lawsuit has become a growing feature of crisis communications management and response. In the wake of many (if not most) crises or other negative company events, plaintiffs' lawyers will often assert damages on behalf of consumers, employees, or shareholders. What was once a two-day or perhaps week-long crisis now has a "long tail," with negative reputational impacts related to the incident extending for months or even years.

- **The increasing availability of legal filings and exhibits:** In the old days, a reporter or other interested party had to physically go to the courthouse to pull a hard copy of a legal filing to see information related to a case or receive the copy directly from one of the lawyers (or litigants) in the case. Today? With PACER, the federal government's docking system, anyone with an account can pull up any court filing related to any legal action within minutes. In addition, any party to a litigation can post a legal document to their website using a Scribd editor or similar technology, including TMZ, *The Wall Street Journal*, or *Business Insider*. Want proof? One of the biggest legal issues in fall 2015 in the United States involved litigation related to the falsification of emissions data for diesel vehicles sold in the United States by German automaker Volkswagen. Want to see the latest motion to consolidate the various court cases into a single MDL (multi-district litigation)? I just found it while sitting here drinking my coffee on a Saturday morning. It took less than four minutes.

When viewed in this light, it is little wonder organizations sometimes decide it makes sense for the Chief Crisis Officer of an organization to be the General Counsel or one of his or her assistants and *not* the head of corporate communications or public affairs, some might expect. As we learned in Chapter 2, though, this can have highly negative ramifications for an organization's overall crisis communications response, since (to state the obvious) lawyers are trained as *lawyers*, not *communicators*. This is another reason why companies must have a crisis communications infrastructure in place—including the systems, tools, and personnel—to ensure that the appropriate

"PR mindset" drives what are increasingly becoming legal decisions. Public relations practitioners and crisis communicators may not like this growing intrusion of legal concerns on the practice of our craft, but with the growing trend toward law and regulation impacting every aspect of our lives, they'd better get used to it.

Essentials of Litigation Communications

I've mentioned several times that my earlier book, *In the Court of Public Opinion*, deals specifically with litigation communications in all its facets. My understanding is that it's considered a pretty good book on the topic; if you're interested in learning more, I advise you to pick up a copy.

For the purposes of this book, however, let us take a 10,000-foot look at various aspects of litigation communications in the broader context of the modern crisis. Since all crises now have at least some legal elements to them, we must understand the way the structure and protocols described in this book are applied (or misapplied) to the legal process, so that we can better coalesce the various disciplines into an organized whole for the Chief Crisis Officer and his or her core crisis communications team.

In the Court of Public Opinion

"Your Honor, we feel the trial failed to deliver on its pretrial publicity."

Levity is not usually associated with the legal process, but let's use the cartoon above as a way to frame our discussion.

There is an elemental reason why most litigation doesn't live up to pretrial publicity: Most cases settle (in the civil contexts, estimates run as high as 95 to 98 percent of cases, in fact). Most cases never see a trial and rarely see the inside of a courtroom. The ultimate resolution in most cases isn't the stuff of TV melodrama, with the jury foreman dramatically rising to proclaim the verdict. Rather, the vast majority of legal matters are fought in the pages of motions, briefs, and other documents buried in some legal docket, and behind closed doors during settlement discussions (and those settlements, by the way, are often sealed or otherwise confidential). As a result, the only place where legal issues and legal crises are debated and "decided" is in the proverbial court of public opinion.

This creates a couple of interesting issues. First, even if the case is resolved favorably after the crisis has faded and the news cameras have gone away, there's no guarantee that the media and/or the public will perceive the resolution as a victory for the company involved—since no definitive judicial determination exists upon which to hang one's hat. In many cases it is only the public that determines winners and losers—and, thus, a party to a lawsuit can do much to influence perceptions by properly communications the resolution to that lawsuit (in an agreed-upon settlement press release, for example, or in subsequent interactions with the public). In the event of a negative resolution, there may be ways to minimize the impact if the crisis communications team is working closely with legal team on the proper framing and description of the case and its ultimate result. Thus, managing litigation communications is a *process* and not necessarily just isolated crisis events, one after the other, until the legal issue goes away. And the work of managing perceptions sometimes goes on long after a settlement or other resolution is reached.

Definition of Litigation Communications

Let's back up a little. What is litigation communications? What is the textbook definition? My definition is as follows:

> *Litigation communications is the process of managing communications throughout the process of a legal dispute (as opposed to a crisis event) in a manner that benefits both the case itself and the reputation and business interests of the company or organization.*

But isn't litigation communications just like crisis communications? You prepare as well as you can, then work to minimize or mitigate damages when news of the legal events or litigation occurs.

This is sometimes true, but unlike crisis communications, a *proactive* element exists in litigation communications—that is, there are times when putting a positive message before your target audience can influence the way legal issues are framed in the mind of various stakeholders. In most crisis communications, where reaction and response is the norm.

You May Want Your Story Out There

Let's consider this notion of proactive communication in greater detail.

My mother used to ask me what I did for a living as a PR consultant, and I'd tell her: "I get people in the newspaper, and I keep them out of the newspaper, depending upon what day of the week it is."

This is particularly true in the litigation communications arena, far more so than in the general practice of crisis communications.

For example, during a legal dispute, *you* may be the party that wants to get the news out. You may, in fact, be the aggrieved plaintiff (corporations are often the plaintiffs in suits involving such issues as commercial contracts, intellectual property or anticompetitive behavior). Even as a defendant, there may be various elements of the litigation, cross-claims, and counter lawsuits that you want to promote to give the public more facts surrounding the incident that led to the litigation—and therefore, presumably, more of the truth. Indeed, there may be times during litigation communications, as opposed to crisis communications, when a company or organization is actively trying to make the story bigger, rather than smaller.

Public Perceptions of Lawsuits Affect All Manner of Behavior

> *"I rob banks because that's where the money is."*[2]
> — Willie Sutton, bank robber

Beyond the proactive litigation communications that you might undertake if you are a plaintiff or a defendant with a counterclaim, during litigation communications, you must bear in mind that effective communications may not just impact the reputation of your company or organization but also the progress of the case itself—including the way your adversaries behave—in the current case, and potentially cases to come.

The way you respond publicly in the initial stages of a lawsuit, for example, can have a huge impact on its ultimate resolution: Since we've learned that the vast majority of cases are resolved before trial, this usually means the ultimate cost of a settlement when you sit down at the bargaining table.

Specifically if a party has been beaten up publicly for days, weeks, or months in relation to the litigation, the settlement number will be a whole lot different than if they've managed the crisis elements of the litigation properly during the course of the lawsuit.

Particularly when you are a defendant, the way you respond publicly—and the skill with which you handle the public aspects of the litigation—can impact other areas as well—for example, encouraging or discouraging copycat lawsuits on the same, or even different, issues. The cold, hard fact is that plaintiffs' lawyers are like the bank robber Willie Sutton: They go where the money is. If plaintiffs' lawyers view your company as an easy target, they pile on just as surely as sharks circle chum in the water. They may join the current litigation— particularly in a mass tort or a class action—or file other sorts of cases, including antitrust or shareholder derivative actions, based on the same information. They may even look at other areas of the company's operations, viewing the company as "an easy touch" for potential settlement dollars down the road. In essence, just like in the crisis communications context, the way you respond impacts whether the litigation is contained or begins to spin out of control.

You must then consider regulators, prosecutors, politicians, the investment community and so forth, all of whom believe what they read online and in magazines and newspapers as well—and who have the ability to impact your company and the issue at the heart of the legal dispute. Politicians, prosecutors and regulators? If they see an opportunity to score clear points at the expense of a fumbling defendant, you can be sure they'll take it.

Or as famous defense lawyer once said to me: "What's the difference between the plaintiffs' lawyer and a state regulator? A public pension!"

We'll look at a specific example of the difficulties in facing off with public prosecutors further along in this chapter. My overall point is that if you're not managing the legal crisis in a manner that makes everyone think your company or organization is a "hard target," regulators, prosecutors, politicians, and other audiences will see a real opportunity—an opportunity to score and make a name for themselves.

Responding Effectively to the Crisis Elements of Litigation

What are the key elements and strategies surrounding litigation communications that crisis communicators should know to allow them to respond effectively during this particular subset of crisis issue?

A few general guidelines follow:

1. **Understand the unfolding nature of litigation.** If you are a defendant company or organization, you're at a natural disadvantage when facing

off against plaintiffs' lawyers or prosecutors, because they can usually trot out a sympathetic victim in front of the cameras, or in press releases and other filings, to show the wrong you've done. For example, in the case of a product liability lawsuit, the injured party might be wheeled out in a wheelchair for a press conference or sit down for a tearful one-on-one with *60 Minutes* or one of the morning news programs. In a criminal prosecution, the prosecutor might put forth a presentation of "facts" at a press conference when they file an indictment, attempting to frame the issues out of the gate: Specifically, they want to impart to the public that you or your company are outlaws, and they are the white hat riding into town to clean up Dodge.

The best way to counteract such attacks is to meet the enemy on the battlefield: Frame the issues with key media outlets before they sit down for that teary interview or attend the incendiary press conference. This is hard to do during the initial phases of a lawsuit, when there's a complaint and not much else, but it can be done. Particularly in litigation, remember the following: The other side may get the first bite of the apple . . . but it's a *big* apple. There will be plenty of opportunities to fight back, given the unfolding nature of litigation itself.

During a lawsuit, there will be many events and opportunities to fight, such as the filing of an answer, a motion to dismiss, the discovery process (which goes on for months or years and tends to involve dozens of individuals court filings), a motion for summary judgment, trial (if there is a trial), and appeals. Although the complaint is often the crisis event that catches a company or organization unaware and sets the issues in motion, opportunities exist at various points in a lawsuit to frame the issues with various stakeholders *before* the next filing or event occurs. The core crisis communications team and Chief Crisis Officer should be working with the legal team to figure out when and where those points of inflection exist and use them to properly frame the issues in the minds of the various stakeholders. The filing of a complaint, even with all the attendant emotion and hoopla, is just the opening inning of the ballgame.

2. **Create the "Mantra of the Case."** In doing the above, you're creating what I call the "mantra" of the case: the one or two lines that explain what's really going on in this litigation—messages that become short-hand for media and other audiences when describing the litigation as it moves forward.

Describing "what's really going on" is key. The facts and the law that are at the heart of the story behind the case are usually buried in thousands of pages of legal documents. Deep inside those court filings are core messages that should become your mantra. Digging through those nuggets to find those key elements . . . aye, there's the rub. If you find those nuggets and present them in a compelling fashion—using the facts and the law to tell a story rather than just a procedural play-by-play—you will begin to create a mantra of the case that is repeated over and over again during the course of this particular crisis.

3. **Engage Third Parties Who Are Writing the "History" of the Case.** Who is telling the story? Who is writing the history of the case even as it's going on? The Chief Crisis Officer and the core crisis communications team should be working with the lawyers to engage influential individuals across a variety of disciplines—media, the investment community, politicians, other policymakers, and so forth—who will influence the way the case in perceived now and in the future. Do they understand your story? Are they framing the issues and your side's position in the right way? Engaging third-party commentators who are, quite frankly, telling people what to think about your legal issue can go a long way to establishing, or rewriting, the history of the case.

And as in establishing the "mantra" of the case, the key is to be reaching these audiences on a regular and sustained basis even as the legal crisis is unfolding over months and sometimes years. This can make a difference in saving (or salvaging) a reputation even as the case is fought separately, deep within the pages of voluminous court filings on the docket, in most cases, far removed from the public arena.

A Continuing Process of Communication

Given the above, the Chief Crisis Officer and the core crisis communications team should be working with the legal team throughout the litigation to ensure that a coordinated, proactive system of media outreach is in place. This should be happening at all phases of the litigation, particularly in between the individual filings, so that you are properly framing the issues with various audiences.

Thus, effective litigation communications is not necessarily event-driven. At its most elemental, litigation communications is *not* the stuff of broad press releases and statements posted on company websites, but rather the "hand-to-hand combat" that organizations must engage in to ensure that media and other key audiences fully understand the case and the story behind the individual legal events that occur during litigation process—each with the potential to be its own individual "crisis"—so that the company frames potential rulings in the proper context in terms of impact on the overall litigation and the company's business goals.

There is a simple reason for this proactive posture between court action and other legal events. In most cases, it is difficult, if not impossible, for a legal journalist to understand the overall context of a legal issue from your organization's standpoint *after* the most recent ruling has occurred. There just isn't enough time. The reporter in question has to file a story on the ruling or other court action often within minutes of the event itself. If you haven't been in communication with that reporter all along and haven't provided him or her with a steady flow of information that describes the *real* story of the litigation, how can you expect that media outlet to get the story right?

You can't.

Therefore, your rapid response team must be preparing and reaching out to media in advance of key rulings to give them a complete picture of the case. In many cases, it is highly unlikely the other side is doing just that—particularly if you are up against a sophisticated plaintiffs' lawyer or public prosecutor. In the end, you are doing your client a true disservice if you do not consistently engage your public audiences throughout the litigation process.

Prosecutors and the "First Bite of the Apple"

It's important to remember that although Corporate America rails against plaintiffs' lawyers on a regular basis, prosecutors and regulators often wield the biggest publicity bat against Corporate America—and they do not fear using it in all manner of specious cases to bludgeon unsuspecting defendants into civil or criminal settlement.

I interviewed famed litigator Theodore ("Ted") Wells, Jr., in 2009 on the role of media and public perception in the criminal process. He had the following to say about prosecutors and the way they use media throughout the legal process:

> *"Someone should go back twenty, twenty-five years," he said in an interview in his Sixth Avenue office in Manhattan, "and review prosecutors' indictments over that time."*
>
> *What they'd find, Wells said, is that today's indictments have become little more than press releases with legal captions, "Twenty five years ago, an indictment was a legal document. You read an indictment these days—that's the prosecution's press release right there," Wells said. "It has a huge negative impact on a defendant's ability to get a fair trial."*

As an example, consider Abacus Federal Savings Bank, a minority and family-owned community bank based in the Chinatown neighborhood of Lower Manhattan that I worked with in recent years. The tale of this small, minority-owned bank highlights the ability of prosecutors to use the publicity process to seek conviction "in the public arena" long before a case ever goes to trial, and the ability of an innocent defendant to rewrite the story over time.

With much hoopla, the Manhattan District indicted tiny Abacus, with six branches and little more than $250 million in assets, for mortgage fraud in May 2012. Although no evidence was offered to implicate senior executives or the owners of the bank (who were not charged), Abacus was indicted as an institution—along with a handful of former employees of the bank. Thus, this small bank earned the distinction of being the only bank in the United States indicted as an institution for mortgage fraud in the aftermath of the 2008 financial crisis.

That's right: In the wake of all the subprime shenanigans and interest-only insanity allegedly undertaken by some of the biggest players on Wall Street, a conservative little community bank serving minorities in a corner of a single city was the only bank prosecutors chose to target for criminal prosecution. This is despite the fact that Abacus had—before, during, and after the financial crisis—one of the lowest mortgage default rates in the country: less than 0.5 percent, compared to a national average of more than 5 percent. To quote an article on the case in *BusinessWeek:*

> . . . *while subprime mortgages did have respectable default rates during the housing boom, even then they defaulted at higher rates than other mortgages (hence the name subprime). Abacus' loans, conservative fixed-rate mortgages with high down payments, maintained their minuscule default rate even during the worst of the recession.*[3]

In his indictment (with an accompanying press release and YouTube video, naturally), the DA took quite a victory lap, excoriating the bank as emblematic of all that caused the mortgage crisis, while the individual defendants were needlessly shackled and paraded in a public hallway outside the courtroom before arraignment—in front of a media corral set up specifically for the occasion (this is even though three of the 11 defendants had been charged previously and were already out on bail).

Yet the facts of the indictment didn't exactly match the press event's hype. Only 31 allegedly fraudulent loans were listed in the indictment, and four of those had already been paid off. Of the remaining 27, only one was delinquent. Moreover, these loans were years old; it is well known in mortgage-related circles that the vast majority of questionable mortgage loans fail within the first year.

The kicker? According to court filings, the loans in question had earned at least $174 million for Fannie Mae and its investors during the period in question.

In other words, these loans never hurt anyone. In fact, in stark contrast to the Countrywide's and Wachovia's of the go-go mortgage run-up, little

Abacus loan portfolio consistently made Fannie Mae (and, indirectly, the American taxpayer) money.

According to *BusinessWeek*:

> *In* [Manhattan DA] *Vance's description, Abacus's fraud epitomizes the reckless behavior that swelled—and then burst—the U.S. housing bubble. But Vance was understating the uniqueness of the case . . . If the point was to send a message to Wall Street, the bank was a curious choice. Few people outside the Chinese-American community have ever heard of Abacus. Compared with the whales of global finance, its plankton, with roughly one ten-thousandth the assets of JPMorgan Chase.*

Despite this initial barrage of negative publicity, the bank had the foresight to work month-by-month, piece-by-piece to rebuild its credibility and restore its reputation, both in its local community and the wider banking community. News coverage of the bank's side of the story appeared in *BusinessWeek* and *Crain's New York Business*, among other media outlets. The bank also worked with Matt Taibbi on his 2014 best-selling book, *The Divide*, which feature the Abacus story in a chapter on the way small banks were punished while the big banks walked.

As the case went to trial, it is fair to say that few I spoke to in the close-knit legal community in New York believed that the bank or its leadership had done anything wrong. The case was seen as a bald-faced play for publicity by the prosecutor.

And while it is unclear whether the publicity itself had any direct impact on the case, in June 2015, Abacus Bank was acquitted on all counts. As Gretchen Morgenstern stated in the *New York Times*:

> *Much has been written about the failure of state and federal prosecutors to pursue criminal cases against mighty institutions and high-ranking figures after the 2008 financial crisis. This is a different story, of a powerful prosecutor relentlessly pursuing a speck of a bank that for 31 years has prudently served an immigrant community in New York City.*[4]

Here is the broader lesson: Communications and public perception surrounding litigation unfolds over time. It ebbs and flows, just like the activity in the case itself. Although a flurry of media coverage will follow an indictment or the filing of a criminal or civil complaint, this is only the opening round of the fight.

In Abacus's attempt to ensure that a balanced representation of the case and its issues was given publicly throughout the case's three-year odyssey, I am reminded of the opinion of Justice Anthony Kennedy in a seminal U.S.

Supreme Court case regarding a defendant's right to protect himself publicly against prosecutorial statements that skew perceptions:

> *An attorney's duties do not begin inside the courtroom door. He or she cannot ignore the practical implications of a legal proceeding for the client. Just as an attorney may recommend a plea bargain or civil settlement to avoid the adverse consequences of a possible loss after trial, so too an attorney may take reasonable steps to defend a client's reputation and reduce the adverse consequences of indictment, especially in the face of a prosecution deemed unjust or commenced with improper motives. A defense attorney may pursue lawful strategies to obtain dismissal of an indictment or reduction of charges, including an attempt to demonstrate in the court of public opinion that the client does not deserve to be tried.*[5]**

What Is This Case All About?

How do you describe what a case is all about? This comes back to the message.

As we learned in Chapter 5, constructing the proper message—one that is compelling and doesn't fall back on tired clichés—is often given short shrift during crisis communications response. Sometimes during litigation, given the vagaries of the legal process itself and the particular training of the legal team, the quality of message suffers even further. As in Chapter 5, I can't reiterate enough how important a strong, succinct, and quality message is to winning the public battle, particularly during a legal crisis. If you want to compel, you have to be compelling.

Thus, it is highly inadvisable to fall back on tired clichés during high-profile legal matters. You can't spout bromides like "We do not comment publicly on litigation" or its equally vacuous variant "These charges are without merit and we will defend ourselves vigorously" (as if a party might announce it *wasn't* going to defend itself vigorously) and expect these statements to have positive results. These statements are the litigation communications equivalent of the hand-over-the-camera-lens "No Comment"—they are knee-jerk clichés, built up over years of misuse by ill-informed legal counsel. If you engage in such cliché mongering, don't be surprised if your response to particular litigation winds up buried toward the bottom of an article, or ignored entirely. The legal reporter on the receiving end of such a response knows it's a load of crap, as does the public.

---

* An excellent documentary on the Abacus case, entitled "Abacus: Small Enough To Jail," is set for theatrical release in May 2017.

Where Legal and PR Concerns Conflict

Indeed, there a lot of areas where "standard legal practice" can have an enormously negative effect on the perception of a legal case in the eyes of the public or other relevant audiences. Legal writing buried deep within the court docket can sometimes find its way to media and other public audiences—often in a very negative way. Moreover, many legal arguments and other statements considered "boilerplate" in court filings are shockingly tin-eared when it comes to the court of public opinion. The Chief Crisis Officer and his or her team must be in close contact with an organization's legal department—and any outside attorneys working on a particular legal case—to ensure that the messages conveyed in court filings and other legal documents don't "blow back" in the court of public opinion, causing reputational damage far in excess of any potential legal advantage.

To highlight this, let's look at two examples—one involving a company that we already examined in Chapter 5: Wal-Mart.

Wal-Mart Blames Tracy Morgan

On June 7, 2014, a Wal-Mart tractor-trailer on the New Jersey Turnpike crashed into comedian Tracy Morgan's limo, critically injuring Morgan and two members of his entourage while killing another comedian, James McNair. A month later, Morgan and the others sued Wal-Mart for their injuries in federal court.

Wal-Mart responded with a court filing of its own, which provides an example of the way practicing lawyers sometimes don't consider the reputational impact of the arguments they make in legal documents that can inevitably wind up in the public's hands. In its court filing, Wal-Mart claimed Morgan's injuries were, at least in part, his own fault. This is the legal concept of "contributory negligence," and it is considered pretty standard in a court case. However, in this particular case, the public response to the legal argument was anything but standard.

The claim was immediately picked up by national media outlets and made headlines for weeks. CBS News.com, for example, blared a headline reporting that "Tracy Morgan: 'Can't Believe' Wal-Mart Blaming Him for Crash Injuries."

Again, to be fair to Wal-Mart, claiming the victim may be responsible for his or her injuries is a standard "affirmative defense" in personal injury lawsuits. Lawyers plead these defenses routinely, even if there is no current evidence to support them, because they can't add the defense later. The legal team hopes that during the discovery process, they'll find evidence to support their claims. If don't find any evidence, they just drop the claim—no harm, no foul.

Unless, of course, your plaintiff is a famous comedian, and media of all kinds are closely watching the case.

Here's the point: Wal-Mart and its lawyers should have known that Tracy Morgan's personal-injury lawsuit was not your typical tort claim. Morgan's celebrity made the case extremely high profile and placed every court document and filing under the microscope. Part of the discussion between attorneys and media professionals should have been whether the negative reputational fallout from invoking such an affirmative defense outweighs any possible legal gain.

By following the standard legal procedure and asserting the affirmative defense, Wal-Mart gave Morgan's lawyers all the ammunition they needed to paint the company as an unfeeling corporate giant. This enormously damaged the company's public image, as headlines ricocheted to all corners of the media and social media landscape for more than a week.

And Morgan and his legal team knew how to use these headlines to their benefit. "After I heard what Wal-Mart said in court I felt I had to speak out," Morgan said in a statement. "I can't believe Wal-Mart is blaming me for an accident that they caused."

His attorneys also issued a strong statement attacking Wal-Mart, which further fed growing support for their client. "Tracy Morgan is struggling to recover and they answer and blame him and the other victims for what they caused," they said. "That's despicable."[6]

Wal-Mart's response? Tepid and legalistic: A Wal-Mart spokesperson said that "Walmart filed its official response to the plaintiffs' lawsuit earlier today, and the company continues to stand willing to work with Mr. Morgan and the other plaintiffs to resolve this matter."[7]

This weak response probably didn't do much to counter negative perceptions. In fact, the next day the company responded again issuing a slightly longer statement that sounded a little more human (as we have seen throughout this book, the "second press release to clarify the first" is a sure sign of a weak crisis communication response): "Walmart is committed to working to resolve all of the remaining issues as a result of the accident. While we were required to respond to the lawsuit, we have also taken steps to encourage settlement discussions."[8]

By following standard legal tactics for an atypical case, Wal-Mart created a PR mess for itself and gave Morgan additional ammunition to force the company to settle on highly favorable terms in early 2015. Since this case was headed toward settlement anyway, there can be little doubt Wal-Mart should have had a keener eye toward potential media scrutiny and tailored its legal tactics accordingly.

When Legal Principles Conflict with Corporate Principles

Or consider this example, from another recent case: In January 2015, New York–based retailer Saks Fifth Avenue dealt with a similar media assault that also became a teaching moment. This case underscores the fact that the legal team must fully understand a company's position on public issues. In the Saks case, routine legal strategies began to wreak havoc on the company's reputation as LGBT-friendly, which the retailer had painstaking built up in recent years. Saks's standard legal approach to a discrimination claim came back to haunt the company in a very big way.

The story: Leyth O. Jamal, a transgender woman who worked in a Saks store in Houston until 2012, sued the company, claiming she was discriminated against by being referred to as "he," being forced to use the men's bathroom, and being pressured to look more masculine, among other things.

Jamal's suit, in federal court in Texas, did not get much media attention when it was initially filed. That changed once Saks responded.

In a December 2014 Motion to Dismiss, Saks stated that Jamal had no case, because although Title VII of the Civil Rights Act of 1964 protects against sex bias, it doesn't protect against gender-identity bias. To put it more legalistically from the motion itself, "transsexuals are not a protected class under Title VII."

This is where Saks's reputation woes began. Human Rights Campaign, a Washington, DC-based civil-rights group for the LGBT community, decided to go all-out promoting the lawsuit and Saks's response. On Jan. 8, 2015, the group said it was taking the "rare step" of suspending Saks from its Corporate Equality Index (on which the retailer previously received a highly positive score). It laid out the details of Jamal's case and attacked Saks for its legal argument. This led to a spate of articles with headlines like *Businessweek*'s "Saks Claims It Has the Right to Discriminate Against Transgender Employees."[9]

Much of the coverage mentioned that although courts are split as to whether Title VII protects against gender-identity bias, both the U.S. Department of Justice (DOJ) and the U.S. Equal Employment Opportunity Commission (EEOC) have said it does. But as *Businessweek* pointed out, EEOC rulings and DOJ memos don't have the force of federal law or federal court decisions.

Saks found itself in a difficult position. Lawyers' standard operating procedure is to try to get a suit dismissed in its initial stages by arguing that, even if we accept all the facts in the plaintiff's complaint as true (as a judge must do in deciding a motion to dismiss), the allegations don't give rise to a legal case.

In legalese, there is a "failure to state a claim upon which relief can be granted." Saks argued that relief could not be granted to Jamal because Title VII doesn't cover transgender rights.

Again, although that is a legally sound approach, organizations would be wise to be aware of and prepare for potential reputational fallout. *Buzz-Feed* quoted Jamal's lawyer, Jillian Weiss, as making a statement that while legally dubious (given the split in the courts), underscores how a company can become a punching bag, "I don't have any problem with Saks strongly defending this case, but that doesn't require them to make statements that transgender people are not protected from sex discrimination."[10]

Weiss added: "They can't both be a defender of LGBT equality and argue that there should be no LGBT equality."

In their initial response to the media torrent, Saks issued a statement stating that it didn't discriminate, and that the facts didn't support Jamal's accusations of bias. "Saks maintains a long history of policies and practices that are fully supportive of the LGBT community and our LGBT Associates," it said.

Reporters pressed on one question: Does Saks believe Title VII covers gender identity? Saks responded: "We have no further comment."

Shortly thereafter, Gerald L. Storch, CEO of Saks parent Hudson's Bay Co., echoed Saks' contradictory responses in *The New York Times*. Storch told the reporter that the company didn't discriminate against Jamal: "It's preposterous to think that in any way Saks Fifth Avenue is anything but a strong advocate for LGBT rights."

He then refused to discuss the now hot-button issue of its legal strategy. As with earlier statements, the company had to follow up with another statement to the *Times* in which it said it believed Title VII protects everyone from sex bias, but Jamal isn't claiming that—she's claiming gender-identity bias (there's that second statement again, explaining earlier responses!). Saks said it would follow court precedent that gender identity isn't covered "until it is modified by the courts or the legislature."

Storch's *Times* interview compelled Human Rights Campaign to issue a press release over PR Newswire headlined "Saks Fifth Avenue Doubles Down on LGBT Discrimination." In it, the group again excoriated the company's legal strategy. Compounding the reputational damage, on January 15, New York State Attorney General Eric Schneiderman opened an investigation into the company's treatment of transgender employees.

"Mr. Storch's abhorrent decision not to renounce that position is not only morally wrong, but wrong on the law," Schneiderman wrote, quoting Sarah Warbelow, HRC's legal director, and citing the EEOC and DOJ stances.[11]

The PR blowback was so fierce that, less than a week later, Saks reversed course and finally placed its reputational needs before its legal strategy. On January 26, Saks withdrew its Motion to Dismiss entirely. It is extremely rare to see public backlash affect a legal strategy so dramatically, but Saks seemed determined to defend its reputation as an ally of the LGBT community.

Saks' statement explaining the withdrawal of its motion to dismiss vehemently denied the company discriminates against transgender people.

> *"Our position is, and always has been, that it is unacceptable to discriminate against transgender individuals," the retailer said. "Saks does not, and will not, tolerate discrimination and legal strategy should not obscure that bedrock commitment."*[12]

The company said that it would now fight the suit on the merits.

Saks was clearly trying to repair the hit to its reputation, ultimately deciding that the legal strategy wasn't worth the damage to Saks business and prestige.*

Action Points

- All crises now have a legal component to them, so the Chief Crisis Officer and his or her core crisis communications team must have an understanding of litigation communication and how it differs from traditional crisis communications.

- Prosecutors and plaintiffs' lawyers now have myriad outlets for disseminating information about legal disputes—most are skilled and ready to use the public arena as a platform to present their side of the case directly to audiences.

- The true story of your case is often buried deep within the docket, and if you are not careful, you will let the other side frame the issues in a manner that can be highly damaging to your company's reputation and its case.

- Issues must be framed and explained to media and other audiences throughout the course of the litigation—not just when individual events, rulings, and filings attract the public attention.

- The crisis communications team must be in continuous communication with a company's legal team and outside lawyers to ensure that both sides have a thorough understanding of the way litigation issues may be perceived by various public audiences.

---

* Many thanks to my colleague Thom Weidlich, and former colleague, Rachel Gamson, who originally reported on the Wal-Mart/Tracy Morgan case and the Saks Fifth Avenue case for our CrisisResponsePro.com software product.

Technology and Crisis Communications

Throughout this book, we've talked about the need for speed in crisis communications. More than any other factor, the ability of the Chief Crisis Officer and his or her crisis communications team to move quickly in the early stages of a crisis can, quite literally, mean the difference between a crisis that is contained and one that rapidly begins to spins out of control. Thus, as we learned in Chapter 2, the Chief Crisis Officer must be the type of professional who is decisive and has the authority to act. In Chapter 3, we learned the importance of having an effective crisis communications plan in place—a playbook, of sorts, to ensure you are not making it up as you go along.

But how do you further ensure your crisis response protocols have the necessary velocity to ensure success? Technology can provide the key. With the right technology in place, particularly in those critical early phases of a crisis, the Chief Crisis Officer and his or her team can assess and share information about the events unfolding before them, draw on resources and messages tailored to the situation at hand, and collaborate on strategies and tactics to ensure a crisis is managed effectively and efficiently despite the chaos of those opening moments.

> *"Software is the catalyst that will remake entire industries during the next decade. We are single-mindedly focused on partnering with the best innovators pursuing the biggest markets"*[1]
> — Marc Andreessen, venture capitalist and inventor of Netscape

This chapter examines technology and how it will one day change the practice of crisis communications.

"But Jim," you ask, "with social media, brand monitoring, and other software being used every day in the crisis communications industry, hasn't technology already changed crisis communications?"

The answer is a firm "Yes, but . . . " In my view, we are currently nibbling around the edges. Big changes are ahead. I believe that in the next decade you will see a wholesale reinvention of the crisis communications landscape—from crisis communications planning to monitoring, execution, and after-incident reporting. In this chapter, we will look at the state of technology in crisis communications, some of the roadblocks and failings in making current technology applicable to the challenges and rhythms of crisis communications, and the amazing places I see cutting-edge technology going in the years to come.

Predicting the Future

> *"Before man reaches the moon, your mail will be delivered within hours from New York to Australia by guided missiles. We stand on the threshold of rocket mail."*
> — Arthur Summerfield, U.S. Postmaster General, 1961[2]

There is always a risk, of course, in making predictions: You can be spectacularly wrong and wind up looking silly in the process. Moreover, even when discussing the current state of technology, you can date yourself pretty quickly. Consider the following passage from my 2009 book, *In the Court of Public Opinion*, which looked at the role of technology in the litigation process:

> *Web sites. MySpace. Blogs. Twitter. These are among the newest tools of modern communication . . . I have yet to explore the possibilities of Facebook and MySpace . . . but it's clear that blogging, social media, and other forms of Internet-based, interactive communication have had an enormous impact on the court of public opinion, and it's only going to grow.[3]*

Rather quaint, no? It's only been a handful of years since those words were written, but I sound a little bit like that Postmaster General from 1961 with his discussions of "rocket mail."

In other words, this chapter could become real outdated, real quick. That said, I recently went back and reread that 2009 chapter, titled "Navigating Cyberspace: Social Media and Other Internet-based Technologies," and while some of the particulars are a bit off (too many mentions of MySpace as the most glaring), the underlying themes and conclusions are sound: Social media, websites, and other Internet-based technologies have taken a leading role in the process of adjudicating high-profile legal disputes, and lawyers communicating about their clients and cases must adjust.

Even Postmaster General Summerfield was on to something in 1961, since today you can send mail to Australia—not within hours, but within seconds: email, of course.

Technology Changes, but the Song Remains the Same

> *"A lot of nominated shows this year are actually on Netflix.* House of Cards. Orange Is the New Black. *Enjoy it while it lasts, Netflix. Because you're not going to be feeling so smug in a couple of years when Snapchat is up here accepting Best Drama."*
> —Amy Poehler, host of the 2014 Emmy Awards

The point I'm trying to make is that technology is moving so fast that many of the specifics I refer to in this chapter will seem outdated in no time at all. So while I will refer to specific products and services, I'm also going to stick to general—what I would call immutable—concepts regarding the use of software in crisis communications, so that even if the technologies change, the analysis contained in this chapter will still be of value. Although the names of companies and services might be different in the months and years to come, and new technologies might emerge that we did not anticipate, the basic themes of this chapter should still hold.

Now throughout this book, we've learned the basic elements essential to the effective practice of crisis communications. These include:

1. Understanding and **monitoring** issues, incidents, and events that might trigger a crisis communications response;

2. Designating a **Chief Crisis Officer**, a core crisis communications team, and ensuring the proper collaboration between team members;

3. Creating a **crisis plan** that is a living document that actually can be used by the Chief Crisis Officer and the crisis communications teams during a crisis event;

4. Developing **rapid response** systems for coordinating response; and

5. Ensuring consistent, coherent, and compelling **messages** during a crisis.

So in that spirit, let me start off by suggesting that technology in crisis communications, generally speaking, takes the following forms:

- Technology to monitor media and social media before, during, and after a crisis;

- Technology to create the crisis communications plan, and that will keep the plan a living, effective roadmap for action;

151

- Technology to bring the crisis communications team together and provide the tools needed for effective and efficient response;

- Technology to assist in developing effective messages at the speed of the modern crisis; and

- Technologies to deliver messages to various audiences during a crisis or other event.

We will look at each of these technologies in this chapter, consider how they work together, and examine why the tools created for other aspects of public relations—including brand management, product publicity, and event management—sometimes don't work all that well in the context of crisis situations.

As you consider all of this information, keep an eye on the future: Although these technologies currently exist in separate "silos," performing distinct functions as if the others did not exist, my feeling is that it won't be that way much longer. I see a technological singularity on the horizon in the crisis communications field, where machine learning and artificial intelligence (AI) technologies weave these separate and distinct functions together to the benefit of the Chief Crisis Officer, his or her team, and ultimately the organizations confronting crises. In other words, in the near future, technology will:

- Not only monitor issues and trends on social media, but also deeply analyze the results and alert the team of the issues that are becoming crises, as well as point out the type of responses that worked best in the past for other companies when addressing similar crises;

- Gather the right team for a particular crisis based on this analysis—including members of the core crisis communications team and particularly suited to the crisis at hand;

- Provide a central, virtual meeting place for the team to assemble and put the plan in action;

- Assist in the preparation of messages, and execution of the response plan, using advanced AI that informs the content-creation process; and

- Create, refine, and update the crisis communications plan based on what actually worked for the organization during its most recent crisis and what both the crisis communications team and the technology have learned in crisis communications training and the course of managing prior crises.

In other words, like the shipboard computer in *Star Trek*, technology will one day take the Chief Crisis Officer by his or her hand and lead him or her through the steps we've outlined in this book for effective crisis communications response. This does not eliminate the need for the "human touch"—in this case an effective Chief Crisis Officer and team—any more than the shipboard computer eliminated the need for Kirk, Spock, McCoy, and the rest of the *Star Trek* team. Rather, it will break down the walls between the various technological functions in the current crisis communications response environment, along with a lot of the guesswork regarding the strategies, tools, and procedures that allow organizations to move quickly and decisively in the wake of negative reputational events.

Again, we're not there yet, but we're inching closer.

In the rest of this chapter, we will quickly review some of these "silos," where they exist as of this writing and how they apply to the specific needs and idiosyncrasies of the crisis communications environment. In truth, I could spend a whole book on this topic, so some of my descriptions will appear passing at best. But in each section, consider the broader lessons that apply specifically to crisis communications—particularly when discussing tools that have been created *not* specifically for the crisis communications field, but for the broader public relations and brand management industry.

Media and Social Media Monitoring: Effective Use in Crisis Communications

What is media and social media monitoring? It's the process of reading, watching, and listening to everything out there, including major media articles in *The New York Times* and the *Washington Post*, news outlets like CNN and NBC News, blogs and other websites, and social media like Twitter, Facebook, Instagram, and other platforms. This information is then taken, reviewed, and analyzed in a variety of ways to help inform organizations as to how things are going; what the media and the public are saying about you, your company, and its product; and how well your particular messages are resonating with these audiences. When done well, this process is designed to give you exactly what you need to gauge the effectiveness of your marketing or public relations program and point you in the right direction moving forward.

Traditionally, such service has been divided between those monitoring media (which currently includes "traditional" media sources like those outlined above, as well as blogs and other "new media") and those monitoring social media (what members of the public are posting directly about you on various social media platforms). Recently, cutting-edge platforms have emerged that combine these two functions into a single monitoring platform that collects and presents all of this data to the client at once—usually with the ability to drill down into the various components, and ideally to the level of the original communications, whether it be an article, Tweet, or Facebook post.

As of this writing, some of the major services for media and social media monitoring include Cision, BurrellesLuce, Brandwatch, Meltwater, and Critical Mention. New platforms pop up on the scene daily: All claim to do things better and all have sophisticated, high-tech dashboards that promise to give you a snapshot of sentiment—both media and social media—at a glance.

Sounds confusing, huh? This is an awful lot of information for the Chief Crisis Officer and his or her team to digest, particularly in the context of crisis communications, where speed is everything. Therein lies the problem: The sheer volume of data monitored by social media monitoring and other software services leaves much of it unusable in the crisis communications environment. A real problem in Corporate America is that a massive fire hose of data is flowing into organizations each day, with no way to analyze its true meaning and figure out what to do with this data in real time. In the crisis communications context, where decisions have to be made in a split-second, drowning in such data can be deadly.

The symptoms of this data overload are easy to see. I've been in meetings with Fortune 100 clients where hour-long presentations are made, replete with 60-slide PowerPoint decks that describe the current state of media and social media reaction to a crisis or issue. Invariably, any actionable intelligence that could help the company deal with the crisis is buried on slide 37 or so of that deck, but no one can see it through the word clouds, diagrams, and other measurement indicia that get brand managers and advertisers excited and leave crisis managers twitching.

I think to myself: This is all fine folks, but we've got a crisis happening outside this conference room door *now* and a public that needed reassurance 10 minutes ago. To quote the *Saturday Night Live* character Jebidiah Atkinson: "Wrap it up!" Moreover, the quality of the analysis can sometimes be suspect, in a "garbage in, garbage out" sense. In other words, what you see on that fancy tech dashboard of yours is only as good as the inputs and the judgments made regarding what comprises those inputs. (This "framing" of inputs is sometimes the result of computer algorithms—which, of course, have their own framing context problems as well.) With the wrong inputs, you can wind up with skewed data that provides little, if any, insight into exactly what is happening. In the worst case, it provides the wrong information upon which to base your strategic decisions.

An example from my crisis communications work will give you a sense as to how monitoring works . . . and how, sometimes, it doesn't.

We were working on a very contentious issue during the summer of 2015 an entertainment company that was in a difficult, adversarial negotiation with one of the largest online retailers in the world. Put bluntly, the retailer was putting the screws to my client in ways that only a true monopolist can. The crisis was playing out day-to-day before the deeply opinionated stakeholders in this community: first in the trade media, then in major media, such as *The New York Times* and *The Wall Street Journal*, and social media.

The battle was bloody, but we were winning. We came into the fight a little late but had worked hard on our client's behalf to ensure our position was well framed and reasonable. We enlisted third parties to rally to the client's defense and decry the heavy-handed actions of the retailer.

We also engaged a media and social media monitoring service to better understand public sentiment—in as close to real time as possible—as the issue played out in the *Times* and the *Journal* and in key trade publications covering the industry. As discussed, the monitoring service collected all mentions of the crisis across a range of social media platforms. The service we used was automated, utilizing what we thought were sophisticated algorithms to sift through the enormous quantity of social media posts.

On this particular day, however, my colleague—one of the social media experts in our office—came to me with the most recent monitoring reports from one of the leading social media monitoring agencies. Something was wrong, she told me.

I looked at the numbers and something was indeed wrong.

She showed me a pie chart with a breakdown of social media sentiment into three categories: Positive, Negative, and Neutral (so far, so good).

The strange part was that the neutral comments, by far, dominated the numbers. Indeed, more than two-thirds of the social media contact on Facebook, Twitter, and other social media outlets was neutral, with positive and negative comments about evenly split in the other one-third.

This data made no sense. We worked on at least four major media articles in the week prior, all of which were positive. We made our case quite well and ensured that the right messages had gotten out effectively and in language that was straightforward, compelling, and reframed the way audiences would look at the crisis.

That should have been reflected in the numbers. Indeed, given the public tempest over this particular commercial negotiation, one would have assumed that very few "neutral" parties existed in the first place. After all, on so contentious an issue, why would someone who is neutral be posting about the topic anyway? Presumably, the neutrals wouldn't care one way or another. Hmmm . . .

The answer became abundantly clear after we drilled down, taking a look at some of the so-called neutral social media sentiment: The monitoring service mismarked the results—not out of negligence or ineptitude, but because the criteria they set up (automated, following an algorithm) for measuring the positive or negative aspects of this issue was faulty. More specifically, they failed to take into account that most of those who posted on Facebook, Twitter, or other social media were linking to one of the articles we'd placed the week prior.

The problem? The analysis did not consider the underlying tone of the individual articles being forwarded, and the headlines and synopses of those articles were usually neutral in tone. Clearly, a Tweet of a positive article is positive, right? If you read the article and agreed with its underlying argument, you tweeted it. In this case, if the tweet didn't include positive commentary on my client's position, the resulting tweet was characterized as "neutral" rather than positive. There was no way to pick up the overall characterization of the dispute without taking a closer look at the tone of the underlying article being tweeted.

We went back and broke down the results; this was no small task considering the thousands of social media posts related to this issue. As it turned out, instead of two-thirds of the social media being neutral, neutral sentiment was less than 20 percent. (Truthfully, I thought it might be even lower than that.) Positive tweets, by far, ruled the day.

The positive social media sentiment was in large part thanks to our client's hard work over the preceding several weeks. Indeed, most of the social media activity consisted of tweets containing links to the articles and blog posts we'd worked on, which were of a highly positive nature. As a result, we knew that what our client was doing was working and that we should keep it up.

But if we hadn't gone through the social media monitoring to painstakingly analyze each post, there was no way to know that. With that sort of error, we might have made strategic choices based on faulty data. The client might have assumed that a more aggressive public posture, including giving interviews in the media, was not valuable. They might have shifted strategies entirely.

Going forward, we overlaid a process to effectively drill down on social media posts to better understand the exact impact of our efforts and changes in sentiment related to the dispute based on the various PR tactics we were using. It wasn't easy, but the client was very pleased with the results.

There's a lesson here that underlies this chapter. An enormous number of tools are available to the public relations and "brand" industries, most with sophisticated user interfaces and highly touted methodologies for gauging sentiment. Unfortunately, some give you reams and reams of data, but not the information you actually need to *win*—particularly during a crisis, which tends to be far faster moving and (as we've learned throughout this book) different from other forms of public relations, such as general brand management or promotional efforts. By the time you blow through the smoke-and-mirrors and realize this, it may be too late. So you must understand going into the process what exactly you need for effective crisis communications response to properly evaluate the tools assembled before you.

Media and Social Media Monitoring Were Not Designed for Crisis Communications

Why didn't the social media monitoring software described above work in gauging sentiment in this particular crisis situation? Because it wasn't designed to.

Rather, it was designed to measure consumer sentiment in the most general sense—that is, not specifically during a complex crisis being played out as much in the pages of *The New York Times, The Wall Street Journal*, CNBC, and *The Washington Post* as in social media posts. The monitoring service took a far more simplistic view of social media when considering whether a Tweet of Facebook post was positive or negative.

And make no mistake—dig below the slick graphics, fancy logos, and space-age charts of some of these technology offerings, you often find a less-than-sophisticated approach to monitoring social media—one that doesn't lend itself well to crisis communications and other complex forms of reputation management. In this particular instance, when we've probed a bit, some of the account representatives for social media monitoring agencies told us that the criteria they used to judge whether a particular post is negative or positive was facile at best. One representative told us that they simply look for Twitter posts that say blatant things like "Company X sucks" or "Check out this awesome deal" to determine whether or not a social media post is positive or negative. The algorithms cannot differentiate nuance or "gray" areas—in this instance, the content of an article linked to a post.

As a result, neither could the client.

Creating Something That's Actually Useful During a Crisis

Is there something about the crisis communications process itself that makes it particularly not suitable to the use of technology? After all, there are now wonderful new technologies for media buying and project management in the advertising and public relations fields, media monitoring and social media monitoring, and mass distributing a press release to thousands of media markets worldwide. There are also tools for mass crisis notification offered by various vendors—for example, when a university needs to alert all of its students to an incident of violence on campus (the "shelter in place" notifications that you see in active shooter incidents) or an oil exploration company needs to notify all of its employees of an explosion on a rig in the Gulf of Mexico. (Obviously, this is not "crisis communications" in the sense we use in this book but more "emergency notification"—although there are elements of overlap between the two.)

Additionally, in the legal field, there are new technologies for legal research and e-discovery (the electronic collection and analysis of the thousands of pages of documents and other materials that form the basis of modern corporate litigation) as well as services like LegalZoom for the preparation of legal documents. The financial industry has had its Bloomberg terminal and other technological resources for years.

Yet, there's very little technology specifically designed for the crisis communications field. There are a number of reasons: First, vendors in various markets often gravitate toward the largest segments of those markets (as do the investors that fund startup investments in new technologies to address such markets—as we see in the Mark Andreessen comments that open this chapter). So they are constantly expanding, rather than contracting, the definition of markets—creating tools that can be used by the largest audiences possible. Crisis communications, as a result, becomes a sub-market of public relations, which becomes a sub-market of advertising and marketing services. Broad tools are then created with mass appeal for the entirety of these audiences.

Although the crisis communications market is big by most measures, it is still a small segment of the overall advertising, marketing, or PR budget of a major corporation. As we've learned throughout this book, crisis communications can have a big impact on the reputation of a company or organization and its overall success. But given the smaller overall size of the market, there's little incentive to create specific technological tools to service this very distinct animal.

Put more simply: Why create a collaboration tool for 1 percent of the overall marketing and communications field, when you can create Slack or Box or Dropbox and serve multiple segments of the industry? Why create a social media monitoring service specifically keyed to crisis communications when you can create a "Brand Monitoring" service that monitors media and social media activity for the largest brands in the broadest sense of the word?

This is not to knock any of these services, by the way. Some are extremely good at what they do for the bulk of the audiences they service. Rather, it is to point out the obvious: Tech companies and their investors are like the bank robber Willie Sutton (whom we discussed in the last chapter). They build big, broad tech solutions "because that's where the money is."

More on Why Technological Solutions Are Often Unusable

Here's another reason why some cutting-edge technology is mostly unusable in the crisis context: I'll be 50 years old when this book is published. Depending on who is reading, this number will either sound very old or relatively young. If you're in the technology field, an advertising agency, or a PR firm, you probably think I'm ancient. As in: "What's this old man doing telling me about technology, even if it is in an area where he has 'domain expertise'?" If you're a corporate executive or leading lawyer, I'm a contemporary or perhaps a bit younger.

This is important because it says something not just about the readership of this book, but also about how young the tech world skews. Whereas the software engineers and other Silicon Valley-types who create technology might view a professional at 50 as really, really old, most in positions of power in the corporate world, who ultimately use this technology, do not.

Here's the point: Sometimes those who create technology are not the users of that technology. A huge knowledge gap exists, particularly when it comes to a specialized, "experiential" specialty like crisis communications: Those creating software for the field have never actually managed a crisis. They've never been forced to confront the negative reputational ramifications of an unexpected and fast-moving event. Sure, they might have done some public relations along the way—maybe some proactive publicity on behalf of clients, for instance, or Tech PR, or event management. But crisis communications? They've heard about it or read about it, perhaps, but I'd wager that the vast majority have never been on the front lines as a crisis was unfurling before them.

That's not to besmirch anyone. There are a lot of smart young people who have done all sorts of wonderful things in the PR field. My point is that there is a disconnect, which, at least partially, explains why you don't see as much great software for the crisis communications field as you do for brand management, positive publicity, event management, or other disciplines that fall into the marketing/PR arena. They simply do not have the experience.

Back to Monitoring

Ok, so now I told you an awful lot about what I don't want and don't need in monitoring, whether it be social media monitoring or monitoring of major media and blogs. Let us now discuss what I do need as a crisis communication consultant and what, I believe, the Chief Crisis Officer needs for similar success.

My monitoring needs are as follows:

- A way to identify issues, on a day-to-day basis, that may become crises, and—more significantly—determine whether social media and other "chatter" is trending upward over time.

- A single dashboard that shows me both media and social media content on one screen in real time. I don't need fancy charts, word clouds, and diagrams. I need to see what the Tweets and Facebook posts look like as they come in, what major media stories have been written about the issues surrounding my crisis, whether a petition has emerged on Change.org and whether it's garnering signatures at a rapid pace, and so forth. I need something I can glance at quickly before making rapid-response-style decisions on what crisis protocols to follow and what responses may be required to effectively handle the crisis or issue.

- I need the content of major media articles and blog posts at-hand (presumably as a click-through on the dashboard I've described above), so that I can understand exactly what is being said about this issue, rather than relying on Tweets and posts of headlines.

- I need a *concise* daily report of the latest developments in both social and other media, preferably one or two pages (or the electronic equivalent), so that I can show to my superiors (as a consultant, my clients, in the case of the Chief Crisis Officer, the CEO). In other words, I need a report for members of the team who are not inclined to sign on to some funky dashboard, so that they can tell at a glance where this crisis is going and what may happen next.

And that's it. That's what is needed from my media and social media monitoring in the crisis communication context. More is not better. More will just gum things up while we're trying to move quickly and respond effectively during the initial stages of a crisis.

What service do I use? The answer is several . . . and none. In other words, my company pulls information from a variety of media and social media monitoring sources, but we don't stop there. Using our own protocols and methodology, we compile this information daily in a form tailored specifically for crisis communications response. In other words, we combine the latest technology with a lot of hard work to get exactly what we need. The result is actionable intelligence to inform the Chief Crisis Officer and the crisis communications team.

That said, my software company (which you'll learn about below) is in the process of developing technologies to provide this type of automated tool specifically for crisis communications response. For now, we hustle to put this stuff into usable form for rapid response in the crisis context, even as technology is moving closer and closer to the point where machine intelligence and AI will bring us there.

Software for Collaboration and Crisis Plans

In a way, this sets up the next part of our technological discussion, which deals directly with online services for crisis and litigation communications. Services like CrisisResponsePro (www.crisisresponsepro.com), a company we started in mid-2015, can address many of the "silos" I outlined earlier in this chapter, including: notifying the right team for a particular crisis; providing a central, virtual meeting place for the team to assemble; assisting in the preparation of messages and execution of the response plan; and ensuring the crisis communications plan is a "living" document, rather than a binder that sits on a shelf. In addition, from any browser, smartphone, or tablet, the right software solution will bring the crisis communications team together and provide the tools and resources for a more effective and efficient system of response.

A caveat: I use CrisisResponsePro in the examples that follow, and as you might imagine, I am a little biased in favor of our particular technology. Regardless, the Chief Crisis Officer and his or her team must find a collaborative technology that solves the major roadblocks to crisis communications that we've described throughout this book: getting the team together and getting them all on the same page quickly. Whether it's your proprietary technology, a Sharepoint-style software that lives on your corporate servers, or a specialized subscription service, every company should use some type of collaborative/storage platform to ensure their team is responding fast and well when a crisis occurs. This is because, as you now know, the bottlenecks to effective crisis communications often lie in the frustrating early stages of an issue or event, when the client is unable to:

1. Alert the team fast enough;

2. Get a handle on issues and events fast enough; and

3. Get the proper messages and responses approved and before the public . . . you guessed it, fast enough!

As we saw in Chapter 4, new advances that speed the delivery of cardiac services have made a huge difference in heart attack survival rates, even though the underlying substance (i.e., the science and medicine behind cardiac intervention) hasn't changed. In the crisis communications arena as well, technology can provide the critical speed necessary to ensure effective crisis communications response, regardless of the underlying nature of the crisis and the strategies and messages being executed.

Specifically, here are some of the attributes you should look for in any collaborative software you've identified to serve as the backbone of your crisis planning and response protocols:

- **Speed.** As we have discussed throughout this book, when a crisis hits, time is of the essence. The collaborative software your crisis team uses should be built with speed in mind. Our CrisisResponsePro system, for example, is built on the "Virtual WorkRoom" model: You open a new Virtual Workroom for each crisis and issue you face, assemble the right crisis response team for that particular assignment, notify each member of the team via email and text, and get to work.

  You must also know where your crisis software exists on your server if it's going to be used, which sounds elemental, but you'd be amazed what an impediment this can be to effective action. As detailed in Chapter 3, I've actually been in meetings with Fortune 100 companies where members of the crisis communications staff have gotten into arguments over where a particular crisis plan exists on their corporate servers. Is it on the "N" drive or the "K" drive? Nobody seems to know—including those who are supposed to be using the system on a day-to-day basis! My experience with Sharepoint and similar software that reside within the walls of the corporate computer infrastructure is that all too often they exist in some lonely corner of the corporate servers, unattended and virtually unused—like a dying Rustbelt town with unfamiliar streets and out-of-date shops and services. No one wants to go there.

  For that reason, our CrisisResponsePro crisis communications software is subscription-based, updated on a daily basis, and housed in a private cloud for immediate access from any computer, tablet, or smartphone. It is highly secure (as you'll see below), but there's no software to update and maintain by your company's IT department (another roadblock, to be sure).

  This brings me to an important point: There are two ways to host and store data in a crisis communications system—on your corporate servers or in a hosted environment. Our argument is to avoid corporate servers. Your crisis software must be accessible immediately, intuitive, and attractive to use, which means it can't be stale, confusing, or convoluted. If members of the crisis team have to "work to get there," they won't *get there*, I can assure you. The collaborative software the Chief

Crisis Officer and crisis communications team uses must conform to the way you work. If it's too slow, hard to understand, and difficult to update and maintain, everyone will move back to email and other ill-suited technologies. Speed suffers, and inevitably so does the effectiveness of the overall crisis response.*

- **Efficiency.** The ideal crisis communications software should have all of the right tools at your fingertips in a highly intuitive fashion. Usability is key. You should be able to collaborate, review, and initiate your crisis communications response protocols from any desktop, laptop, smartphone, or tablet. Ideally, without hours of training and instruction, the Chief Crisis Officer and his or her team members should be able to collaborate, assign tasks, and report on latest developments without burying your data deep within a complicated interface or—even worse—your email inbox. For example, our service allows us to research what other companies have said in similar situations using a comprehensive Public Statement Database (which, as of this writing, contains more than 10,000 public statements issued by other companies and organizations during a crisis). You can download the templates you need, edit them to fit the particulars of the crisis or issue, and upload finished statements for quick and efficient review by the entire team. There are areas to incorporate monitoring reports and background documents to ensure your fingers are on the pulse of both traditional and social media.

- **Security.** A word about security, which I mentioned above in the bullet point on speed: Simply put, if your software is going to exist in the cloud, it must be secure. You can't just slap together some software, host it on a public cloud service like Amazon Web Services (AWS) or Microsoft Azure (two of the dominant public cloud hosting services at the moment), and open for business. Rather, if you are going to house your crisis communications software outside of your corporate servers (as we recommend), you need to ensure your provider delivers a level of security that exceeds that of most corporate environments. Ideally, you are looking for a secure, private hosting facility (sometimes called the "private cloud"), with physical security on-site, controlled access, nightly back-up to multiple server locations, and

---

* We haven't even addressed the type of crisis that knocks out your corporate servers in the first place—such as a natural disaster or other physical event. You don't want to be sitting around waiting for you organization's redundancy plan to kick in before your crisis communications plan does. You customers, shareholders, employees, and other important stakeholders won't wait for that. All of this argues for a solution that is not internal, but rather is housed outside of an organization's corporate computers.

regular intrusion detection and security audits. Further, third-party services should feature NSA-level, 256-bit, two-way encryption (in transit and at rest); two-factor authentication; and non-recoverable password protection for all documents. This is a long list and a list that may change as data security improves, but the point is clear: An effective system should be as safe as (if not safer than) the corporate servers in your office.

Technology in the Creation and Upkeep of Crisis Plans

As we learned in Chapter 3, to create a crisis plan that is actually used, you've got to A.C.T. in a continuous loop—that is, you must:

- **Assess** the current state of your crisis communications system and the risks facing your organization;
- **Create** a living, breathing document that provides a roadmap for action, a way to bring the team together and the tools and resources that give the team a starting point for effective communications response; and
- **Train** against that document, so that you understand whether it works during a crisis.

To complete the loop, you assess again—both after training and in the wake of a crisis event (i.e., the after-action report, or "hot wash," that emergency response consultant Tom Mauro will discuss in our Afterword). You find the holes in your current plan, figure out what worked well and what didn't, and update your crisis plan accordingly.

The ideal software solution would take you through each of these steps. We envision something like TurboTax or LegalZoom, which would lead you through the process of creating a crisis plan for your organization in the first place and store it somewhere accessible from any laptop, tablet, or smartphone on-the-fly. Done right, the same technology would also allow you to update that plan regularly, as personnel changes take place and new issues, approaches, and best practices develop.

To my knowledge, nothing like that exists . . . but we're working on it.

As of this writing, the technology we use allows for a client's crisis plan to be seamlessly integrated into their customized portal and updated whenever needed. In our software, the living, breathing crisis communications plan you created in Chapter 3 is uploaded and viewable through all of your Virtual WorkRooms—wherever you are and from whatever device you are using. Moreover, from a smartphone, you can reach any team member via phone or email, and submitting updates to your crisis plan, your scenarios, your templates, and other materials are easy.

In addition to the enhancements I mentioned above, we're also planning an automated update system that prompts our clients periodically to supply updates to their crisis plan—not only to update key contact information, but also company locations and resources and other information. We are also currently exploring technologies to refine and enhance the actual crisis plan in real time, as our clients discover what works and what doesn't for their particular company, the types of scenarios they face on a regular basis, and best practices throughout the crisis communication discipline. (The Chief Crisis Officer and core crisis communication team can tease out many of these enhancements through training exercises, as well as through the team's actual response to crisis events.)

It's not the onboard computer from *Star Trek* I mentioned at the beginning of this chapter, but it is a definite step in that direction.

Putting Crisis Collaboration Software to Work

How does the right technology work for the Chief Crisis Officer and his or her crisis team in actual practice? Let me give you a few examples, drawing from our actual experiences with the technology we use. Again, these examples are designed to give you a sense for how the right crisis communications software can address many of the issues we've been looking at in *Chief Crisis Officer*, in terms of bringing the team together, harnessing the tools of crisis communications, and responding in a manner that addresses the issues before you with the type of speed that contains a crisis rather than allows it to grow. Although the focus is on the software we use, the lessons apply to any system you are using.

First example: I was leaving a meeting with a financial client in Midtown Manhattan in mid-2015. I received an urgent voicemail from a small manufacturing client: His plant was on fire, and media was already arriving outside the facility, eager to learn what was happening. I quickly jumped into a nearby Starbucks and opened a Virtual WorkRoom on the CrisisResponsePro software, inviting the client's CEO and the plant's facility manager onto the site. (Thankfully, this being Manhattan, there's a Starbucks on nearly every corner.) In the collaboration area of the Virtual WorkRoom, we exchanged details on the fire and a strategy for proper response. We quickly researched CrisisResponsePro's database for statements issued by other companies and found a few that dealt with the same situation. We also found a downloadable template to fit our needs, which gave us a model to use. At the touch of a button, that template could be converted to talking points, an employee email, and a draft Twitter post. With the details inserted, I uploaded the draft statements to the Virtual WorkRoom's DocVault, which my client reviewed and approved from his iPad. (While I was in a Starbucks, he was working in a McDonald's across from his facility—he couldn't get into his office, obviously!) With final approval of the statement, we made it available on the company website and to any media who called or showed up at the site.

The entire process took about eight minutes!

This is the kind of velocity that the right collaborative software can bring to the crisis communications environment. And, again, whether you choose CrisisResponsePro or some other solution, or create one on your own servers, the tool you use should bring this kind of speed to your Chief Crisis Officer and his or her team.

A few more examples further flesh out best practices in this arena:

- A logistics company in New Jersey we were working with suffered a fatal truck accident on a major interstate at rush hour. The driver, a 20-plus-year employee of the company, was killed. Reports indicated there might be other fatalities as well. The company's PR team had already left for the day, and the company General Counsel was at a convention on the West Coast. (Indeed, at the moment of the accident, the General Counsel was on a crowded tour bus with other industry executives on their way to the event.) A major accident with fatalities bringing traffic to a halt just outside a large metropolitan area was going to be big news.

  Despite the fact that the crisis communications team was gone for the day, our team was collaborating within minutes: They downloaded and edited a statement expressing condolences, highlighting the excellent driving record of the driver and mentioning that an investigation was ongoing. With a district manager joining the collaboration from the site of the accident, the team was also able to determine that there was only one fatality: the driver. The crisis communications team was able to get this information into the first stories that appeared on local media websites about the accident—with information about the number of casualties and the driver's excellent driving record up to that point. This helped squelch additional questions, follow-up stories, and speculation. The team also prepared a quick employee message to ensure internal audiences were informed, which put an end to rumors and speculation about what was actually occurring. Even though the accident tied up traffic for hours on a major thoroughfare at rush hour, the issue disappeared as a public concern by the next morning.

- One of our clients experienced a protest outside their building by radical activists. We were able to position one of their people outside the facility and upload images of the protest to our software solution in real time. Our goal was to determine how big the protest was, whether media was in attendance, and the amount of disruption that was being caused in the local neighborhood. Team members were collaborating and getting reports from the scene without overlapping emails, confusing text photos, or incomplete voicemails. Everyone on the team learned firsthand—and at the same time—the extent of the disruption; therefore, they could make informed decisions as to the degree of response required.

- A financial company faced legal action brought by an overly aggressive and publicity-hungry regulator. Legal and PR teams both inside and outside the company used technology to collaborate, store key background documents, and create and edit materials for proper response to media, employees, customers, and other audiences. As often happens when facing a legal or regulatory issue, public attention died down for several weeks, then spiked up again when the regulator issued new information to the public. Thanks to the document storage capabilities of the software solution, the team had immediate access to the prior materials and messages, as well as a record of their collaboration on prior strategy.

These are just a few examples of the ways the right collaborative software can make a big difference in the speed and effectiveness of crisis communications response and, in doing so, fulfill the requirements we've given throughout this book. Moreover, the right system works not just for large corporations, but for any organization that wants to respond better and faster to sensitive issues and events with potential reputational impacts. And particularly for mid-sized and smaller organizations, maintenance and upkeep of the system is easy. Again: Nothing kills technology faster than the sense that it is stale.

Wide-scale Dissemination of the Message

Finally, a word about getting your messages to the various audiences you are trying to reach with your crisis communications response. I haven't focused on this area much for one reason: This is not where the real bottlenecks and delays occur in crisis communications response; therefore, it is not where technology can have the greatest impact. As we've learned throughout this book, it is in collaboration, notification of the crisis communications team, and ready access to resources and materials where technological solutions can provide the Chief Crisis Officer and his or her team with the greatest advantages.

That said, a variety of software is available to disseminate your messages during PR events, including crisis communications. This can include software that:

- Pushes out press releases, statements, and other materials to media and bloggers that may have an interest in the event—the most popular of these are paid newswire services like PR Newswire, BusinessWire, and GlobeNewswire (owned by NASDAQ);
- Social media dashboards that allow you to post to Twitter, Instagram, Facebook and other social media sites in a timely manner;
- Software that creates crisis-related websites and new pages in the newsrooms of existing corporate websites. These are called "dark sites"— they are created beforehand and go live in the event of a crisis; and
- Emergency notification systems that allow companies in crisis to broadcast information to a variety of audiences in the event of a crisis, including media, constituents, and other stakeholders (usually through text, voicemail or other direct communication).

Each of these systems have their relative uses and misuses, which have been documented in many other PR and crisis response trade publications, so we'll spend less time on them here. The big thing you should remember and watch for is, as we described in other parts of this chapter, the applicability of each software solution to crisis situations, where the goal of effective communications is often to *minimize* and *mitigate* reputational damage when a crisis occurs. (Quite frankly, you must remember this point when dealing with any software you might use in crisis communications.) Sometimes this involves getting information about what is happening to the broadest possible audience, such as in a natural disaster or a product recall. Other times, the goal is to minimize, which is a very different marching order than you would find in proactive publicity.

In crisis communications, a delicate balance exists: You're trying to inform the public each step of the way, while also ensuring that you don't amplify the event or incident—risking a crisis that might spin out of control. In those situations, a press release distribution service that gets your message out to thousands of media outlets at the same time may be less effective than a personal response to the five or six reporters—the "lead steers" as we call them—who will report on your response in the right way and get it in front of the right audiences at the right time. This is often key to ensuring that the negative reputational impacts of your crisis are contained.

This is an inherent limitation of most, if not all, crisis dissemination software. It's great if you want to reach thousands of markets across the globe; it is less great, and less useful, if that is not your goal.

Media Lists, Media Databases, and Other Directories

In the beginning, there was Bacon's and Burrelle's. Back in the dark ages—say 20 years ago—before the advent of the Internet and online services, we had these things called books: hard copy directories of reporters on a shelf in our offices. When you needed to reach a reporter, you'd pull down a directory and find the page for a particular publication—say, *Fortune* or New York's *Daily News*—and scan through the list of reporters by department or beat until you found the one you needed. Then you'd build a media list.

Preparing the list and sending your information to a reporter (usually via fax or snail mail) was a slow, arduous process. In the meantime, the reporters you dealt with on a regular basis would be ensconced on your Rolodex for ready access with a specific pitch (or, as time went on and we approached the "modern age," your Personal Digital Assistant).

Times have changed. Bacon's is now Cision, which describes itself as providing "media intelligence to power your story," and Burrelle's is now BurrellesLuce, which is dedicated to "improving the way you capture, measure and connect with media." There are many, many other media databases out there, as well as online resources like Leadership Directories that offers a database of media, as well as lists of senior leaders in business, government, nonprofits, law firms, and lobbying organizations.

We use these directories every day, and they are very useful. Indeed, virtually every PR practitioner knows how to use a media database to find contacts in various markets around the United States. In the end, as with press release distribution services and the rest, the effectiveness of these databases depends on your goal.

But, as we have discussed above, remember: In many crises, you don't need a comprehensive media database of thousands of markets across the United States or around the world. You have a crisis . . . the media is coming to you! Most organizations know immediately the dozen or so top media they need to reach, and their information, in many cases, is already collected as part of the crisis plan. Media lists and databases supplement this effort, of course, but they are not central to overall crisis communications response.

Indeed, when crises occur, the software that finds the right reporters tends to be the same software that is monitoring and tracking who is already covering the crisis via media and social media. In many cases, our first media outreach is to those outlets that have already posted their initial stories online (or Tweeted developing news), as well as those who cover the organization as part of their beat.

So by all means, have that media list at-the-ready and subscribe to a good media database, but don't make it a crutch. When a crisis erupts, finding who is interested in your story is usually the least of your worries.

The Road Ahead . . .

There is much, much more I could have said in the pages of this chapter regarding various technologies that impact the practice of crisis communications, and therefore the work of the Chief Crisis Officer. I apologize if I've given any particular technology or service short shrift. As with all of the material in this book, I want you to use the descriptions, stories, and arguments contained herein not as a particular prescription or set of instructions, but rather as a *conceptual framework for ways of thinking during a crisis*, to allow you to make the right choices about an action plan moving forward.

Whatever technologies you choose for crisis communications monitoring, collaboration, materials creation, and dissemination of your crisis response messages, the key point is to make sure your technology is shaped and attuned to the task at hand, rather than trying to shoehorn your crisis communication needs into software and other technological solutions better suited for product marketing, brand management, and proactive publicity.

As for the future, the Chief Crisis Officer should continue to watch for technologies that could radically change his or her ability to create and execute the crisis plan, bring the crisis communications team together more effectively, and systematize collaboration on messages and protocols for response. And as with most innovation, technology moves slowly at first, then takes off with the speed of one of Postmaster Summerfield's letters rocketing toward the Australian coast. The incremental technologies described in this chapter will one day lead to an environment where the more structural and logistical elements at the heart of the crisis communications managements techniques are facilitated by a thinking, learning, and collaborative new technology designed to specifically serve the crisis communications team.

Action Points

- Technology has only just begun to the change the practice of crisis communications, and you can expect AI and machine learning technologies to foster rampant change in the ways the Chief Crisis Officer and his or her team respond to crises in the years to come.

- Media and social media monitoring technologies are sometimes ill-equipped to handle the particular needs of the crisis communications team.

- Collaborative technology exists today to allow the crisis communications team to come together quickly, exchange ideas and strategies, and respond effectively to a crisis event.

- Using technology to create, store, access, and execute the crisis communications plan you created in Chapter 3 is the new technological frontier. The right communications technologies are being created that will allow not only for the storage and access of the plan, but for the continual updating of crisis contacts and protocols in a fast-changing environment.

- Distribution services, media directories, and other tools for the dissemination of crisis messages proliferate. The trick is to know which services to use and how to use them to ensure that the crisis is addressed and mitigated without unintentionally escalating attention.

Chapter

8

Putting It All Together: The Chief Crisis Officer in Action

This chapter is shorter than the rest, but there's a reason for that.

With a thorough grounding in the structure, leadership, and technology needed to make your crisis communications program a success, I wanted to devote this final chapter to a single hypothetical example of what I view as the ideal crisis communications response.

In the pages of Chief Crisis Officer, *we've learned quite a bit: Why effective crisis communications is so important, who the right Chief Crisis Officer is, the team and plan that should be in place for effective crisis response, and the tools and technology that make it all work. Now let's put it all together.*

After our example, we'll consider some final lessons that can be applied to crises of any kind, whether physical or virtual, real-time or regulatory, exploding or unfolding. We'll look at the common objections that corporate executives often use to avoid proper crisis response planning and the need to adjust your plan as the circumstances warrant. Like a boxer heading into the ring or a General heading into battle, the Chief Crisis Officer knows that he or she is going to take some lumps, but understands that—with the proper training and technique—they can withstand any assault and emerge the victor.

Building on everything we've learned in previous chapters, let's imagine an organization's Chief Crisis Officer leading his or her team through the initial stages of a state-of-the-art crisis communications response. Working from a well-conceived and accessible crisis communications plan, with all of the tools and resources in place and updated, we will model the execution of crisis response protocols working smoothly, efficiently, and decisively as a crisis event moves forward.

Nothing is ever this perfect, of course, but for the purposes of this hypothetical, we're modeling the ideal response. Bear with me . . . there will be plenty for cynics to chew on further along in this chapter.

For this exercise, we will use a scenario that is difficult to think about, but one that is all too common in our business and personal lives these days: the Active Shooter. You are the Chief Crisis Officer of a retail store chain, designated by your company to lead the organization's response to unexpected events with negative reputational ramifications. You've worked hard to develop a crisis plan for your company that is a true action plan for responding to a variety of scenarios, including an active shooter.

We will also assume that you've availed yourself to a cutting-edge technological solution for collaboration and the creation of response materials, as discussed in Chapter 7. You've got a crisis communications machine hitting on all eight (going back to when there were eight-cylinder cars) . . . and you are about to use it.

Active Shooter!

It's Monday morning; you're sitting in your office, staring at an Excel spreadsheet. It's 11:30 a.m., and you need to get a better handle on these budget numbers for a meeting taking place just after lunch. Some of your team's numbers just don't make sense. You scratch your head and lean back in your chair.

The first email comes in from the head of security for the company:

> *Jim,*
>
> *We've got a situation at our store in Phoenix. Gunshots. Police on scene. Active shooter—may still be underway. Don't know more, but we need to be ready.*
>
> *Phil*

Gunshots . . . crap! This could be a bad one. You let the budget committee members know that you won't be making the meeting this afternoon.

Significantly, you already trained for this type of situation at an off-site crisis communications retreat with video-conference connections from the other regions of the company. "Active shooter" was one of those scenarios you trained for, although at the time, quite frankly, you didn't feel like going. Now you're happy you did.

The first step is your crisis plan. You access your crisis plan immediately.* You review an initial checklist for an active shooter scenario. It tells you to do two things immediately: Assemble the team and collect information at the scene so that you can understand exactly what is happening. You are on it.

In your crisis plan, you have a matrix of key contacts throughout your company for the various types of crises your organization might face. "Active Shooter" is easy to find. Phil (the head of security who sent you that email) is one of the members of your core crisis communications team. You also have the regional vice president covering the retail location in Phoenix, a company lawyer, and two members of the company's public relations team (one of whom is your expert on social media). There may be some vacations in there, but at least you know who you are after.

Using your company's crisis management software, you immediately notify the team and gather them together virtually. Each member of your core crisis communications team receives an email and a text alerting them to the crisis and telling them to sign on to the crisis communications tool for response. You give a short description of what has happened: "There's been a shooting at our store in Phoenix. We have no information yet, but need to be ready to respond."

Within a few minutes, messages and details are already beginning to stream into the system from both the crisis location and other members of the team (who are spread out across the country).

As mentioned, the Active Shooter checklist in your crisis plan tells you must do one other thing immediately: You need to start getting a steady stream of accurate information from the crisis site—the "front lines"—to make the right decisions about the proper level of response. (At various points in this book, we've discussed the importance of getting the proper information in the initial stages of a crisis, as it's been my experience that that the first information you get on any crisis is mostly wrong.) You immediately communicate with the regional vice president on your crisis team— Sally Jones—who's charged with the responsibility of getting exactly that information stream going. She says she'll get on it and within a few minutes you have the assistant general manager at the store location in question providing details from the scene.

Ideally, your crisis communications software has eliminated the confusing flow of overlapping emails that you've seen during past company crises,

---

* If you haven't created or subscribed to a tech solution for the management of crises, you may be using a written plan, perhaps one supplemented by the Crisis Flash Sheet described in Chapter 3, and word-processed templates stored on your company's servers.

which often led to chaos in the opening stages of the event, as bits-and-pieces of information dribbled in to various members of the crisis team amidst the reams of email that fill each member's inbox each day. With your new crisis plan and protocols in place, the team is already working, and it's only a few minutes into the actual crisis.

Next, according to the checklist, you need to get control over the site of the crisis—not just from a physical standpoint, but from a PR standpoint as well. Store security is already working with local law enforcement and other first responders. Phil, your national security director, reports that he's in contact with both local police and your own personnel.

The latest news from the scene: Customers and employees may still be in the store. There's no information on fatalities. It's an active shooter situation, so the danger appears to be ongoing. No word yet whether it is a robbery, an incident of terrorism, employee-driven workplace violence, or some other issue.

Sally Jones posts a message to alert the team that media has already begun showing up at the site. The flow of communications needs to be established immediately to both the media on the scene and those calling the local store and your headquarters in Dallas. Reporters should not be walking around the crisis site indiscriminately, gathering a detail here and fact there, out-of-context, and broadcasting it on Twitter or Facebook. This could give the public a highly distorted view of what is happening.

There's no local PR person on-site at the store in Phoenix, so—per the crisis plan—the assistant general manager, Herb, has been designated to identify the media onsite, reach out to them, and begin the process of getting them the right information on what is occurring and what might happen next. Access to the store has been cut off, but your manager on-scene can see the crisis plan and checklists via his smartphone and is collaborating with you and the crisis communications team for guidance on what to do next.

> *Herb,* you write on the crisis communications portal, *Phil tells me law enforcement has locked down the scene? From a PR perspective, we need to make sure media, employees, and others aren't roaming around while all this is going on. We also need a location to interact with media so that we can get them information when it becomes available.*

Herb replies less than a minute later:

> *Site's been locked down by Phoenix PD. Store wasn't open yet—all employees were evacuated through the rear doors. We're pushing media back and asking all media to remain at the north end of the facility so that they can receive information as it becomes available. Phil is also*

coordinating with local police, so they know exactly what we're doing. We'll have more as soon as we get it.

At nearly the same time, a post from Phil gives the entire team the first concrete details of the actual shooting:

Just spoke with local P.D. There was a radio station event setting up at this location this morning as part of a local charity promotion. Someone walked up and just started shooting. Latest information is that shooter is still at-large. Three people shot, including an employee and one of the hosts. No word on fatalities, but not good.

Not good indeed.

Given the severity of the situation, you know two things: You must get something out on social media quickly and the CEO and executive leadership team needs to understand the situation.

First, you contact the executive team, starting with your CEO, Sue Miller. At some organizations, a couple of levels of management are between the Chief Crisis Officer and the CEO, but not here. You've made sure of that. You get the CEO's assistant immediately and reach the CEO within minutes. Per the crisis protocol, she brings in the COO, Joe Harper, via conference call.

You inform them of the situation and what you know thus far. They ask that Joe Harper be added to the collaboration software to monitor developments for the CEO. You do that.

Monitoring! That's next on your list. You assign two staffers in your office with the immediate task of monitoring both social media and local news radio in Phoenix, as well as other media websites that might pick up the story first. A few Tweets have already appeared—some from the general public and one from a local television news station in Phoenix that Tweeted:

Reports of a shooting at a local retailer. @Action11Phoenix is on our way and will report from the scene shortly.

This brings you to the next item on your checklist: social media. On the company's crisis communications portal, you post:

What's our social media strategy?

Jeff Hunt, your social point person, writes back immediately:

We need a Tweet right away, per the crisis plan. Also need to consider Facebook. We'll need to activate the dark site on our website as well for emergency information and to give us a place to direct the public for information. We have no idea how long this situation is going to last, so we may need multiple updates.

You respond:

Go for it. But Phil—you'll need to make sure the police and first responders on the scene know and are comfortable with what we are saying.

Phil jumps back into the conversation:

Absolutely. I'll show the police commander the draft statement on my smartphone as soon as it is uploaded to our crisis communications site. He knows it's coming. No problem.

Next, you must provide a statement. From the crisis plan's online resources, you search for a template that will serve as the model for the company's first public response to the shooting. It is very short and simple—since facts have not been confirmed at this point, you will only report on what you know. You've learned it's critical not to speculate. It's a fine line, but even a statement that doesn't say much sends a message: The company is aware of the crisis, on the scene, and collecting information and will report back to the public as soon as possible.

Here's the template you find on your crisis communications site:

This [morning/afternoon/evening], there was a shooting at our facility in [LOCATION].

[DESCRIBE WHAT IS KNOWN ABOUT THE CIRCUMSTANCES OF THE CIRCUMSTANCES OF THE SHOOTING AND THE RESOLUTION OF THE INCIDENT].

[DESCRIBE WHAT IS CURRENTLY KNOWN ABOUT INJURIES OR FATALITIES].

Police and emergency response crews have responded and are investigating. The facility remains closed to both the public and our employees.

Our thoughts and prayers are with the victim(s) and [his/her/their] family(ies) at this time.

We are working closely with law enforcement officials and will continue to update the public as more information becomes available.

With a few edits, this message will be ready for upload to the crisis communications portal for review by the CEO and COO before posting on the site. The final looks like this:

This morning there was a shooting at our retail store at 1000 Anywhere Drive in Phoenix, Arizona.

Initial reports indicate that the shooting occurred as a radio station was preparing to broadcast from outside our store. Police indicate that this is an active crime scene and there are injuries

Police and emergency response crews have responded and are investigating. The store remains closed to both the public and our employees.

Our thoughts and prayers are with the victims and their families at this time. We are working closely with law enforcement officials and will continue to update the public as more information becomes available.

The message is complete and approved. Herb will also download the statement on-scene and make it available to local media that have convened on site. Meanwhile, Jeff finds a template Tweet on the portal. With minimal editing, the first Tweet is out:

> *There has been a shooting at our store in Phoenix, with injuries. We have few details, but will alert the public as soon as we can. Go to http:// tinyurl.com/psbab4o for updates.*

A similar short statement is created to post on the company's Facebook page.

Less than 20 minutes have passed since that first hurried email from the security director, and you have reassured the public that you are aware of the incident, in control, and thinking about the victims, their families, your customers, and you employees. This prevents a small crisis from becoming a big one and reinforces the reputation of your company as caring, responsive, and prepared.

Now that you've coordinated effectively with the team and gotten your first public communication out there, you need to start thinking about what comes next: An active shooter may be on the loose near your store; there may be fatalities; or more may be happening on site. This is a very fluid situation—it could only be the beginning of a very long afternoon. Just as you are thinking that, a new message from Phil is posted on your crisis communications site:

> *Ok, new update from Phoenix P.D. This information has been confirmed: Suspect has been apprehended—he was hiding in the store. P.D. reports it was a small caliber handgun used in the attack. Two people were shot, not three: a disk jockey and a production assistant. No employees of our company were hit, although one was injured in the melee. A medical*

crew is on the scene—the injuries are not life threatening. No motive yet, but the shooter appears to have known at least one of the radio station employees.

This message provides some additional clarity, and thank God the situation wasn't worse. The active incident is over, although you suspect it will be a day or so before the store will reopen.

You must update your statement and social media posts with this information. You must then upload the updated statement to the website and send it to local media. It's also time to send an internal email and text to employees in the region, letting them know what is happening—particularly those who were evacuated from the store and might be wondering when they can get back to work.

A final post to the crisis portal comes from your COO, Joe Harper, conveying a message from the CEO, Sue Miller:

Sue says nicely done everyone.

❄ ❄ ❄

"Everybody has a plan . . . until they get punched in the face."
— Mike Tyson

This quote from Mike Tyson is substantially true, as is a similar quote from 19th-century German military strategist Helmuth von Moltke that states: "No battle plan survives contact with the enemy."

But don't mistake either quote as an endorsement of no planning at all. Yes, your plan may change as a result of unforeseen events or new challenges (i.e., after you get punched in the face—metaphorically, I hope), but that doesn't mean you don't have a plan. I've yet to meet a general who goes into battle without a plan, even if he or she knows the plan is going to change substantially when the bullets start flying. This is also true in crisis communications. If you do it right—as we've learned throughout this book—your crisis plan is a living, breathing, learning document that changes as new facts come to light, new crises are uncovered, and talent and practices perfected.

In other words, this stuff works.

Unfortunately, I often find a cynical strain of thinking in the hallowed halls of Corporate America related to crisis communications, driven by a fear of taking any steps that could influence events so chaotic and uncontrollable. A knee-jerk sense exists that:

- You can't control when a crisis occurs, who it affects, or how the media and other public audiences perceive it.

- Whatever we create in terms of systems plan and processes will just be to pacify the CEO (or board of directors). We'll rarely use it after it is created.

- There's just too many things that can happen to our company to plan for them all. Therefore, the planning itself is a waste of time . . . just too many gaps!

- I know it's important, but in terms of priorities, I've got five other things I'm working on now that are as important or more important. I just don't have the bandwidth to prepare for events that may not happen.

At its worst, this negative viewpoint leads to rejection of the process entirely—from appointing a Chief Crisis Officer, to designating the core crisis communications team, to creating an effective crisis communications plan, to providing the tools, resources, and technology to properly put the plan into action.

After reading *Chief Crisis Officer*, I hope you take away one thing (and excuse my repetition): This stuff works.

That's the point of the scenario above, and in the end, this book as a whole. It is the message I want to convey to the Chief Crisis Officer, his or her team, the CEO and top management at organizations that struggle with effective crisis communications response, and others who may be peripherally involved with coordinating response to negative reputational incidents— including the exploding kind of crisis outlined above or an unfolding crisis like a regulatory investigation, lawsuit, or social media rumor that threatens to undermine your company's product or service.

So while we're all entitled to our opinions, bear this in mind: I've been doing this for nearly 25 years—all day, every day. I know better. I've seen it over and over again, hundreds of times, at organizations of all sizes—from small businesses to the biggest of the Fortune 500.

This stuff works. It doesn't work perfectly, and sometimes you get punched in the face. In the end, though, all of the tips, tools, and tactics contained in this book can have an enormous impact on the way a company or organization handles a crisis, which ultimately impacts their reputation, operations, and bottom line.

But, it only works if you believe. Senior management needs to be committed to this, and take steps before your next crisis to put the proper structure and leadership in place.

So find yourself a Chief Crisis Officer, assemble the core crisis communications team, develop the plan, and put the right technology in place to ensure it is accessible and actionable.

It will quite literally mean the difference between a crisis that is managed . . . and one that manages you.

Action Points

- The ideal crisis communications response brings the team together in a timely and efficient manner and gives them all the tools they need to make the right communications choices even as events are unfolding before them.

- Whether the crisis involves an active shooter, product recall, accident or legal issue, checklists, templates, and a clearly defined crisis response team eliminates the need to "make it up as you go along."

- Effective crisis planning works . . . but only if cynical attitudes are avoided and the proper priority is given to crisis planning, developing the team and utilizing technology to ensure effective response.

Afterword

Perspectives on Crisis Communications Response

Throughout this book, you've gotten more than an earful of my views on crisis communications: what makes an effective Chief Crisis Officer, the tools, technologies, and team he or she needs to be effective, and the strategies and tactics that need to be at-the-ready to ensure a fast and effective response. While I like to think I know everything, I also realize that other viewpoints and perspectives exist that are, perhaps, even more insightful than my own. As such, I thought a chapter of interviews with other professionals with expertise in crisis communications response in all its various forms would be highly valuable to the Chief Crisis Officer, the core crisis communications team, and anyone else with an interest in these issues.

In this section, you'll meet several crisis communications consultants who have been on the frontlines of major corporate crises. You'll also hear from a former crisis communications professional, who now heads public affairs for one of the most prominent associations of in-house lawyers in the nation, and a former New York City police captain, who now advises corporations on emergency response. Finally, we'll get insight from the Chief Content Editor of our CrisisResponse-Pro technology software, who spends each day analyzing what works and what doesn't in the area of crisis communications response.

Harlan Loeb

Global Practice Chair, Crisis and Risk
Edelman PR
Chicago, Illinois

> " . . . the more conservative position is to lay low and wait for that
> near-death experience before finding religion and good health. "

About Harlan Loeb

*With more than 20 years' experience, Harlan Loeb is an attorney and nationally
recognized expert in corporate enterprise risk, including issues and crisis management, crisis training, and litigation communications. Harlan's background includes:
strategic counsel and execution across a broad range of operational, strategic, and
financial crisis management engagements, high-profile litigation communications
assignments, and comprehensive public strategy campaigns. His work spans all
business sectors from health to technology and from manufacturing to finance. He
has worked closely with a variety of governmental entities to develop issues and
crisis management protocols and training guides, including work with the U.S. Air
Force Academy, the DOJ, the U.S. Air Force, and the EEOC.*

*A former practicing lawyer with experience in nonprofit, public interest law,
Harlan is a graduate of Vassar College and earned his law degree with honors from
the University of Minnesota. Harlan is also a faculty member at Northwestern
University Law School.*

**For many people, PR is about products, parties, and press releases. But the
work of a crisis communicator is quite different. Can you describe what
you do in the field of crisis and litigation communications?**

Sure, I think we are the field generals and the surgeons for companies that
face destabilizing risk. And in that capacity, we help companies and other
entities navigate the unnatural environment that they're thrust into in either
high-profile litigation or crisis, which is fundamentally a different business
challenge than most companies are equipped to handle.

How are they ill-equipped for such things?

If you look at a crisis, it throws senior decision makers and other corporate executives into a series of non-linear, non-quantitative events, which is really not the
background and comfort level for most senior executives. It's just the contrary.
Most really relish control. They have records of success and achievement. And
in some sense, more instant results, and instant data and confirmation.

In crisis, it is just the opposite—it's not linear, it's fundamentally dynamic, with things going in many different directions. And unless you've been through it and have developed what you and I would probably term, "experiential intuition" or "experiential intelligence," it fundamentally forces a default to instinct, which generally leads them the wrong way.

So things start coming at you in a dozen different directions, and you're ill-equipped to respond. Is that right?

That's right. And what we see quite a bit is that executives in companies default to commoditized approaches, where their comfort level is nourished. "We should get a press release." "We've got to put out this fire." "We've got to put out that fire." Rather than engaging proactively, or engaging on the issues in a very robust way.

There's also a "hide" instinct, and brain studies confirm it. They hide behind the lawyer's counsel to do no harm, which obviously does matter in some cases. But sometimes—many times—it is the wrong advice.

So, many times, they focus on the tools instead of the strategy. Is that a fair assessment?

Well said. It becomes very tactical. I think many companies find it hard to see the forest for the trees, look above . . . out at the horizon a bit . . . and that's fundamentally where we come into play.

And risk, candidly, is never been more fragmented and more destabilizing than now, given all the tools—I call them social exposure tools. We see it in crises, in the context of litigation, and we see it in politics frequently. And so, companies really are operating in what I would call a new age of crisis and risk.

In the old days, the "cyanide-in-the-Tylenol" is the example of the old-fashioned kind of crisis, or your plant blowing up. And these days, it's not so event-driven, and it's not so specific. Is that right?

Correct. I think there's greater—what I would call—"ambient" risk. Unknowns. For example, you've got companies with global supply chains that could face disruptive risk in the form of cyber hacking, *force majeure*—any number of things—as well as quality issues and corruption along the supply chain.

They know that those things are possible, but have very little control over it. And years ago, perhaps, they weren't so exposed. Supply chains weren't as robust. And now almost every global company has a supply chain, and regulation making them responsible for every stop along that train ride.

Do you think business executives and lawyers are getting it? Understanding the way the world is changing in that regard?

I think they understand the world is changing. I fundamentally don't believe they know what to do about it. I think they struggle with the significance of digital, struggle with proactive engagement, because it does require a level of risk to manage risk.

So, naturally, the more conservative position is to lay low and wait for that near-death experience before finding religion and good health. And fundamentally, as you and I know, it's $50,000.00 to put together a plan and develop a capability, or $500,000.00 later to clean up the mess.

Particularly because it can come at you now from so many areas, it's unwise to think that it is going to pass you by. Is that fair?

I think it is. I think that in the days of old, crisis risk used to be a low-risk but high-impact. I think it's skewing to moderate, and in some areas like cyber security, between moderate and high-risk. And so while also a qualitative proposition, companies fundamentally don't have a choice but to be prepared on some level.

Because the notion of crisis management in any context, whether it's litigation, financial fraud—whatever it is—the notion of crisis management is somewhat oxymoronic, because once it happens and you're ill-prepared, there's no way to manage it.

And legal elements now affect every sort of modern corporate crisis, correct? Because law and regulation is everywhere?

Right. There is not a corporate crisis I've seen that was not either preceded by or generated litigation. So it's either on the front end, the middle end, or the back end, but litigation hovers quite closely.

Switching gears a bit: Tell me a little bit about how you got into this field and what you like about it. You were a lawyer, so that's a nice fit.

It's a good question. Part of it is I'm always a bit of an accidental tourist. I was working pretty aggressively and prominently in the nonprofit world, doing appellate litigation for significant constitutional issues. And, as a result, a lot of media work associated with some of the cases we were in, a lot of policy work on employment issues, hate crimes.

And as I began to think about what the private sector adjunct of that position was, somebody had footnoted the notion of working in litigation communications. At the time, I wasn't really sure what that meant. And, after considerable examination, evaluation, I'm still not sure what it means! But it's really been a very creative way to use a law degree . . . you can affect strategy in very different ways than you might as a lawyer. I always say to friends, "It's the fun of being a lawyer on a strategic level without the hours and the detail that go into some of the mundane activities that our colleagues that are practicing law do every day."

And in a way, some of those day-to-day activities of lawyers make them ill-prepared to respond during a crisis, right?

Right, and it gets to your point about tools and tactics. As high-achievers, senior executives, lawyers, whomever it is, we naturally default to our comfort zone, that which we know, that's what's worked for us in the past. And as you and I both know, that default, while comforting on some levels, is highly ineffective.

Just like it would be ill-advised if you and I decided to perform open heart surgery—we just simply don't have the experience, training, or understanding. It does not make sense to manage a high-profile crisis, be it litigation or whatever source or cause without the experience.

And—as you know—what we do is highly experiential. It's an immersion-based training protocol. And years in doing it matter, and I don't say that as a sales pitch. I say it as—I wouldn't pick a heart surgeon off of a brochure. I'd want to interview the person. I'd want to get a sense of what they know, how they've handled situations—how they handle confusion and complexity.

And I think there's too little of that experiential skill set in this world of increasing complexity.

That they've been in the operating room before?

Correct.

❋ ❋ ❋

Eric Rose

Partner
Englander Knabe & Allen
Los Angeles, California

> *"In a crisis, speed matters, and silence is always the most toxic strategy. We're in an environment starving for news, and if you don't fill that void with information . . . someone else will."*

About Eric Rose

Eric Rose is a skilled crisis communications consultant I've had the pleasure of working with for more than a decade. Based in Southern California, Eric has advised corporations, government entities, nonprofits, and individuals in all manner of crises for more than 25 years—both across the United States and internationally. He's also active in politics, public affairs, and government relations. Eric has experience in virtually all major industries, with a specialty serving unions representing police officers and other public safety professionals. He has been a counselor to numerous Fortune 500 companies, trade unions, and other organizations, interacting with senior leadership and advising them on corporate issues management, executive exposure, and media relations. Eric has worked for both political and public sector clients in industries including higher education, healthcare, energy, transportation, consumer goods, hospitality and leisure, and environmental management.

Eric, who attended Cal State Northridge, comments regularly in the media on communications issues and has been a guest lecturer at the University of Southern California as well as before groups of PR professionals.

Tell me, Eric, how did you get into this field?

Accidentally, like most of us, I guess. I worked for elected officials for most of my life—well over 20 years—and I was a government executive for a while, having been a deputy chief of staff for a city council member, and a press secretary or spokesperson for highly visible elected officials. One day I got a phone call from a very senior representative of a PR company who asked: "Do you want to go to lunch? I think you should go into public affairs and crisis management." I told him I have no skill set in that area. He replied: "What do you mean? You do . . . but you just don't know it."

And he was right . . . therefore launching me into this career. At the time, I didn't realize the parallels between handling and working for a highly visible elected official who's always under the microscope—essentially, always in crisis—and dealing with crises for corporate clients. Working through crisis and other issues—if you're doing it right, the strategies and techniques are quite similar. Often, it comes down to, interestingly enough, understanding how others view an issue, being a good writer, and being able to articulate your position.

Indeed. Do you see differences in strategies between the crisis communications and public affairs? Why don't you define the two, just so our readers will understand?

Sure, I define it this way: Public affairs is managing the daily issues that corporations deal with that have a public or governmental face to them. A crisis, on the other hand, is an unexpected emergency. It requires immediate attention—and left unattended, it can fester and become a critical incident. For a publicly traded company, it can affect stock price or the way the company is viewed by consumers. If it's not handled properly, it could damage the brand and take a long time to recover.

Also, I think a difference is speed. In a crisis, speed matters, and silence is always the most toxic strategy you're trying to overcome. The lawyers will often advocate for silence because they're fearful of the repercussions from a legal standpoint, the liability, for any action a company takes. What I preach in my work with responsible companies is that there's no rationale for silence. Silence becomes the focus of the coverage even if the actual response to a crisis, whatever it may be, is perfect.

In other words, even if the crisis is handled well, silence will paint another picture?

Right. If you have an operationally perfect response, but you are silent, you are setting yourself up to be fundamentally hurt in a very significant way from a reputational perspective. I cannot emphasize strongly enough that retreating to a "no comment" stance at the start of a crisis is almost always extremely harmful to the overall goal of getting a company through a crisis and regaining public confidence in its product or service. The lawyers involved are going to urge everyone to say nothing. My advice: Ignore that advice and do not go "radio silent" in a crisis. People need to hear from your company.

I tend to divide crises into two categories: the exploding and the unfolding. What do you think of that?

I like that. I like that a lot. And there's also a matter of degree that needs to be assessed, and you need the proper tools to do that. I've actually developed a chart for companies to measure the severity of a particular crisis—because part of what you have to do is avoid escalating a minor incident into a major crisis. And while this is an art, not a science, there are certain measurements I believe that you can take to help determine whether an incident is actually a crisis, or if it is just an incident that bears watching.

Time and again, consumer product crises show that having a clear game plan can make the difference between a brand's protection and its destruction. Moreover, we have seen that a plan based on open and straightforward communications, backed by a commitment to do the right thing for consumers, is a necessity in matters involving public health and safety.

So some incidents and events rise to the level of watching, but not necessarily need a full-fledged crisis response, correct?

Yes . . . 100 percent. I think that's exactly right because there are all sorts of elements to consider. When, for example, do you want to get senior management involved? When do you escalate it? Who becomes the leader of the response effort? Who becomes the spokesperson? There's all sorts of things that happen once you determine that a crisis has occurred.

It was actually challenging to put my chart together, because it was one of those times where you say something to the client and it's so obvious they say "Oh yeah . . . I know that . . . " but when you actually ask them to articulate what makes an incident rise to the level of a crisis, they're like "Uhhhh. . . . ." And I've had situations where clients call me and say "We have a crisis!" But when we walk through a series of questions or exercises that I ask, it turns out they don't have a crisis at all—they just have a situation that the crisis team should be monitoring because it may become a crisis. It's one of those things that I'm always careful about: not making a non-crisis a crisis.

What do you think of the role of crisis planning in this process, and how well do companies do that?

I think good companies understand the critical elements of planning. You can't plan for everything, so you have a crisis preparedness plan in place and you have holding statements. And they are invaluable as guideposts. Because, inevitably, things are going to change, but you need that guide-post. Having worked on, and with, airlines in crises, I think they probably understand it the best because they all have comprehensive standing crisis plans in place. They have prepared statements. What most people don't realize is that when there is an aircraft incident—such as a crash—the first three to five press releases are already pre-written. And I've worked directly for airlines, and I have worked on crisis communications for airlines. People may think, wow, that's cold . . . but it's reality. We're in an environment starving for news, and if you don't fill that void with information, someone else will.

In a crisis, the companies that do best—especially in preserving their brand reputation—are those that do two things well: show they care about their customers and openly and quickly share the facts—good or bad—with the public.

Do you think airlines understand it better, and do it better? Are airlines the type of company that others should look at to learn how to do it right?

I think airlines are among the best at handling crisis communications. I think that you have companies in all industries that do it well, but from a sector perspective I think that they do it the best, because they have to. Specifically, a crisis plan has the best chance of success when the main objectives are to:

- provide as much information as quickly as possible to consumers, customers, employees, shareholders, and the media;
- help the public understand what is occurring;

- structure contact with the media to eliminate potential dissemination of misinformation; and
- put out as much factual/positive information as possible and counter-act any negative response.

You mentioned you come out of politics and government. I sometimes feel that political types see everything like it's a campaign, instead of a crisis to be managed and minimized. What do you think?

I think you're right. Communications professionals who come from politics have an old saying: There are no Wednesday's in politics, which means after the Tuesday election, it's over. You've won or lost, and all that's left to do is to measure your success and what's been learned. But in crisis communications, that might not be so bad either—it teaches you to measure success. Because the product we offer is not tangible. So I take a page from politics: Did we accomplish our goal? What was our definition of success? Because you and I may—just for example—look at it and say: "Well, I was able to get the CEO on major national television programs and help explain the issues, thus getting back to normal business practices. And that's a success." But the CEO you're working for may say: "No. Not until the stock price rebounds," or some other variation. So in a way there is some value from the political world in that a lot of things in politics are measurable and there's deadlines for elections, for passing legislation, and other tasks. So I do take a page from that book, but I also think that you're right. You just have to be careful not to get caught up in all those traditional, political issues.

You can, though, see political consultants get caught up in the "message of the day" and things like that, correct?

I'm not a big believer in the message of the day. But what I am a big believer in is message. The message is the hardest thing. This is where I completely differ from some of my friends in the political world who are more concerned about media buys and fundraising and rallies. More important is message. It is about consistency, clarity, and frequency.

Honing the message is important. It goes without saying that what a company says and how it says it, particularly in the first 24 hours of a crisis, can determine the ultimate outcome. As you have seen, the wrong message articulated at the wrong time in the wrong way may well set the course for how a company performs for the duration of a crisis. Having said that, we already know from research that it takes an average of four to five times for a person hearing a message for them to be able to retain it, so while I'm not a big believer in the message of the day, I'm a big believer in the message and repeating the message over and over again—to the point that the CEO or spokesperson is sick and tired of hearing the message.

I mean, look again at the political world: the most successful politicians at the national level, they have a stock campaign speech and the only people who are bored with the stock campaign speech are the members of the media who have to hear it *ad nauseam*. But the people who hear it for the first time, it's new to them. So if you take another page from that book of politics.

I have another theory, by the way. I call it the theory of three. People for some reason remember things when there's three. I often joke with my clients that the Ten Commandments would have moved better if they were the Three Commandments. More people would remember . . .

And maybe stop breaking them!

Exactly! Yet, some of the most unsuccessful crisis management people have too many messages and want to change them too often. I would add that when a crisis is under way, it is critical that messages be reviewed and updated as appropriate as the crisis evolves.

And long, elaborate position papers for reporters who don't have time to read them?

Yes. The media—and the general public—have attention deficit disorder. And I remind people that, in interviews, thousands and thousands of words may be spoken, yet only a few are ever used. So your goal really is to be able to ensure that you use the right words, the minimum amount of words, the most important words you can use.

So I'll talk to a client. We'll go through media training and maybe they listen, but not all the way. Then they see the interview and remark: "Wow. Of all the things I said, the reporter picked up on that. That wasn't the most critical point." And I tell them that's because the spokesperson wasn't disciplined, because he or she gave them too much.

I will often tell a client: "You had a good conversation, but a bad interview." Because they try to educate and explain and convince, when what they're really supposed to be doing is sending a message.

I often hear: "Eric, that was a horrible interview. I was boring. I was repetitive. After about five minutes, the reporter said, 'Okay. I have everything I need.'" I'm going to tell them that's probably a homerun interview. If you tell me that you spent 20 minutes, the reporter has a complete handle on the situation and understands your perspective and you feel good about the interview, I'm going to say it's a horrible interview. You gave them too much information.

I argue in this book that what is really missing from crisis communication management is not necessarily the tools, the website, Twitter feed, etc., etc., but the structure, the logistics, and the leadership of crisis response. Where people most get screwed up is that they don't have a structure in place, and they don't have a person in charge when a crisis occurs nor a plan to respond. What do you think?

I agree with you 100 percent. You and I are on the same page. It's speed and leadership every time. There's no excuses for not countering the negative imagery that comes from a crisis. That's why you've got to be ready. There are right ways to do it and there are wrong ways to do it, but there's no excuse for silence. The only actions you can control in a crisis is what you say and sometimes what the public sees.

I would say a close second—a very, very close second—is empathy: caring for the victim. You can have the most perfect response in absolute terms, but if you're not showing you care for the victim, you're interrupting the sensitive impacts that the crisis has caused on the community, the neighbors, and employees. In real time you are going to be unsuccessful with controlling the crisis.

How often do you feel lawyers will dissuade clients from appearing to care because they feel it somehow exposes them to liability?

I would say 90 percent and they're completely wrong. You have to come in with the assumption you're going to be sued, but companies that do the right thing will always prevail, so you can. There's nothing wrong with saying, "I'm sorry." Apologies are critical and just because you apologize does not mean you are admitting guilt. Fundamentally, the public wants to know three things: What happened? How did it happen? And what are you doing about it, or what are you doing to prevent it from happening again? And sometimes you will have to use the "s" word: Say you're sorry, just because it is the right thing to do, and you know it in your heart.

I've actually had situations where clients have been afraid to say, "We love our customers." They just can't bring themselves to say it in response to the crisis, because the responders—including lawyers—tend to be very technically oriented, and love is not a measurable attribute of their product. They therefore feel like they can't say it, or there's something wrong with saying it, and the lawyers are telling them: "Well, instead of love, why don't you say you meet the needs of the needs of the clients in all instances . . . " or some pabulum like that.

Right. And the imagery is critically important. In a crisis, you often have people who are hurting. There's nothing like having someone out there actually helping, wearing the company uniform or logo and showing that the company really cares.

You get all the credit for caring and people don't get that because lawyers stop it.

I have been the outside consultant on crisis management teams involving fatalities or serious injuries, and in preparing a written statement or briefing the CEO for an interview, the question will inevitably be raised about using the word sorry. The argument against saying "we're sorry" is usually voiced by an attorney, who protests that "an apology complicates litigation," because it may be construed as an admission of guilt or culpability. Simply put, they are wrong.

How often do you feel executives play kind of "ostrich syndrome": That if they just ignore something or say as little as possible, maybe it will go away?

Too often . . . way too often. Frankly, the best tool nowadays to show them that this won't work is social media coverage. Most executives I find are now in their 50s. So if you're an executive of a company now, you're probably middle-aged, right? And you haven't grown up with social media and so you don't understand how strong it is and so I think if you show them the social media coverage—and I'm talking everything from Twitter to Facebook and YouTube, all the different social media tools out there—then they kind of get it to see it. Most executives I work with don't see the negative coverage because they are not seeing it in a newspaper or on television . . . but it's happening.

I showed some social media coverage to one client about six months ago, in an instance where there wasn't a lot of traditional media coverage, so they thought there wasn't a problem. So we looked at YouTube, and there were more than two and a half million views based on a blog posting. And the CEO had never even seen the video, because their media department was only showing the CEO what was important to the CEO, which is what appeared in the mainstream media.

So CEOs need to understand that the world has changed from what they grew up with—and even from the early stages of their careers?

I think the job of a "Chief Crisis Officer" is convincing—showing through evidence that the event is real and impacting the company. Most executives I work with love research and evidence, so when I show them the social media coverage of their incident, they then tend to say: "Okay, we're going to say something." Then they tell the lawyers: "Help us to say what Eric wants to say without getting sued." Then we're in the driver's seat.

Unfortunately, the sad part of most crises that spin out of control is that they're always preceded by that initial week, or two weeks, of mishandling, where no one believed what was actually happening, no one recognized that the crisis was growing and getting out of hand. And then eventually things go bad, maybe they call in a crisis communications firm with expertise in this, and eventually everyone gets religion and starts doing things the right way. But by the time that happens so much time has passed, the crisis damage may be irreparable.

❋ ❋ ❋

Derede McAlpin

Chief Communications Officer
Association of Corporate Counsel (ACC)
Washington, DC

> *"The biggest mistake most companies make when responding to a crisis is slow response. In this media environment, you have about 15 minutes or less to determine the appropriate response. It's unfortunate, but it's the media environment we live in."*

About Derede McAlpin

Derede McAlpin, vice president and chief communications officer at the Association of Corporate Counsel (ACC), is a crisis management expert with a special focus on high-stakes litigation and reputation management. Throughout her career, Ms. McAlpin has served as a trusted advisor to CEOs, Fortune 500 companies, high-profile figures, and senior executives. Some of her most memorable projects include leading international communications on behalf of the nation's first full face transplant recipient, working on the landmark U.S. Supreme Court First Amendment case Snyder v. Phelps, and high-profile trials, as well as managing crisis issues following data breaches and scandals. In her current role, Ms. McAlpin oversees all of ACC's communications, research, branding and publications functions, and provides executive-level counsel and direction for ACC and its Board of Directors.

Prior to joining the ACC, she served as vice president of Levick Strategic Communications, where she led strategic communications, litigation, reputation management, and marketing campaigns for Fortune 500 companies, law firms, associations, and other professional service organizations. In that role, she served as lead communications counsel for global clients facing crisis and litigation issues, including regulatory matters, class actions, whistleblower cases, data breaches, and sports and entertainment issues, among others.

After graduating from law school, Ms. McAlpin served as a judicial law clerk in the Superior Court of the District of Columbia where she gained extensive experience in trials, hearings, and other court proceedings on the civil, criminal, and family law calendars. Early in her career, she worked on the news team of Philadelphia's leading 6-ABC WPVI-TV, where she covered local and national news stories.

Ms. McAlpin earned a Juris Doctorate degree from the Temple University School of Law and a Bachelor of Arts in communications from Howard University. She also studied international law in Rome, Italy, and completed the Yale Publishing Course (YPC, which is advanced leadership training for book and magazine professionals).

How did you become a crisis communications consultant with a legal background?

It's funny . . . I never planned it. You never know what your destiny is going to be. I officially started my career at 6-ABC WPVI-TV—an ABC-owned and operated station in Philadelphia, in the station's public affairs department as an intern and then moved to the news department after graduating from college to work as a member of the news team—where assignments ranged from presidential elections, governmental scandals, to trials and the biggest news stories of the day. My most memorable work includes a breaking news story involving Gary Heidnik, a serial killer whose case inspired the movie *Silence of the Lambs*, and the trial of Nicodemo (Little Nicky) Scarfo, a member of the American Mafia who was later convicted on RICO charges in federal court in Philadelphia.

After working in the media, I attended Temple University School of Law. After graduating from law school, I worked as a judicial law clerk at the Superior Court of the District of Columbia, which provided invaluable insight into the inner workings of the court, judicial reasoning, and legal process. It was the clerkship that really inspired me to combine my communications background and legal background. As a former member of the press, I particularly enjoyed working with journalists and anticipating quotes and the next day's coverage. I must say it was quite fulfilling to sit through a Felony 1 or civil trial and accurately predict news angles and coverage.

After my clerkship, I decided to combine my communications and legal background and experience into a niche career rather than pursue the practice of law. Working behind the scenes in the media and law created a perfect foundation for me to direct media strategy on high-profile trials, Supreme Court cases, amicus filings, and bet the company litigation. And that evolved into a whole practice of litigation and crisis communications work.

I made an argument in my last book that litigation communications and crisis communications were two very different disciplines, but I've actually

come around in my thinking a bit because crisis communications is now so intertwined with legal issues, no matter what the particular crisis happens to be. What do you think of that?

I would say that litigation and communications do intertwine, but they're still quite different disciplines. Traditional crisis response tactics can run afoul with the Model Rules for Professional Conduct, as well as the ethical constraints for litigating in the court of public opinion. A litigation strategy also requires careful evaluation of the potential risks and benefits of engaging with the media. It's a delicate dance that requires balancing the pros and cons of being responsive to media inquiries with the overall litigation strategy.

So your sense is that sometimes people who are traditional crisis communicators aren't seeing the whole playing field when they go to give recommendations in litigation situations?

I would say that it can be a "blindside" and disservice to a client. It's like reaching for a Tums to make the pain go away, when you actually need heart surgery. Why? Litigation is a very specialized subgroup of crisis communications. It requires a different skillset, which includes an intimate knowledge of the court system, working knowledge of the ethical rules, and knowing how to advance your client's or your organization's position while playing by the rules. It also involves having the understanding that in litigation, media often don't understand the process. There's often an automatic presumption of guilt, which means the fundamental guarantees of fairness under the law and our judicial system mean absolutely nothing in social media and the court of public opinion.

What are the skills needed for these various types of crisis?

There is not a one size fits all when it comes to managing crises. It all comes down to subject matter expertise and hands-on experience. The top five traits of an effective crisis manager include being an active listener; thinking outside the box; the ability to triage and come up with solutions on a dime; and the capacity to handle stress and remain calm while under fire.

Ultimately, you want someone at the table with crisis management experience—and in most cases it should *not* be someone in the corporate communications role.

Why is that?

Someone with only corporate communications experience might not have the skills needed to manage a crisis. Another factor is privilege. If you're relying on your internal communications person and then you're sending memos, all communications are subjected to discovery.

Very good point. How often in crisis matters do you find that the legal department drives the process more so than the communications department?

In my experience, the corporate communications department rarely drives the response. It is usually outside counsel along with the General Counsel. Why? General Counsel are no longer simply lawyers. They increasingly serve as guardians of the enterprise. This is supported by ACC research, which finds that chief executive officers and boards of directors are increasingly expecting General Counsel to "see around corners," address potential legal and regulatory issues, and mitigate risk.

So it is the case that the General Counsel or one of the top assistants becomes the Chief Crisis Officer within the organization and is working directly with the outside consultant?

Yes, in most instances General Counsel are the protectors of enterprise. They serve as the gatekeeper. Based on research from the ACC, we are finding that the role of an in-house lawyer has expanded from traditional legal work to one that wears three hats: leader of the law department, counselor in chief, and strategist.

How well do you think in-house lawyers understand the process of responding publicly as opposed to just legally?

I think with more and more high-profile cases, there is a much higher appreciation for the need to respond. Attorneys by nature are risk-averse, so it goes against their nature, but they know it's necessary and you see the reputational harm that happens to other companies when they fail to respond. As a result, there are fewer that go for the "No Comment" option—but it's still part of the instinct.

What about outside lawyers at law firms who are actually litigating the cases?

Outside lawyers with experience on high-profile issues often use the press as a strategic tool. I find litigators are most skilled and great in this area. They know the importance of good communication and how the court of public opinion can turn a case that has very minor legal issues into a crisis. At the end of the day, the actual outcome in the court of public opinion could be worse than the outcome in the legal system.

What's the role of planning in this? Some companies have a crisis plan. Has it been your experience that when things start happening they don't even use it?

I would say the biggest mistake most companies make is that, despite the fact that they have a crisis plan on the shelf and they have a robust team, they don't respond fast enough. There's just a lack of preparation and training within a team to respond fast.

Another problem is that the crisis plan by itself gives a false sense of security. There might be general outline—especially if you're managing a big brand or a product—of certain things that could happen inside a plant and the protocols to respond. But there are things that can happen that fall outside of the plan. Lack of training and testing also leads to failure.

I often find that when people put together a crisis communications plans, they have in mind only gigantic events: A product gets recalled, there's cyanide in the Tylenol, that sort of thing. And that may well happen, but there's all sorts of events that fall under the definition of crisis and need to be attended to that no one has thought of so they start making up a response.

That's true, there are just things that could happen that you don't anticipate. Maybe you planned for the explosion but you didn't plan for the disgruntled employee that's disparaging your company online. You have to have a discussion with stakeholders and key parties in all of the different departments. There's no quick fix, but you might find that you can address these issues in the social media policy, you can train employees and improve overall communications within the organization. As an organization, you shouldn't be sitting down to discuss an issue for the first time after something has happened.

Exactly right. How often do you in your current role get involved in crisis communications issues?

For the ACC, my experience is particularly relevant to the members we serve. I do workshops on crisis management, and we hold conferences on data breaches and other emerging trends.

How often do you get a call from a General Counsel asking: "We really have something bad happening, how can you help us?"

All the time. I get these calls for recommendations for crisis professionals, or members come up after they've done training and say: "Oh, I didn't see that this was relevant then, but this is my problem." In my role here I don't represent clients, but I do know the space well and people with the right experience.

So it sounds like you believe legal, rather than a company's communications department, should take the lead on a core crisis communications team. That the crisis communications functions should exist primarily in the legal department, with representatives from brand PR and corporate

communications as members of the team but not driving the process, right?

If you leave it to your company's PR department, it might be someone with only experience in "regular" PR or social media . . . things like that. You really need someone with the right experience, someone who can call the shots and will know how things will play out to make the right recommendations. You just can't make those recommendations if you're only a person that writes corporate Tweets. However, during a social media crisis, you definitely want someone in place with social media expertise.

I think that's a very good point. A lot of companies don't have a gigantic corporate PR staffs, and they're doing all sorts of other things. You can't do a real estate opening on Monday, a new product announcement on Tuesday, then a crisis, or a legal issue, Wednesday. You simply don't have the skills and experience.

Right, because at the end of the day, legal is going to be, in many cases, driving the response. It's all about the strategy. The General Counsel is going to be the key advisor to the CEO.

Tell me about the importance of speed in crisis and litigation communications.

The biggest mistake most companies make when responding to a crisis is slow response. In this media environment, you have about 15 minutes or less to determine the appropriate response. It's unfortunate, but it's the media environment we live in. You start out your day thinking you're going to be working on one thing, then all of a sudden you get a phone call about an issue and you are in crisis mode. It is all about readiness.

And it's very often the lawyers who are thrust into the lead role, and in this current environment they should be, it sounds like.

Yes, absolutely. Crisis happens—it is not an issue of if, but when. General Counsel play a primary role when it comes to risk management and crisis management—they are the ultimate protectors of the brand.

❄ ❄ ❄

Thomas Mauro, Jr.

Senior Director of Corporate Security
Metro One LPSG
New York, NY

> *"Media relations creeps into every crisis, and you can either be in front or behind it."*

About Thomas Mauro

Thomas Mauro has a unique background for this book—but one that is of great value when understanding the role of communications in effective crisis response.

Mauro is currently a consultant with Metro One LPSG, which provides a full range of protective services for corporate complexes, high-risk industrial sites, retail and education facilities. Mauro's current role builds upon a 20-year career with the New York City Police Department (NYPD), where he rose to the rank of captain, assigned as executive officer of two precincts in Brooklyn and serving as incident commander (duty captain) for the boroughs of Brooklyn and Staten Island. He also spent seven years as the director of exercises and training for the Office of Emergency Preparedness and Response at the New York City Department of Health and Mental Hygiene (DOHMH). During emergencies, he led the agency's planning efforts as planning section chief. During Hurricane Sandy in 2012, he was DOHMH incident commander for a high-rise building search operation in the Rockaways section of New York City. He is a subject matter expert in Active Shooter Planning, a certified National Incident Management System (NIMS) Incident Command System (ICS) instructor, a Federal Emergency Management Agency (FEMA) Master Trainer, and a certified Master Exercise Practitioner by the Department of Homeland Security.

Tom holds a master's degree in Criminal Justice from the State University of New York at Albany and a bachelor's degree in English Education and is an adjunct professor at St. John's University and Wagner College.

So you got started in crisis response at the New York City Police Department, correct?

Yes, I was with the NYPD for 20 years. Several years of my career were spent in training, from training recruit officers at the Police Academy, conducting leadership and management training for NYPD supervisors using hands-on scenario-based training, to providing Executive Development Conferences for police department executives.

That must serve you well in your current job.

Oh yeah. And I've continued my educational growth by obtaining additional credentials in the field since retiring from the NYPD. I am able to support agencies, private sector, faith-based groups, and non-governmental organizations with their preparedness efforts using a cycle that includes planning training, exercising, and evaluating. When training is needed, I am able to use my formal education, NYPD training, and personal experience to develop customized training programs to meet clients' performance needs.

And at that time you were with the NYPD, did you have a communications role? Did you deal with the media and other public audiences?

Oh, all the time. As a precinct executive I needed to work closely with neighborhood newspapers as well as the city dailies and TV media. That is how the precinct advertised its community relations programs and also answered questions about crime and other incidents that occurred in the precinct. It was a very two-way relationship with the media. When the media needed information from me, I would provide it—and when I needed to push out my own programs and messages, I would ask them to run an article or attend precinct events, such as police awards ceremonies. It was reciprocal relationship built on trust.

So even though that wasn't your primary role, it sounds like it was a major part of your job.

Yes, it was an important part of my job because when an incident occurs, when an emergency or a crisis occurs, we have to rely on the media to get information out to the public in a timely manner, and also to push the agency's messages out. We could only do that by developing relationships with the media. I think that's one of the keys to a good media relations strategy— developing relationships in advance of a crisis.

And how do you go about doing that?

As a precinct executive, it was not uncommon to physically visit the neighborhood newspaper media outlets. I have arranged meetings with reporters that covered my areas exclusively. In the private sector, my company arranged meetings with the press to talk about current events, and new initiatives that the company has developed to help agencies, organizations, and the public become better prepared. We see a relationship with the media as an opportunity to open dialogue with the public and let them know what to expect during a crisis and how they or their agencies and companies can be better prepared. It's important for the public to know how information will be communicated during a crisis and strategies they can put in place so that they are informed and prepared.

Most media outlets are now competing with social media, and we all know how quickly social media pushes out information. The problem is, social media is not always accurate. So if agencies can push out accurate information quickly to media outlets—and the media knows the information is reliable because they have a relationship with you—then they can better compete with social media.

Do you find that social media is the bane of your existence these days?

No, not at all. In fact, I think social media can be used to an entity's advantage. Social media provides information that we couldn't get through other channels. Social media allows us to know what people are thinking in real time. Another good strategy is to stay ahead of social media by monitoring it. Monitor Twitter feeds, Facebook posts, Vines, any other similar outlets. I won't embarrass myself by trying to name all the social media feeds that my kids use, but you can subscribe to a service where you monitor Twitter and other feeds that are coming into a defined geographic location. That's a strategy presently used by many governmental agencies. Agencies and businesses will know what information is circulating and if the information is inaccurate, we have the chance to correct it by providing accurate information.

Do other ideas come to mind about what people should do in terms of getting ahead of a crisis?

Well let's go back to the problem with social media regarding rumor control. When you read what people are thinking and saying in real time, much of the information will not be truthful, so if you have a good social media strategy, you can push out accurate information to the people that are reporting information, and to the groups that are reading the rumors. So getting in front of the traditional media channels and keeping up with the social media channels are always important. Press conferences are important because official and accurate information that we have at that time will be relayed to the public through a number of media outlets: traditional television and newspaper sources, on-line, and through social media. It is important for officials to inform the public specifically what they should do or not do, so the public may begin taking steps to protect themselves, if necessary.

Right, so now tell me what you do in your current job, your main focus.

I provide the tools to help agencies and businesses prepare for emergencies and disruption of services through planning, training, exercising, and evaluating. The key to crisis management is having a plan: a plan that everyone involved has been trained in and has practiced through some type of exercise. When a crisis occurs, it's important that we use the plan as we have trained and exercised. It's great when companies take the step to write a plan, but it's equally critical to take that plan and use it and practice it and not just let it gather dust on the shelf. It is also critical that the information contained in the plan is shared with those who will be tasked with the responsibilities of implementation. An agency's leadership is often involved with planning and exercising, but we need to ensure that the people that will be on the front line know the plan and have been trained. I have experience in all phases of the planning cycle including the operational implementation, so I am able to provide my clients with planning, training, and exercising, that will be realistic and practical when the plan is needed for a real-world event.

Now, in the work that you do, is it right to say that your main focus is on the emergency response and business continuity rather than the communications side?

Yes, but communications is always a component of every emergency. Communication is always the first area in need of improvement when we conduct "hot washes"—after action reviews of how well we dealt with a real-world incident or performed during an exercise. There should always be an honest review conducted so that when the crisis is winding down, those involved may gauge how well they did and what areas need improvement. I find that most often, intra-agency and inter-agency communications require improvement. During the after action review, I will ask the participants, what could have been improved? You got through this emergency, but what can we improve for the next time this happens? The number one concern is always communications. What information do you need? When do you need it? Who needs to have it? Plans should include a notifications section listing positions and contact information for persons requiring the information and identify who is responsible to make the notifications. Written documentation that the notification occurred is important so that the responsible person may prove later on that the notification was made. During the review, participants also need to ask, do we have a plan? Did we follow the plan? Maybe we need to rewrite our plan.

You said the number one area that needs improvement is always communications. Why do you think that is?

Because people always feel that they did not have the information that they needed when they needed it. They were either not notified or not brought into the loop early enough. Also, the mechanisms of communication may have failed—such as cell phones not performing as expected, radio frequencies being underutilized or overutilized, or user errors such as being unfamiliar with equipment or technology. Also, interagency communication is often a failure point. We need to work on our mechanisms to keep all the partners informed during the emergency so everyone involved has the same information at the same time.

And in terms of media relations during a crisis, this internal communications breakdown affects what's being said to the media?

Exactly, and what is key to navigating the media during a crisis or an emergency is for everyone involved to be on the same page. It is critical that each different agency or participant in an emergency is sharing the same information, especially with the media and the public. The media will report the information provided by a source, so without a consistent message the public will end up confused and then involved agencies will need to devote resources to correcting inaccurate information. Everyone involved needs to be on the same page. We have to avoid a single entity going off-script and the script needs to have accurate information. All persons handling information for their organization need to be informed about relaying the same information provided for the incident and that no individual should add information to that script or invent information that doesn't exist. All agencies and other partners need to speak with one voice.

Are there any examples that you can think of where that was a problem?

There are examples of this from 9/11 at the World Trade Center site. One that stands out in my mind during the first few days was the complete chaos after a message went out through media that anyone who wanted to volunteer can come down to ground zero and lend a hand. This was not an official message, coordinated and approved by the fire and police commanders in charge of ground zero, but a single person speaking off-script to the public through mainstream media. Volunteers showed up and there was no mechanism in place to check them in. Most came down with good intentions and were carrying buckets of rubble alongside responders. Some volunteers dropped off donations of clothes, equipment, and food. But unfortunately, a few people who showed up with other intentions, and walked off with responder equipment, including firefighter coats and helmets.

Aside from the stolen property, this was dangerous on many levels, especially having untrained civilians without proper respiratory equipment working in a contaminated area. I think it was day three or four when police took control of the perimeter, had a fence erected along Canal Street, and allowed access to the site to only pre-assigned, credentialed responders and construction workers. The public message changed then and the police were able to begin bringing control and coordination to the chaos.

Do you think you have a different take on the media relations aspect than somebody who's just focused on media relations?

Well, a lot of times, governmental agencies see the media as an adversary. I think just the opposite is true. As a former police captain, I provided interviews and information to members of the media and that information was reported inaccurately or with a political slant. Significantly, this only happened with members of the press I had not met prior to them covering an incident. I had no rapport with them. Reporters who I worked with regularly reported the facts accurately for the most part. There's a lesson in this: you need to embrace the media, develop relationships, and come up with a plan for working together during an emergency. Mainstream media has a stake in making this work as well, because they're in competition with social media channels. During large-scale emergencies, where there is information coming in from numerous sources and places, it is beneficial to have a single-point for collecting and coordinating the information and crafting public messages. Usually this person or office is called the Public Information Officer (PIO), and each agency probably has their own. Bringing the PIOs from different agencies and businesses together to share information and agree upon the accuracy of content going out to the media improves communications during emergencies.

Here's a quick story about a time when I was actually pleased to have a good relationship with the media. A local cable news reporter I work with in the past—on *New York 1* (the local 24-hour news channel) interviewed me about a car accident when I was an executive officer of the 63rd precinct in Brooklyn. The accident involved fatalities in the Marine Park section of Brooklyn. The camera went on and he asked his first question—and I was not able to answer the question as articulately as I wanted to. I just messed it up. So the reporter actually stopped the interview and let me start over. I attribute that to having a relationship with the person in the past. He didn't want to embarrass me on camera, so he allowed me a "second take" . . . I don't know if that happens often, but I was certainly grateful.

Since media relations is not your primary role, have you been in situations where you've been frustrated with the way media is handled?

Absolutely, and this is why agencies and other entities need a plan for public messaging and understand the importance of providing timely information to the public. When the media calls an agency's press office requesting information about an incident and its effect on let's say, public health, if the agencies involved do not provide a statement, the media will go ahead with a report anyway, using sources that are not reliable. This provides inaccurate information. I don't think it's intentional because they have their deadlines to meet, but the result is the same. Agency leadership needs to work toward drafting and approving public messages in a timely manner, so that accurate information is relayed through the media. A specific frustration that I had was when the PIO had drafted an accurate message for the media but agency leadership would not take the time to approve the message. Instead (and as I predicted), media interviewed "subject matter experts" located across the country with no grasp of our situation, and they painted an inaccurate picture for the public, which caused unnecessary concern and alarm.

In terms of your preparation and training work, is there a crisis communications aspect in terms of dealing with the media and other audiences?

Yes, I direct functional exercises to help clients manage communication with agencies, responders in the field, and with the media, as well as our governmental officials. Functional exercises are designed to simulate realistic conditions because a good scenario will make the exercise participants feel as though the incident is unfolding for real. The exercise planners spend many hours and days designing "injects," which are scripted questions, for the players. For each inject there is an expected action, usually based on an existing plan. The action taken is evaluated and if the expected action is not performed, there is usually a training issue or an issue with the plan itself. Both can be corrected before the plan is needed for a real emergency. Among the injects are those written for players that involve media questions or the need for a public message. Exercise controllers will make an actual phone call or send an email to a targeted player requesting the information. This is a good way for agencies to practice drafting public messages and dealing with the media under simulated conditions.

How do all these levels of communications—with media, interagency communications, internal communications—work together in a crisis. Do you see the media relations as separate and distinct area?

Absolutely not—it all works together. It's not separate at all. What needs to happen first is that all the entities and stakeholders involved come together to figure out what has happened. What are the facts? What is the truth? And the facts could be good or bad, but facts are facts. And once you've gathered this information, you figure out who needs to know it, and when they need to know it. So during an incident involving more than one entity—let's say a corporation or public authority, local law enforcement, regulators—there should be a meeting taking place at a joint information center. A joint information center is a place where agency PIOs will convene to share information, to share what they know with each other and with the official in charge, whether that be a mayor or a commissioner, or the CEO of a business.

Once everyone is brought up to speed about what the facts are, then there needs to be a selected person who is a single point of contact for the media. That person needs to take the information and prepare a press release and then provide it to the media.

Do you have advice on who that single point of contact should be?

It should be the person whose job it is to deal with the media as part of their day-to-day position. Their job description should include interfacing with the media. It should also be someone who's been trained in media relations and also public speaking. A problem many entities face is that some of their top leadership have no experience speaking in front of a camera, or to a group of people, and public speaking is not something that everyone has the skills to do. Public speaking can be developed through training and practical experience. In 2002, the NYPD sent me to the FBI National Academy program in Quantico, Virginia, where I took a course in public speaking. The instructor, Penny Parrish, was excellent and used, at the time, modern technology to video our presentations so we could watch ourselves presenting, see our mistakes, and correct them.

The single point of contact needs to be someone specially selected, with public speaking skills, who understands how to gather information and then cull it down to a series of messages and then work with the media to push the information out to the public. It is beneficial for this single point of contact to represent one of the key agency stakeholders, or even come from the local mayor's—or other elected official's—office. The person needs to be a credible source for the media and for the public, and be able to speak as an authority on the nature of the emergency. It is helpful to identify the persons who could fill this role in advance and include them in plan writing, training, and exercising.

You know, it's interesting, I started out thinking that the media relations might not be central to what you do, but from everything that you're saying, it sounds like I'm wrong, that it is pretty top-of-mind in the training that you did. Is that accurate?

It's definitely accurate, yes. Absolutely. Media relations creeps into every crisis and you can either be in front or behind it. The way to get in front of it is to pre-identify your media relations leaders, establish a joint information center to gather information from every partner with a stake in what's happening, and then ensure a single point of contact to manage the information and public messaging so that the message is consistent across agencies and jurisdictions. Often when agencies are working to bring an incident under control, their focus is on operations—so communications and media relations relating to public messages may not be a priority. Pre-identified professionals performing this role and working with operations to obtain accurate and timely information will allow operations to focus on life-safety and incident stabilization, while the media professionals ensure that the public receives the information that they need to ensure their safety. My days of being in the middle of operations may be in the past, but in my current position, I have enjoyed being able to use my experience and training to work with agencies and strengthen their communications capabilities through plan development, training, exercising, and evaluating.

❊ ❊ ❊

Thom Weidlich

Crisis Consultant and Chief Content Manager
CrisisResponsePro, Inc.
New York, New York

"It's unusual to see a company that really has it together . . . it's one of those situations where you're spending a lot of money preparing for something that may happen only infrequently. But it can have a huge impact when it does happen."

About Thom Weidlich

An accomplished journalist and crisis communications consultant, Thom Weidlich servers as chief content manager of CrisisResponsePro, the online software for crisis and litigation communications. In that role he writes about crisis communications and also oversees the creation and collection of a wide range of content on the site, including templates, public statements issued by other companies, and crisis planning materials.

As a crisis communications consultant, Thom specializes in litigation communications, crisis management, and media-relations strategy. Before beginning his tenure at CrisisResponsePro, Thom was a consultant at Sitrick & Company, a nationally known crisis and bankruptcy communications firm. Prior to this, he was a longtime reporter for Bloomberg News, where he covered the trials of Enron's Kenneth Lay and Jeffrey Skilling and media mogul Conrad Black. He also covered bankruptcy, securities cases, structured-finance litigation, and the federal courthouses in Manhattan and Brooklyn.

A journalist for more than 20 years, Mr. Weidlich previously had been a reporter at The National Law Journal, *where his beats included law firms and employment law;* PRWeek *magazine, which covers the PR industry; and* Direct, *a direct-marketing publication. He also had been a freelance journalist, writing for the* New York Times, ABA Journal, *and other media outlets.*

Thom holds a master's degree in History from Columbia University and a bachelor's degree in Liberal Arts from The New School in New York. He was a 2010 fellow in the Journalist Law School program at Loyola Law School in Los Angeles. In 2001, he won the Bertrand Russell Society book award for his book on the British philosopher, published the previous year.

So let's start by discussing your background and how you got into this field. How did you find yourself in crisis communications, and particularly as the chief content manager of CrisisResponsePro?

I had been a journalist for many years, 20 years, mostly covering legal issues. My last seven and a half years were at Bloomberg, where I was on the legal team—so mostly what I covered was adversarial situations. I always had it in the back of my mind to go into high level PR, although at the time I really thought it would be more in the area of financial PR. I've been an editor at *PR Week* magazine and wrote about the industry in some detail. Then, I got much more interested in crisis communications because I thought it would be more strategic. And, of course, litigation communications, since I was a litigation reporter for so many years.

Eventually, this brought me to Sitrick, and then to PRCG, another crisis communications firm,* and to CrisisResponsePro, which was a software created by PRCG that was just being rolled out. One of the big attractions was working on the software. When I first went into crisis communications, I thought that there had to be some sort of software to automate crisis communications and get people organized. So, I was really surprised to learn that there really wasn't anything like that on the market.

How do you define crisis? Obviously, a lot of crises are legal, but what's the definition you would use?

There are different types, but I would say any kind of incident where a company's reputation is at risk, and the reputation risk can really affect the bottom line.

So, anything that affects reputation in that sense would be a crisis, you think? Or are there certain types of events that are more likely to be crisis— the immediate or unexpected threats?

Well you have the quicker crises, such as fires or accidents, and other events that might develop more slowly, such as litigation or, I would say, even issues management.

You spend a lot of your time analyzing what companies do and don't do during a crisis. What do you think, after doing this steadily for several years now? How well do companies respond during a crisis?

It's depressing, to tell you the truth. I think companies are shockingly bad at this. It seems such a waste in a way. There's a trend of people writing about the problems of being overly optimistic, and I think that's one of the problems here is that companies don't want to admit that they might run into problems—which they, of course, they will, because there will always be problems in any company above a certain size. So, they don't prepare and aren't organized beforehand. When a crisis hits, they seem to be just making it up as they're going along.

So more companies mishandle things than handle them well?

I would say it's more that they mishandle things. It's unusual to see a company that really has it together, or has someone in-house dedicated to crisis. It's one of those situations where you're spending a lot of money preparing for something that may happen only infrequently. But it can have a huge effect when it does happen."

---

* PRCG/Haggerty LLC, the author's firm.

So, as a former reporter, did you think companies had it all together?

Yes, I really thought they were far more organized than this. I often say that, as a reporter, when I would call a company in the morning about a lawsuit, about them being sued, it would take them all day to get a statement saying simply: "We're gonna fight this lawsuit vigorously." All day! Now, I understand why. It's because they have this incredible bureaucracy that keeps them from responding quickly.

So, you've been reviewing companies and analyzing their crisis communication response. What types of companies or industries do a really bad job? Anything jump out?

Well, there's been a number of crises in the healthcare arena in 2015 and 2016 that were particularly poorly handled. Valeant, the pharmaceutical company, had problems with their financial disclosures and pricing. I don't think they've been particularly transparent about that.

Then, there's Theranos, the blood testing company. They became very belligerent when *The Wall Street Journal* started writing about them in the fall of 2015, alleging that there were problems with their testing equipment and protocols. It turned out that nearly everything *The Wall Street Journal* reported was true. The CEO now cannot manage a blood lab for two years, and the entire business is in jeopardy. I don't think they handled that very well, and they've gotten a lot of criticism for the approach. We just recently wrote about a piece in the *San Francisco Chronicle* comparing Theranos' response to their crisis with the response by Zenefits, the employee benefits startup. A crisis at Zenefits developed when, among other things, it was discovered that their employees were not properly licensed to sell the insurance they were selling.

How did Zenefits' response differ from Theranos'?

Zenefits really appeared to have done a better job. They immediately admitted there was a problem—the exact opposite of what Theranos did. The CEO stepped down, unlike at Theranos, where the founder and CEO (and one-time media darling Elizabeth Holmes) is still running the show. It looks like Zenefits is settling with state regulators over these issues and really trying to change. That makes a difference.

I have a theory that the public will forgive mistakes, even egregious mistakes, so long as you properly handle the aftermath. Is that your sense?

Yeah, I think owning up to the problems is really one of the most important things a company can do when facing a crisis. And be genuine about it. In Theranos' case, I think they may have genuinely believed in the early stages that they weren't the problem, that they just had a PR issue. But in retrospect, it seems crazy that they viewed it that way.

Well there's a school of crisis communication response that says "Admit nothing, lawyer-up and try to scare the hell out of the media outlet. At the least, you'll get a better story." Theranos has proved that wrong, haven't they?

Yes, Theranos really went after the *Journal*, and the *Journal* didn't back down. The only thing I can guess is that the *Journal* felt that they really had the goods on this company.

In a way, Theranos protested too much?

Yeah, right. Exactly.

Tell me about what you see in the area of apologies and how companies handle that.

Well, it's funny. Apologies are actually a whole academic area. How to apologize, including on the corporate level. Again, it just seems people don't want to 'fess up to mistakes that they've made. It's very difficult to admit that you were in the wrong. But it's clear in the cases that we follow that in many cases you have to make an apology and own up to the mistakes that you made, you have to say what you're going to do to make amends. A lot of companies don't do that.

Do a lot of them issue the non-apology apology, right? As in: "If you were offended, I'm sorry?"

Yes, absolutely: "We're sorry you misinterpreted our bad actions." I actually think companies are getting slightly better at this recently, because the fake apologies, or non-apology apologies, are almost a pop culture thing now. Harry Scherer, on his radio show, even has a weekly segment on apologies of the week.

So are apologies the crisis technique *du jour*?

No, I don't think so. But I think that just as we say most crises involve some sort of legal aspect, a lot of them often involve an apology, too.

The other technique that you used to see on a regular basis is the internal investigation as a PR technique: You'd hire a famous outside lawyer— George Mitchell or someone like that—who'd investigate the crisis or incident and prepare a report, usually months later. You'd appear to be serious about addressing the crisis, but it would be months before the

public would learn anything. Have people begun to see through this technique? What's your sense?

No, I don't think people have begun to see through them, and I do think in some instances it's a genuine attempt to find out what happened. But it is also a valuable crisis communications technique to appoint some sort of an internal committee to show that you are, at least, trying to do something. An internal investigation was launched by Fox News, for example, in the 2016 Roger Ailes employment lawsuit.

The CrisisResponsePro service has a database of thousands of public statements issued by other companies, and as Chief Content Manager, you oversee this. Have you seen some really awful statements issued by companies over the years in response to crises?

Oh, yes. For the most part, we're trying to post good examples of statements so they can serve as a guide to users of our service, so we tend not to post many bad ones. An exception would be for an extremely high-profile story. If the story is big enough, we'll consider posting a statement related to that crisis, no matter how bad it is.

What do you find in the public statements that companies issue? What's your sense of what works and what doesn't?

They really run the gamut. The statements that work well are ones that follow the basic rules of initially—especially an event like a fire or accident—explaining that something has happened, what people need to do to be safe, and what the company is doing to deal with the situation. And, in the very early stages, that they're doing everything they can to gather information about what has happened and convey that information in an accurate manner to the public.

And good statements always have a "human face," expressing sympathy for anyone affected by the crisis.

Right. Sometimes, there is a concern when you express sympathy, that it might sound fake. There's been a recent backlash, in fact, about statements that begin with phrases like: "Our hearts go out to . . . " Are there clichés like that that you think work against a company?

I think it is a big mistake when companies state that "safety is their first priority," because I think people don't believe that. They know a company's first priority is making money. I've seen statements that are much better where a company will say: "Safety is a top priority" or "among our top priorities." I think the reaction is far less cynical.

Ok, so let's say that I'm a company. I want to manage crisis communications the right way. Based on your experience and what you've seen analyzing these issues for quite some time, what should I do?

To me, 90 percent of crisis communications is preparation. Most companies just don't have the systems in place, nor the people in place. So, number one is to have somebody in charge of the crisis—including monitoring potential crises. That person should have a feel for what could turn into a big crisis. Events and issues and other potential crises should be feeding up to that person for proper vetting. Second, you need a crisis team that will assemble when there's a crisis, and for each person on that team to know what they're supposed to do when a crisis hits. Finally, you have a plan in place so that they do know what to do. And you train against that plan.

How well do you see companies doing that?

Again, I don't think they're very good at it because that would require that they recognize that things can go wrong.

Right, it's that optimism thing again. But is it optimism or is it Pollyanna-ism?

I think it's just basic optimism that nothing will go wrong. But also, that companies are so busy doing other things that they don't have time for this—or so they think. It's an opportunity cost question: It is a lot of effort to create a crisis plan, and a team, and have a leader and train on a plan . . . for something that you may only need infrequently. But the problem is that depending on the crisis, it can have a huge effect on your reputation and the bottom line.

Why didn't Target, for example, have a plan for a potential data breach?

Data breaches are very interesting because they're really the crisis *du jour*. So many companies seem to be getting hit with data and cybercrime issues, and they just don't have a plan in place for dealing with them. You often see IT people writing on this, and in the IT community there is a call for a crisis plan specifically geared toward a data breach, and they always recognize that you have to have a communications aspect to that.

Do you feel that IT is driving crisis response in data breaches, where communicators should? Because ultimately, the damage is as much to reputation as to your data and systems.

Yes, I don't think IT has the expertise in terms of communicating with the media and with the public.

So what else should I do? I'm a company who wants to do it right. My lawyers are telling me, "Say as little as possible and get the hell out of the

way. There's no way you can control the media. There's nothing you can do." What do you think?

I think there has to be buy-in from the top that the organization is going to do this and do it right. We're going to have the systems in place. We're not always going to do what lawyers want, in terms of not talking. Some lawyers do get it, but most don't. So, that's an important thing. Culturally, there has to be an understanding that we're going to take this seriously and get it right, because reputationally, the return on investment is there.

There are people who say that a crisis plan doesn't help you because when all hell's breaking loose, nobody follows it anyway. But I don't think that's really true. Obviously, you can't predict everything that's going to happen in a crisis, but if people generally know what their role is and what their duties are, it will go a lot smoother.

Which leads us to technology. How can technology facilitate the process?

The vision behind CrisisResponsePro, again, is to be organized about crisis communications response, instead of just doing it on the fly. And this means organized in a couple of different ways. One is just to have a central place to collaborate, instead of using email. A central place to keep the documents and for version control of those documents. It is truly shocking, in this day and age, that companies still haven't figured out how to keep track of which version of the document is the latest version. I joke that we can put a man on the moon, but we can't institute true version control in a corporate environment. So CrisisResponsePro helps with that.

Technology is being used in other ways, of course—smartphones and social media just being two examples.

Ah, Social media. Older executives and older lawyers and others will say, "Well, that's just a bunch of crazies or teenagers. I can ignore it." Right?

Right, and that's totally wrong, because for a lot of people social media is the main way they're getting their news. And very often, the public first learns of crises through social media as well. And reporters monitor social media closely in their reporting, to find out what stories are out there. So, social media has to be a big part of any crisis plan.

If you could fix one thing about companies and the way they respond to crisis, what do you think it would be?

That they don't think they have to plan ahead. I think that's the biggest mistake I've seen in Corporate America, because I think people just don't understand how quickly things move. I actually think having worked at Bloomberg for so long was good training for this. In fact, we had a saying at Bloomberg: News is predictable. Some news may not be, but a lot of it is.

For example, if you're covering a lawsuit, you know the stages of the lawsuit, you know that a decision on a motion to dismiss is going to happen at some point, so you'd write your templated story ahead of time for any scenario that might happen. Then when the ruling comes down, you just fill in a few blanks and file the story.

It's the same thing with crisis. You know what industry you're in. You know what kind of crises you're vulnerable to. There's no reason not to have templated statements with a lot of blanks in them that need to be filled in. If you generally know what tone you want to take in various situations and what information needs to be disclosed, you can have the templates approved ahead of time. This enhances the speed of response considerably.

If a Bloomberg reporter can do it to help report the news more quickly, it stands to reason that the subject of the stories, the corporations out there involved in crisis, should be able to do it as well.

Acknowledgments

I'm sitting here in my office at 6 p.m. on a Friday in August putting the final touches on this book (which is already many months late) while my wife is at home struggling with kids and visitors (from my side of the family, no doubt!) and God knows what else. Guess who I'm going to thank first?

Elyse DeMayo Haggerty is my love and my inspiration. We've had a road with many turns, but you can't say we haven't kept it interesting. She is a brilliant professional, a dedicated social worker, and an engaging therapist. At various times, I need all three. So thank you.

My two sons have endured the writing of this book as well, and so I thank them too. Liam, now 15, was a newborn when I wrote my first book. Now he's fast becoming my sounding board and consigliere, particularly on matters related to technology and computers. His brother, Conall, alternately known around town and "The Professor" and "Speedy" (and who you met in Chapter 1) will be propping me up soon as well. Each day they are a reminder that I must be doing something right.

I must give special thanks to my editor, Jonathan Malysiak, and everyone at the American Bar Association for their dedication to this project—and for putting up with delays too many to mention.

Professionally, there are too many people to be named. My writing is an extension of the work I've done throughout the course of my career, and a career is built as much by those around you as by yourself. So all of those I thanked in writing my first book, *In the Court of Public Opinion,* are incorporate herein by reference (sorry, that's the lawyer in me coming out). My colleague Thom Weidlich (who is interviewed in the Afterword) is chief content manager of our CrisisResponsePro software product, and his analysis for that product informed several sections of this book. Kudos, as well, to recent colleagues such as Victoria O'Neill, Andrea Garcia and Lindsay Wheeler. My longtime West Coast friend and partner-in-crime Harvey Englander, of LA's Englander, Knabe & Allen deserves a special shout-out as well, as do all who subjected themselves to interviews for Chapter 8 of this book. Their intellect and insight make me look good.

Among my clients, Howard Milstein, Harriet Edelman, and Richard Aborn stand out as mentors and collaborators. I must also thank my friend

Wendy Neu and her late husband John for all their support over the years as well, along with my late DC partner and good friend Jeffery Sandman, who passed away, way too soon, in 2010.

Finally, my parents are gone now, but they still deserve credit for their sacrifice. You can be born with very little in life, but when you watch your parents give and give and give, building a future out of nothing but love . . . well, you were born rich, that's all I can say.

Notes

Introduction

1. Patti Waldmeir, "Why Justice Needs PR," *Financial Times*, June 16, 2003.
2. *In Re Pilot Project For Electronic News Coverage in Indiana Trial Courts*, Indiana Supreme Court, Case No. 94S00-0605-MS-166, Footnote 19, May 2006.

Chapter 1

1. Thomas Lee, "Target strives to patch its image after huge data security breach," *Minneapolis Star Tribune*, December 27, 2013.
2. Greg Keenan, "Toyota to go on media blitz," *Globe and Mail*, January 31, 2010.
3. Ronald D. White, "Company scrambles to defend its image; BP works frantically to contain a public relations as well as an ecological disaster," *Los Angeles Times*, May 1, 2010, 18A.
4. Jack Ewing, "Volkswagen Names New Porsche Chief, Promoting from Within," *The New York Times*, October 1, 2015, B2.
5. Click Detroit, "12 biggest auto recalls," at http://www.clickondetroit.com/consumer/automotive/biggest-auto-recalls/16928110.

Chapter 2

1. Malcolm Gladwell, "The Engineer's Lament," *The New Yorker*, May 4, 2015, http://www.newyorker.com/magazine/2015/05/04/the-engineers-lament.
2. Moriah Balingit, "How Washington Became the Busiest Training Ground for Scandal PR," *The Washington Post*, October 29, 2015, https://www.washingtonpost.com/lifestyle/magazine/how-washington-became-the-nations-busiest-training-ground-for-scandal-pr/2015/10/27/1eb482e6-6b6c-11e5-b31c-d80d62b53e28_story.html.

Chapter 3

1. Gogel, Suresh, Crisis Management: Master the Skills to Prevent Disasters (Global India Publications Pvt Ltd, 2009) page 28.
2. Burson-Marsteller, "2011 Crisis Preparedness Study," http://www.slideshare.net/BMGlobalNews/crisis-preparedness-study-2011.
3. International Association of the Measurement and Evaluation of Communication, "Barcelona Principles Relaunched-Result of Cross Industry Collaboration," September 2015, http://amecorg.com/2015/09/barcelona-principles-2-0-launched-result-of-cross-industry-collaboration.

Chapter 4

1. Associated Press, "Oil rig explodes off La.; 11 missing, 17 hurt," April 22, 2010.
2. United States Coast Guard, "On Scene Coordinator Report *Deepwater Horizon* Oil Spill," https://www.uscg.mil/foia/docs/dwh/fosc_dwh_report.pdf.
3. Maureen Hoch, "New Estimate Puts Gulf Oil Leak at 205 Million Gallons," *PBS NewsHour*, August 2, 2010, http://www.pbs.org/newshour/rundown/new-estimate-puts-oil-leak-at-49-million-barrels/.
4. Jessica Durando, "BP's Tony Hayward: I'd Like My Life Back," *USA Today*, June 1, 2010, http://content.usatoday.com/communities/greenhouse/post/2010/06/bp-tony-hayward-apology/1#.VjtTr-k-vl0.
5. http://www.bp.com/en/global/corporate/press/press-releases/bp-confirms-that-transocean-ltd-issued-the-following-statement-today.html; retrieved from CrisisResponsePro, at https://www.summitas.com/officearticle/20964104.
6. http://www.bp.com/en/global/corporate/press/press-releases/BP-offers-full-support-to-transocean-after-drilling-rig-fire.html; retrieved from CrisisResponsePro, at https://www.summitas.com/officearticle/21964204.
7. http://www.bp.com/en/global/corporate/press/press-releases/bp-offers-sympathy-to-the-families-of-those-lost-in-the-us-oil-rig-fire.html; retrieved from CrisisResponsePro, at https://www.summitas.com/officearticle/23964404.
8. Rebecca Singer, "Hayward tells BBC that PB was making it up day-to-day," *Marketplace*, November 9, 2010, http://www.marketplace.org/2010/11/09/business/bbc-world-service/hayward-tells-bbc-bp-was-making-it-day-day.
9. Monica Langley, "Inside Target, CEO Gregg Steinhafel Struggles to Contain Giant Cybertheft," *The Wall Street Journal*, Feb. 18, 2014, http://www.wsj.com/articles/SB10001424052702304703804579382941509180758.
10. Retrieved from CrisisResponsePro; https://corporate.target.com/press/releases/2013/12/target-confirms-unauthorized-access-to-payment-car.
11. Ibid.
12. Ibid.
13. https://corporate.target.com/press/releases/2013/12/target-confirms-unauthorized-access-to-payment-car; retrieved from CrisisResponsePro, at https://www.summitas.com/officearticle/19901512.
14. Gina Kolata, "A Sea Change in Treating Heart Attacks," *The New York Times*, June 15, 2015, A1.
15. Retrieved from CrisisResponsePro; https://www.summitas.com/officeblog/18385146498337818586.
16. Mike Riggs, "Gunman Killed, Multiple Victims in Mass Shooting at Washington, D.C.'s Navy Yard," *CityLab*, http://www.citylab.com/crime/2013/09/live-updates-shootings-washington-dcs-navy-yard/6901/.
17. Marc Santora, "Doctor in New York City Is Sick with Ebola," *The New York Times*, October 23, 2014, A1.
18. James Haggerty, *In the Court of Public Opinion: Winning Strategies for Litigation Communications*, 2nd ed. (Washington, DC: American Bar Association, 2009), 277.

Chapter 5

1. Louis V. Gerstner Jr., *Who Says Elephants Can't Dance: Inside IBM's Historic Turnaround* (HarperBusiness, 2002), 42–43.
2. William Manchester, *The Last Lion*, Vol. 2, *Alone* (New York: Laurel Trade Paperback Edition, 1988), 32.

3. Ibid., 34.

4. Brent Schlender and Rick Tetzeli, *Becoming Steve Jobs: The Evolution of a Reckless Upstart into a Visionary Leader* (New York: Random House 2015).

5. Jack Ewing, "Volkswagen Reaches Deal in U.S. Over Emissions Scandal," *The New York Times*, April 21, 2016, https://www.nytimes.com/2015/09/23/business/international/volkswagen-diesel-car-scandal.html?_r=0.

6. Frank Jordans, "EPA: Volkswagon Thwarted Pollution Regulations For 7 Years," *CBS Detroit, The Associated Press*, September 21, 2015.

7. David Morgan, "West Virginia engineer proves to be a David to VW's Goliath," *Reuters*, September 23, 2015, http://www.reuters.com/article/us-usa-volkswagen-researchers-idUSKCN0RM2D720150924.

8. http://media.vw.com/release/1064/; retrieved from CrisisResponsePro, at https://www.summitas.com/officearticle/181928509.

9. Retrieved from CrisisResponsePro; https://www.summitas.com/officearticle/201928409.

10. David Barstow, "Vast Mexico Bribery Case Hushed Up by Wal-Mart After Top Level Struggle," *The New York Times*, April 21, 2012, http://www.nytimes.com/2012/04/22/business/at-wal-mart-in-mexico-a-bribe-inquiry-silenced.html.

11. Jessica Wohl and Elinor Comlay, "Wal-Mart Shaken by Bribery Probe, Shares Plunge," *Reuters*, April 23, 2012, http://www.reuters.com/article/us-walmart-idUSBRE83L0C820120424?feedType=RSS&feedName=topNews&rpc=71.

12. Miguel Bustillo and David Luhnow, "Wal-Mart Ups The Defenses," *The Wall Street Journal*, April 24, 2012, https://www.wsj.com/articles/SB10001424052702303592404577364123757598002.

13. http://news.walmart.com/news-archive/2012/04/21/walmart-statement-in-response-to-recent-new-york-times-article-about-compliance-with-the-us-foreign-corrupt-practices-act; retrieved from CrisisResponsePro, at https://www.summitas.com/officearticle/21982004.

14. Aruna Viswanatha and Devlin Barrett, "Wal-Mart Bribery Probe Finds Few Signs of Major Misconduct," *Wall Street Journal*, October 19, 2015, http://www.wsj.com/articles/wal-mart-bribery-probe-finds-little-misconduct-in-mexico-1445215737.

15. CrisisResponsePro (subscription required), https://www.summitas.com/officearticle/23879312.

16. CrisisResponsePro (subscription required), https://www.summitas.com/officearticle/22877712.

17. CrisisResponsePro (subscription required), https://www.summitas.com/officearticle/22879712.

18. CrisisResponsePro (subscription required), https://www.summitas.com/officearticle/11887601.

Chapter 6

1. James Haggerty, *In the Court of Public Opinion: Winning Strategies for Litigation Communications*, 2nd ed. (Washington, DC: American Bar Association, 2009), 275.

2. Robert M. Yoder, "Someday They'll Get Slick Willie Sutton," *The Saturday Evening Post*, January 20, 1951, 17.

3. Drake Bennett, "Mortgage Fraud Prosecutors Pounce on a Small Bank," *BusinessWeek*, January 31, 2013, http://www.bloomberg.com/news/articles/2013-01-31/mortgage-fraud-prosecutors-pounce-on-a-small-bank.

4. Gretchen Morgenstern, "A Tiny Banks Surreal Trip Through Fraud Prosecution," *New York Times*, July 19, 2015, http://www.nytimes.com/2015/07/19/business/a-tiny-banks-surreal-trip-through-a-fraud-prosecution.html.

5. *Gentile v State Bar of Nevada*, 501 U.S. 1030, 1043 (1991).

6. Ken Lombardi, "Tracy Morgan: Can't Believe Wal-Mart Blaming Him for Crash Injuries," *CBSNews*, September 30, 2014, http://www.cbsnews.com/news/tracy-morgan-cant-believe-walmart-blaming-him-for-crash-injuries/.

7. http://www.usatoday.com/story/life/tv/2014/09/29/walmart-blames-tracy-morgan-for-not-wearing-seatbelt/16444487/; retrieved from CrisisResponsePro, at https://www.summitas.com/officearticle/291308209.

8. http://www.cnn.com/2014/09/29/justice/tracy-morgan-crash/index.html; retrieved from CrisisResponsePro, at https://www.summitas.com/officearticle/301312809.

9. Josh Eidelson, "Saks Claims It Has the Right to Discriminate Against Transgender Employees," *BusinessWeek*, January 9, 2015, http://www.bloomberg.com/bw/articles/2015-01-09/saks-and-company-in-legal-fight-over-transgender-former-employee.

10. Chris Geidner, "Human Rights Campaign Takes Action Against Saks Fifth Avenue Over LGBT Policies," *BuzzFeedNews*, January 8, 2015, https://www.buzzfeed.com/chrisgeidner/human-rights-campaign-takes-action-against-saks-fifth-avenue?utm_term=.kkEg48MYJ8#.wijEj8YG28.

11. Human Rights Campaign, "Saks Fifth Avenue Doubles Down on LGBT Discrimination," January 14, 2015, http://www.hrc.org/press/saks-fifth-avenue-doubles-down-on-lgbt-discrimination.

12. CrisisResponsePro (subscription required), https://www.summitas.com/officearticle/261563901.

Chapter 7

1. Matt Lynley, "Andreessen Horowitz Just Raised a 15 Billion Fund," *Business Insider*, January 31, 2012, http://www.businessinsider.com/andreessen-horowitz-just-raised-a-15-billion-fund-2012-1.

2. Robert J. Szczerba, "15 Worst Tech Predictions of All Time," *Forbes*, January 5, 2015, http://www.forbes.com/sites/robertszczerba/2015/01/05/15-worst-tech-predictions-of-all-time/#287c3ee25c19.

3. James Haggerty, *In the Court of Public Opinion: Winning Strategies for Litigation Communications*, 2nd ed. (Washington, DC: American Bar Association, 2009), 241–242.

Index